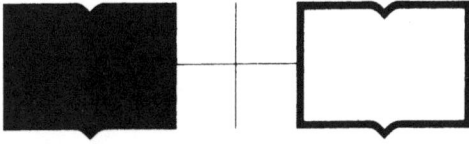

Toronto Reprint Library of Canadian Prose and Poetry

Douglas Lochhead, General Editor

This series is intended to provide for libraries a varied selection of titles of Canadian prose and poetry which have been long out-of-print. Each work is a reprint of a reliable edition, is in a contemporary library binding, and is appropriate for public circulation. The Toronto Reprint Library makes available lesser known works of popular writers and, in some cases, the only works of little known poets and prose writers. All form part of Canada's literary history; all help to provide a better knowledge of our cultural and social past.

The Toronto Reprint Library is produced in short-run editions made possible by special techniques, some of which have been developed for the series by the University of Toronto Press.

This series should not be confused with Literature of Canada: Poetry and Prose in Reprint, also under the general editorship of Douglas Lochhead.

UNIVERSITY OF TORONTO PRESS

Toronto Reprint Library of Canadian Prose and Poetry
© University of Toronto Press 1973
Toronto and Buffalo
Reprinted in paperback 2017
ISBN 978-0-8020-7521-5 (cloth)
ISBN 978-1-4875-9131-1 (paper)

Other editions:
London, Bentley, 1861;
London, Bentley, 1866;
London, Frederick Warne, 1872
'new edition.'

THE

SEASON-TICKET.

'I pity the man, who can travel from Dan to Beersheba and cry "'Tis all barren."'

LONDON:

RICHARD BENTLEY, NEW BURLINGTON STREET.

1860.

LONDON: PRINTED BY W. CLOWES AND SONS, STAMFORD STREET.

TO

CHEYNE BRADY, ESQ.

(OF DUBLIN,)

THIS WORK

IS INSCRIBED BY HIS SINCERE FRIEND,

THE AUTHOR.

MARCH, 1860.

ADVERTISEMENT.

THE following sketches appeared during the past twelve months in the DUBLIN UNIVERSITY MAGAZINE; and the very favourable reception they met with from the public has induced the author to republish them in the present form.

March, 1860.

CONTENTS.

THE SEASON-TICKET.

No. I.

AN EVENING AT CORK.

EVERYTHING has altered its dimensions, except the world we live in. The more we know of that, the smaller it seems. Time and distance have been abridged, remote countries have become accessible, and the antipodes are upon visiting terms. There is a reunion of the human race; and the family likeness, now that we begin to think alike, dress alike, and live alike, is very striking. The South Sea Islanders, and the inhabitants of China, import their fashions from Paris, and their fabrics from Manchester, while Rome and London supply missionaries to the ' ends of the earth,' to bring its inhabitants into ' one fold, under one Shepherd.' Who shall write a book of travels now? Livingstone has exhausted the subject. What field is there left for a future Munchausen? The far West and the far East have shaken hands and pirouetted together, and it is a matter of indifference whether you go to the moors in Scotland to shoot grouse, to South America to ride an alligator, or to Indian jungles to shoot tigers—there are equal facilities for reaching all, and steam will take you to either with the same ease and rapidity. We have already talked with

B

New York; and as soon as our speaking-trumpet is mended shall converse again. 'To waft a sigh from Indus to the pole,' is no longer a poetic phrase, but a plain matter of fact of daily occurrence. Men breakfast at home, and go fifty miles to their counting-houses, and when their work is done, return to dinner. They don't go from London to the seaside, by way of change, once a year; but they live there, and go to the City daily. The grand tour of our forefathers consisted in visiting the principal cities of Europe. It was a great effort, occupied a vast deal of time, cost a large sum of money, and was oftener attended with danger than advantage. It comprised what was then called, *the world:* whoever had performed it was said to have 'seen the world,' and all that it contained worth seeing. The Grand Tour now means a voyage round the globe, and he who has not made it has seen nothing. I do not say that a man must necessarily be much the wiser for the circumnavigation.

It was remarked of Lord Anson, that he had been three times round the world, but never once in it. But, in his case, the expression was used in a two-fold sense, namely, the globe itself, and the people that dwell on it. If travel does not impart wisdom, which it ought to do, it should at least confer the semblance of it, as we may infer from the phrase, 'he looks as wise as the monkey that had seen the world.' Men who miss the reality, ape the appearance. A Fez cap, and an Albanian cloak, have a classical look, and remind you of Byron, and his romantic love for modern Greece, and it is easier to wear them than to quote Gladstone's Homer. A wide-awake, a grizzly beard, and a gold chain, as massive as a submarine cable, smack of the Australian Diggings; and a cinnamon walking-stick, as heavy as an Irishman's shillelagh, shows that the Melbourne traveller has visited

Ceylon on his way home. A Kossuth hat, with a buckle in front as large as that on a coach-trace, a bowie knife, or Arkansas toothpick, inserted like a carpenter's rule into the seam of the leg of the trousers, a pair of long India-rubber boots, and a figured calico shirt-front, half concealed by a Poncho cape, the breast of which discloses a revolver, are hieroglyphic characters, that, duly interpreted, mean California. The French hat, the extreme coat, and the peg-top trousers, bespeak the British raw material, got up at Paris. Everybody wishes to be thought to have travelled, and those who have been unable to enrich their minds, seldom fail to exhibit their foreign spoils on their persons. All this, however, is becoming obsolete. Everybody travels now; and it is no more distinction to have crossed the Andes, to have visited Japan, or to have effected the Arctic Passage, than to have ascended the dome of St. Paul's. There is nothing new under the sun. The visible objects of nature, under their varying aspects, are familiar to us all. We must, at last, turn to what we ought to have studied first—ourselves. 'The proper study of mankind is man.' I have myself lately returned from making the grand tour. I have not seen all the world, but I have looked at a great part of it; and if I am not much wiser for my travels at present, I flatter myself it is because I have not been able to apply the information I have gained, by comparing what I have seen with what I knew before I set out, and what I *find*, on my return, to be the condition of my own country. There are some things not very easy to realize. I find it difficult to believe that I am at last safe at home, and still more so, that I have actually performed this circumnavigation. Here I am, however, at Southampton at last; but every morning I feel as if it was time to move on: the propulsion is on me, and I cannot stop. I go to London, and as soon as I reach it the same restlessness seizes me, and I feel impelled to return. The safest as well as the pleasantest way to ease the speed is to lower the steam, until motion shall gradually cease. I have taken a Season-Ticket, and shall travel to and from London, until the monotony wearies me, and I can again enjoy home. I shall occupy myself in noting down whatever I hear and see, and in studying the characters of those I meet. I shall compare civilized with uncivilized man, and I feel already that the very possession of the means of comparison is of itself one great benefit I have derived from travelling.

Last week I varied the scene, by accompanying my old college friend Cary, to Monkstown, in Ireland. While he was employed in negociating some business of importance, I amused myself by exploring the various objects of interest in the neighbourhood. As I have already observed, I have visited many parts of the world, and seen much beautiful scenery; but take it all in all, or, as the Yankees say, 'every which way you can fix it,' I know nothing superior to that which is presented to the tourist, in a sail from the entrance of Queenstown to the city of Cork. An uninvited and unwelcome guest, on his arrival at a country house in England, expatiated on the splendid views he had seen on his journey thither, and when asked by which road he had travelled, was very significantly informed that he would pass through a much more lovely country on *his return that afternoon*, if he took another, and a shorter route, that was pointed out to him.

Unlike my gruff and inhospitable countryman, I advise you, when at Cork, to remain there, till you have ' done ' the city, and its environs, and then to sail down the river, that you may behold the same objects you had previously

seen, from a different point of view. It is difficult to say
whether the ascent or descent is most beautiful; but on
the whole, I give the preference to the former, on account
of the magnificent panorama which so suddenly bursts on
your astonished view, as you enter the harbour from the
sea. Nor is the climate of this lovely locality less admirable than its scenery; it is so soft, so mild, and so
genial in winter, and so temperate and salubrious in
summer. No foreign watering places that I am acquainted
with are to be compared with those on the Lee for
invalids.

There is only one thing I do not like here, and as I am
a discriminating traveller, and endeavour to be impartial
and just, I must enter my protest, and then pass on
When we cast anchor near the Flag-ship of the Admiral,
I desired a boatman to take me to 'Cove.' 'Sure,' said
he, 'your honour is in Cove now.' 'Yes,' I replied, 'I
know that, but I want to land at Cove,' pointing to the
beautiful town that rose, terrace above terrace, from the
water's edge to the summit of the hill that protects and
shelters the magnificent sheet of water, which it proudly
overlooks.

'Ah, yer honour, it's no longer the Cove any more; it's
Queenstown it's called now, ever since her Majesty the
Queen landed here. Just as the fine ould harbour,
Dunleary, near Dublin, was christened Kingstown, in
honour of the visit of an English king that is dead and
gone. Ah, yer honour,' he said, with a sigh, 'we
hardly know our own names now-a-days.'

I sympathize with poor Pat. 'The Cove of Cork' is
known all over the world. Every map, chart, and
nautical vocabulary contains a registry of it, and no Act
of Parliament, Proclamation, or Gazette, will ever ob-
literate it from Jack's memory, or poor Pat's either. And

besides all this, its new appellation is an unmeaning one. All the towns in the Empire are the Queen's, and 'all that in them is,' God bless her! and in after days the people of this place will know as little which Queen did them the honour to visit them, as my 'Covey' did which sovereign adopted Kingstown as his own. Our North American friends have better taste; they are everywhere restoring the ancient Indian names. Toronto has superseded York, and Sissiboo, Weymouth; even Halifax, forgetful of its patron, desires to be known as Chebuctoo; while the repudiating Yankees are equally ambitious that their far-famed city, New York, should be called Manhattan.

My object, however, is not to detain you longer on the banks of the lovely Lee, but to introduce you to the smoking-room of the Imperial Hotel at Cork.

I like a smoking-room, first, because I am uncommonly fond of a cigar (and there are capital ones to be had at the Imperial, as you may suppose from the numerous friends of old Ireland that reside in America); and secondly, because there is a freemasonry in smoking, not that it possesses secrets of a dangerous nature, but that it incites and promotes conversation. It is freemasonry without its exclusiveness. Its sign is the pipe or the cigar, its object good fellowship. Men sometimes quarrel over their cups, over their pipes, never. The Indians of America always commenced their councils with the calumet. It gave them time to arrange their thoughts, and its soothing effect on their nerves predisposed them to peace. When I was a boy, I always waited till I saw my father in the full enjoyment of his pipe, before I asked any little favour I was desirous of obtaining from him. A man who is happy himself, is willing to contribute to the happiness of others.

To a traveller smoking is invaluable. It is a companion in his solitary hours; it refreshes him when fatigued; it assuages the cravings of hunger; it purifies the poisonous atmosphere of infected places, whether jungles or cities. It conciliates strangers, it calms agitation, and makes you feel all the resignation and all the charities of a Christian. The knowledge of this precious plant, Tobacco, and its many virtues, is one of the advantages we derive from travelling.

Before I proceed further, gentle reader, let me tell you, there are three things I recommend to your notice in visiting Ireland. If you are an admirer of beautiful scenery, go to the Cove of Cork. If you want a good hotel, go to the Imperial; if you want good tobacco, go to the smoking-room there. I may add also, you will find more than good pipes and cigars, for you will meet with a vast deal of amusement, as some droll fellows do congregate there. On this occasion when I visited this 'cloud-capped' scene, two strangers sauntered into the room, and drawing chairs to my table, on which the light was placed, at once entered into conversation, with all the ease of old stagers. They were evidently Yankees. One was a tall, thin, sallow man, at least as far as I could judge of his complexion, for he sported a long beard and a profusion of hair on his face. He was dressed in black, the waistcoat being of a shining satin, surmounted by several coils of gold chain, and his coat, (something between a jacket and a frock,) having capacious side pockets, into each of which was deposited a hard, rough fist. His neckcloth was a loose tie, which was graced by a turn-down collar, and fringed by a semicircular belt of hair, that in its turn overlaid it. His hat was low-crowned, the rim of which curled

into rolls at the sides, and projected before and behind into peaks, not unlike those of a travelling cap.
His boots were canoe-shaped, long and narrow, and
upturned in front, giving you the idea of a foot that
had no toes. As he seated himself at the table, he took
off his hat, and from among some loose papers collected a few stray cigars, which he deposited on the
table. Lighting one of them, he handed another to me,
saying,

'Stranger, will you try one of mine? they are rael
right down genu*ine* Havannahs, and the flavour is none
the worse for not paying duty, I guess. They ain't
bad.'

Then turning to his companion, he said,

'Ly, won't you cut in and take a hand?'

'Ly,' whom I afterwards discovered to be the Honourable Lyman Boodle, a senator from Michigan, and a
colleague of General Cass, the American Secretary of
State for Foreign Affairs, was a sedate-looking person, as
a senator ought to be. He was a smooth-faced, well-
shaven man, with an expression of complacency that
seemed to indicate he was at peace with himself and all
the world. He was dressed like a Methodist preacher,
in a plain suit of black, and sported a whitey-brown
choker of the orthodox shape and tie. It was manifest he
was a person of importance, both wise and circumspect,
a statesman, and a divine, and equally respectable as an
orator and a preacher. It is difficult to imagine a
greater contrast than that existing between these two
countrymen and friends. One was a rollicking, noisy,
thoughtless fellow, caring little what he said or did, up to
anything and equal to everything; the other, a wise and
sententious man, with a mind intent on great things, the

greatest of which was probably the presidential chair of the United States.

'Let's liquor, Ly,' said the tall one; 'what do you ambition? Shall it be whisky, ale, rum, brandy, gin, or what not, for they hain't no compounds here, no mint juleps, cocktails, sherry cobblers, gum ticklers, phlegm cutters, chain lightning, or sudden death. Simples is what they go on, they don't excel in drinks, they have no skill in manufacturing liquids. The Irish can't eat nothing but tators, and drink nothing but whisky, and talk nothing but priests and patriots, ructions and repeals. They don't do nothen like nobody else. Their coats are so long they drag on the ground, like the tail of a Nantucket cow, which is so cussed poor that she can't hold it up, and their trousers are so short they don't reach below their knees, with two long strings dangling from them that are never tied, and three buttons that never felt an eyelet hole; and wear hats that have no roofs on 'em. The pigs are fed in the house, and the children beg on the road. They won't catch fish for fear they would have to use them in Lent, nor raise more corn than they eat, for fear they would have to pay rent. They sit on their cars sideways, like a gall on a side-saddle, and never look ahead, so they see but one side of a thing, and always act and fight on one side; there is no *two ways* about them. And yet, hang me if I don't like them, take them by and large, better than the English, who are as heavy and stupid as the porter they guzzle all day—who hold their chins so everlastin' high, they don't see other folks' toes they are for ever a-treadin' on—who are as proud as Lucifer, and ape his humility; as rich as Crœsus, and as mean as a Jew; talking from one year's eend to another of educating the poor, and wishing the devil had flown away with Dr. Faustus before he ever invented types; praising us for

B 3

ever, and lamenting Columbus hadn't gone to the bottom
of the sea, instead of discovering America; talking of
reform from July to etarnity, and asking folks if they
don't hope they may get it; annoying every——'

'Hush, Mr. Peabody,' said the Senator, casting a fur-
tive glance at me, fearing I might take offence; 'pray
don't go ahead that way, you might, you know, come into
collision, and who knows which may get the worst of that?
Folk don't like to hear their country abused arter that
fashion; it don't convene to good manners, and the
amenities of life. For my part, I think the Irish are a
very sharp people.' 'Sharp,' said the other, 'why there
is nothen sharp on this side the water, unless it's a policeman. Why, stranger,' he continued, addressing me,
'all natur's sharp in America—the frost is sharp, the
knives are sharp, the men are sharp, the women are sharp,
and if they ain't, their tongues be, everything is sharp
there. Why my father's vinegar was so cussed sharp,
the old gentleman shaved with it once; he did upon my
soul. Ah, here is the waiter! I say, Mister, whisky for
three. That fellow don't know the word Mister, I'll be
darned if he does. He puts me in mind of a Patlander,
a friend of mine hired here lately. Last month, Gineral
Sampson Dove, of Winnepusa, married the darter of the
American *Keo*unsel (consul) to Dublin, Miss Jemima
Fox. Did you ever see her, stranger?'

'Never,' I said.

'Well,' he replied, 'that's a cruel pity, for you would
have seen a peeler, I tell you—a rael corn-fed gall, and
no mistake. Just what Eve was, I guess, when she walked
about the garden, and angels came to see her, and wished
they had flesh and blood like her, and weren't so everlastin' thin and vapoury, like sunbeams. Lick! man,
she was a whole team, and a dog under the waggon, I

tell you. Well, they first went to Killarney, on a wedding *tower*, and after they had stared at that lovely place, till they hurt their eyes, they came down here, to see the Groves of Blarney, and what not. Well, the Gineral didn't want folks to know they were only just married, for people always run to the winders and doors, to look at a bride, as if she was a bird that was only seen once in a hundred years, and was something that was uncommon new to look upon. It's onconvenient, that's a fact, and it makes a sensi*t*ive, delicate-minded gall feel as awkward as a wrong boot. So says the Gineral to Pat, "Pat," says he, "don't go now, and tell folks we are only just married, lie low, and keep dark, will you, that's a good fellow." "Bedad," says Pat, "never fear, yer honner, the divil a much they'll get out of me, I can tell you. Let me alone for that, I can keep a secret as well as ever a priest in Ireland." Well, for all that, they *did* stare, in a way that was a caution to owls, and no mistake, and well they might too, for it ain't often they saw such a gall as Miss Jemima, I can tell you, though the Irish galls warn't behind the door neither when beauty was given out, that's a fact. At last the Gineral see something was in the wind, above common, for the folks looked amazed in the house, and they didn't seem over half pleased either. So says he, one day, "Pat," says he, "I hope you did not tell them we were only just married, did you?" "Tell them you was just married, is it, yer honner," said he, "let me alone for that! They were mighty inquisitive about it, and especially the master, he wanted to know all about it entirely. "Married, is it," says I, "why they ain't married at all, the divil a parson ever said grace over them! But, I'll tell you what (for I was determined it was but little truth he'd get out of me,)—I'll tell you what," says I, "if you won't repeat it to nobody,

They are goin' to be married in about a fortnight, for I
heard them say so this blessed day, with my own ears."
If the Gineral wasn't raving, hopping mad, it ain't no
matter.   In half an hour, he and his wife were on board
the steamer for England, and Pat is in bed here yet, from
the licking he got.   It ain't clear to me, if he ever will
see his error, for both his eyes are knocked into one, and
all he can perceive are a thousand sparks of fire before
him, as if he was looking down the chimney of a blacksmith's shop.   Come, Ly, I like your calling such a fellow
as that sharp.   But 'spose we try the whisky.'

In the course of conversation (if such rhodomontade
can be called conversation) allusion was made to Vancouver's Island, which I have always regretted I had not
seen.   I had visited California, but as this new colony
was not then either settled, or much known, I went from
San Francisco to the Sandwich Islands, and it is only since
my return that it has become an object of such universal
interest.   Wishing for information, I applied to the Senator, instead of Mr. Peabody, as I knew he was more
likely to talk to the point than the other.   ' Yes,' he said,
' I have but recently come from there; I can tell you all
about it   It is, to my mind, the most important spot in
the whole world, and will affect and control the commerce
of the greatest part of it.'   ' May I ask,' I said, ' what is
the geographical extent of the island ?'   ' It is as large as
a piece of chalk,' said his tall friend.   ' Do be quiet,
Peabody,' said the Senator; ' there is a time for all things,
but you find time for only one, and that is nonsense.'
' Well, stranger,' said the incorrigible joker, ' if you don't
like a piece of chalk for a measure, and I think it's a
capital one, for it may be as small as what a carpenter
carries in his pocket, or as big as the Leviathan, I'll tell
you its exact size.   It's as big as all out-doors, and you

know how big that is, and if you don't (for Britishers are everlastin' pitikilar), I'll go and get you my map;' saying which, he left the room on his well-meant errand. 'That's a droll fellow,' said the Senator; 'but he is not the fool you take him for; there is more in him than there appears to be. By that free-and-easy way, and his strange talk, he induces people to converse, and while they are amusing themselves with him, he contrives to learn from them all that they know, and all they think upon any particular subject he is interested in. Bear with him, and he will give you information on any subject whatever connected with North America. Vancouver's Island,' he continued, ' is about 270 miles long, and, on an average, from forty to fifty miles broad. Its greatest breadth is seventy miles, and its least twenty-eight; while in one place it is nearly intersected by water, the portage being only eight miles. Its size is, however, of little consequence, as the adjoining territory of the English on the mainland of British Columbia is boundless in extent. It is its position, its harbours, its coal, its fisheries, and its political and commercial importance that render it so invaluable. From San Francisco to the Russian boundary it contains the only secure harbour in a distance of several thousand miles, and even the former is so large, it is by no means safe at all times, as it partakes too much of the character of a roadstead. Whoever owns Vancouver's Island must command the trade of the Pacific and the East; I say nothing of its lying at the entrance of Frazer's River, and receiving the gold from those regions; that is merely a means to an end—I speak of it as the terminus of the Great Inter-Oceanic Railway. The harbour of Esquimault, on the Pacific, corresponds in every particular with the noble port of Halifax, Nova Scotia, on the Atlantic. The railway from the latter to the boundary of New Brunswick, is now nearly finished, and in a year or two will connect with the Canadian line below Quebec, when an uninterrupted communication will be completed from Halifax to Lake Superior. It will then require to be continued from thence to Vancouver's Island, and you will have an overland route from the Atlantic to the Pacific, lying wholly through British territory. Already the Canadians are opening the way through the Red River and Winipeg territory, by connecting the lakes and rivers on the line of traffic, by good portages, by placing steamers on the former and railways on the latter, so as to render the passage short, easy, and expeditious. This is the first step towards the completion of that grand railway line that is to be the route from Europe to China, Japan, the Sandwich Islands, Australia, and the East. The country between Lake Superior and the Pacific is of a nature to support countless millions of inhabitants, while its vast internal navigation, like that of Canada, supplies means of transport unknown in any other part of the world. It is not the size of Vancouver's Island, therefore, that is of importance ; it is its political, geographical, and commercial position that we must regard.'

'Zactly,' said Mr. Peabody, who now returned with the map, and spread it out on the table. 'Zactly, Ly ; now you have hit the nail on head, smack,' and, suiting the action to the word, he hit the palm of his left hand a blow with his right fist, that made a noise precisely like that occasioned by a hammer. 'That's the ticket! Ly warn't born yesterday ; stranger, he has a large mind, sir. It's like a surveyor's tape-box, take hold of the ring, sir, give it a pull, and out comes a hundred yards, all marked and dotted into inches and feet—there is no mistake in him, he is as exact as a sum proved by algebry ; but it ain't every one he lets put his finger into the tape-ring

and draw him out, I can tell you. He knows how to
keep his clam-shell shut, when he don't think proper to
let on. Yes, *Sirree*—he is right. The largest city in
the world will be in Esquimault and Victoria, for it will
cover both harbours, and the neck of land between them.
And see where it lies! not in the frozen North, or in the
brilin' South, but between the parallels 48 and 51 North
Latitude, and in West Longitude between 123 and 128,
which is as near perfection on that warm sea as anything
this side of Paradise can be. For it's tropical enough
for oranges, and North enough for potatoes: and both
are so large, so fine, and so plenty, they ain't to be ditto'd
nowhere. The reason I compared it to a piece of chalk,
stranger, was because I didn't know whether you could
grasp the subject or not, but I perceive you can see as
far into a millstone as them that picked the hole into it.'

' What is the nature of the soil, is that good ?' ' Well,
it's like little England, which the bragging English call
Great Britain, some good, some indifferent, and some
everlastin' bad. But what's good, beats all natur'. I
tried it once, when I was there prospectin, that is, looking
out for land to speculate in : well, the vessel I came in
had been formerly in the guano trade, and I scooped out
of the hold about a handful of that ere elixir of vegetation,
and went and strewed some on the ground, and sowed a
few cucumber seeds in it. Well, sir, I was considerable
tired when I had done it, for I had to walk ever so far
round, like a lawyer examinin' of a witness, not to let
folks see what I was a doin' of; and when I had done, I
just took a stretch for it, under a great pine tree, and
took a nap. Stranger! as true as I am talking to you
this here blessed minit, when I woke up, I was bound as
tight as a sheep going to market on a butcher's cart, and
tied fast to the tree. I thought I never should get out of

that scrape, the cucumber vines had grown and twisted so round and round me and my legs while I was asleep! Fortunately, one arm was free, so I got out my jack-knife, opened it with my teeth, and cut myself out—no easy job, either, I can tell you—and off for Victoria again, hot-foot. When I came into the town, says our Captain to me, " Peabody, what in natur' is that ere great yaller thing that's a sticking out of your pocket?" " Nothin'," sais I, looking as amazed as a puppy nine days old, when he first opens his eyes, and takes his first stare. Well, I put in my hand to feel ; and, upon my soul, I pulled out a great big, ripe cucumber, a foot long, that had ripened and gone to seed there. Now, that's what guano did for the soil, stranger. Capital and labour will do the same for the colony : it will grow as fast as that ere cucumber did.'

' And look seedy as soon,' said I. 'Stranger,' he replied, with a loud laugh, '*you may take my hat*, I owe you a chalk for that. Let's liquor. Waiter, whisky for three.'

' Do be quiet, Peabody,' said the Senator. 'At all times and under any circumstances, sir, this island was so important, that it is astonishing the British Government could have suffered it to remain for so long a period in the paralysing grasp of the Hudson's Bay Company. But now that steam has superseded canvas, where 'else on the whole Western coast of America is there a place to be found, with such harbours, and such extensive and valuable coal-fields? The coal at Ninaimo, which is of excellent quality, is found within a few yards of the water side, and vessels drawing sixteen feet can anchor close to the shore. The coal consists of two seams, each six feet thick, overlaying each other at a short distance, and is in sufficient quantity to supply, for ages to come, all the demands of domestic or foreign consumption, of commerce, or manufactures. There is excellent anchorage in all parts of the harbour of Nanaimo, which is commodious, and sheltered from all winds; and as there is a rise and fall of fifteen feet, at spring tides, and the bottom is soft clay, it forms an excellent careening ground for vessels, and presents many of the advantages of a graving dock. The timber on the island is, in many parts, of a most superior quality for masts, spars, or piles. Many of the trees growing in the rich valleys attain a height of two hundred and fifty feet, and a circumference of forty-two feet at the butt.'

' Pray, what is the name of that tree,' I said.

' It is called the Abies Nobilis.'

' Stranger,' said Mr. Peabody, ' I see you lift your eyebrows at that, as if you wanted an affidavit to the fact. I'll tell you where to prospect for them granadiers. Go to Stoke Harbour and you will find lots of them, as stiff and tall as church steeples. Lord, I shall never forget the first time I see them. I paid a crittur, called Spencer Temple, a broken-down English lawyer, five pounds to show me the locations. When we returned to Victoria, the varmint spent the whole of the money in brandy, until he was a caution to sinners to behold. At last I got him up to my room, and had a bed made for him in one corner. Well, one night the crittur bounced out of bed, in a ravin', tarin' fit, and standin' up in his shirt tail before my sea chest, which he took for a judge, sais he, making a low bow to it, "My lord," said he, "I must apologise to you for appearing before you without my coat and trousers, but a Yankee loafer, of the name of Peabody, has stolen them." "You miserable skunk," sais I, " I'd cowhide you if you were worth the leather, but you ain't. Your mother don't know you. Your skin is too loose for you, the galls

don't like you, and what's more, you are a cussed bad
bake into the bargain. Take that," says I, fetchin' him a
wipe across his back with my shot-bag. With that, he
jumped up on eend till his head struck the ceilin', and
then, fallin' on his knees, and holdin' up both his hands,
he said, "My lord, I plead guilty, and throw myself on
the mercy of the court—I will read an affidavit in mitiga-
tion of punishment." " Into bed with you," sais I ; and I
up with him in my arms, and forced him in, and then
made him swaller a glass of brandy and laudanum. I
had a tempestical time with him, I tell you.'

' The Fisheries,' continued the Senator, ' are on a scale
that is almost incredible. In August and September, the
water is literally alive with salmon, of which there are
seven distinct kinds. They are fine large fish, sometimes
weighing from fifty to sixty pounds, and, on an average,
thirty of them, when cured, fill a barrel. Enormous
quantities are caught by the Indians, who sell them to
the Hudson's Bay Company, by whom they are exported
to the Sandwich Islands, San Francisco, and the Spanish
main. Herrings are also taken in immense numbers,
likewise cod and halibut. In short, as regards the fishery,
Vancouver's Island is to the Pacific what Newfoundland
is to the Atlantic. The native hemp of the country has
been proved, both in New York and New Orleans, to be
superior to that of Russia. To all these advantages,
which would be otherwise useless, we must add the
harbours. I say nothing of those on the Sound and Straits
(and they are very numerous), but I speak of Esquimault
and Victoria, which are only three miles distant from each
other by water, and at one point only separated by a strip
of land six hundred yards wide. Esquimault is a circular
bay or basin, hollowed by nature out of the solid rock.
Sailing through a narrow entrance between two low, rocky

promontories you suddenly enter a land-locked harbour, that looks like a lake in a pine forest. It affords good anchorage, is very capacious, and has a depth of from five to eight fathoms of water. The environs are admirably suited for a city, and the entrance is so constructed by nature, that it can be easily fortified. The adjoining harbour of Victoria, where the capital is situated, though smaller, and not so deep, is admitted by all who have seen it, to present the most beautiful plateau for a city in the world, which, as I have already said, will, at no distant day, cover the whole promontory that separates it from the other and larger port, and present the singular spectacle of a town having two harbours and two entrances. I have told you (but I must repeat it, for it is most important to remember), that these two places, Esquimault and Victoria, or, perhaps, I might designate both as Victoria Bay, offer, with the exception of smaller ones, belonging to Vancouver, the only safe and approachable harbour, for several thousand miles of coast. I have hitherto spoken to you of the Island, without reference to British Columbia; I have alluded merely to itself, its resources, and its climate; but when you consider its position in reference to the main land, the fertile region of Frazer's River and Columbia, the Saskatchewan, the Red River, and the Canadas, and view it as the terminus of a line of railway from Halifax, Nova Scotia, on the Atlantic, and the centre of the trade of the East, you feel as if you required to pause and consider the subject in all its bearings, before you can at all appreciate the influence this young England is to exercise on the destinies of the world.'

' Hear him, stranger,' said Peabody, ' do for goodness gracious sake, now, just hear him; how good he talks, don't he? what a candid man he is, ain't he? Ly, you do beat the devil! Stranger! he is only a bammin of

you ; he knows as well as I do, we must 'nex it ; we can't
help it, no how we can fix it. Go on, and lay your railway, build the city, open the trade, erect churches, and
appoint a bishop, make the dock-yards, construct the forts,
and when you have done, let us know, and we will 'nex it.
We can't afford to let you hold it, no more than we can
afford to let Spain hold Cuby. We want them, and what
we want we must have—that's a fact. It's contrary to the
Munro doctrine, and the American destiny, that foreigners
should plant new colonies in America. The first time
you are engaged in war with some continental power, our
people will go over there in shoals, call a public meeting,
declare the place independent, hoist our noble goose and
gridiron flag, and ask Congress to be 'nexed to the greatest
nation in all creation ! ! We shall then acknowledge the
country as independent, and as a great favour, 'nex it,
and receive its members into Congress, and how can you
stop us ? It ain't in the natur of things you can.'

'My good friend,' I said, ' although I have never been at
Vancouver's Island, I am well acquainted with Canada, its
people, and their loyal feeling. They now number three
millions, which is about the extent of the population of
the old colonies, when they revolted, and achieved their
independence. If at that time you were able successfully
to resist the whole force of Great Britain, I assure you
the Canadians are fully competent to defend their territory, and resolved to do so against aggression. They
have not only no desire for annexation with the United
States, but would consider it a great misfortune ; nor do
I believe the acquisition of British North America is desired by the intelligent portion of your people, even if
it were practicable. There may be some excuse for your
desiring an increase of territory on the south, as your
commerce and peace are both endangered and disturbed

by the repeated revolutions among your Mexican neighbours, who are equally unable to govern themselves, or protect the lives and property of foreigners, who are resident among them. The inhabitants of British North America would deeply deplore a severance of the connexion with Great Britain; and if such an event should ever occur, it will not arise from the annexation or conquest of their country by you, nor from a successful contest with the parent state, but from the natural course of events, in which colonies become too populous to be dependent, and their interests too complicated and important to be regulated otherwise than on the spot, by entire self-government. And be assured, that if they do become independent, it will be by the mutual consent and good-will of both parties, and, let me add, the mutual regret also. Indeed, now that steam has bridged the Atlantic, and the electric telegraph annihilated distance, I cannot conceive how a separation can conduce to the interests of either party. The topic is not an agreeable one ; suppose we discuss it no farther.'

'I entirely agree with you,' said the Senator. 'Noisy demagogues may boast and brag about our destiny, but no sensible man among us desires the incorporation of British North America into our federal union. We have as much territory as we can govern; and, as Vancouver's Island will be the great naval station of England on the Pacific, it will be as easily defended as any other portion of the empire. The system of government in the British Provinces is, in many respects, different from ours; and we may both borrow from each other many instructive lessons. We must take care that a colony does not exhibit more real freedom, more respect for the laws, and more security for life and property than our great Republic; while the Provincial Government must be equally careful that their institutions are of a kind not to engender among its people a feeling of inferiority to their neighbours, or a desire to acquire rights which are enjoyed on the other side of their border, but withheld from them. As it is, your taxes, both municipal and colonial, are infinitely less than ours. We are content, and I am not aware that we could improve our condition. Go on and prosper. The happier you are, the better neighbours you will be to us; and the more prosperous you become, the more intimate and valuable will be our commercial relations. There is room for us both. As a proof of what I have said, so soon as your great railway line shall have been completed from Lake Superior to the Pacific, our China trade will pass through it as far as Red River, where a diverging branch will convey our goods and passengers to St. Paul's, in Minnesota, and from thence diffuse it over the whole Union. We are both equally interested in this route, for all the practicable passes through the Rocky Mountains are in British Columbia, and the only harbours for large ships are situated in Vancouver's Island. One thing is certain, the Australian, Japan, and Sandwich Islands Mails and passengers must pass through this line, as well as the traffic to and from China. But, tell me, please, how could your government have hermetically sealed, for so many years, that fertile and vast country lying between Lake Superior and the Pacific? They tell me that that great hunter, called Bear Ellice, from the number of bears he has destroyed, who rivals Colonel Crockett as a dead shot, and Gordon Cumming for his contests with wild beasts, once a Hudson's Bay Trapper, but now a member of Parliament, is the man who represented the whole territory as a howling wilderness, frozen forty feet deep in winter, and burnt to a

cinder in summer, and frightened Parliament into giving
his Company the monopoly of the trade.'

I could hardly refrain from laughing, to hear this
sensible man talk such nonsense, and fall into such an
absurd mistake. Neither the English nor Americans understand each other ; and both are too apt to give credence
to the most idle reports, and to impute motives that have
no existence but in their own imaginations.

'Mr. Edward Ellice,' I said, 'is no hunter, I assure
you. He is a large landed proprietor in Canada, and a
leading partner of the Hudson's Bay Company, as well
as a conspicuous member of Parliament. He is a man of
great information and much influence, but not distinguished, that ever I heard, for personal encounters with
wild beasts. The sobriquet of " Bear " was given to him
by his Whig friends (who are fond of bestowing nicknames) from a certain brusque manner, and an impatience
of contradiction, though I could never see that he deserved
it more than any other man of fixed opinions.'

'Will you swear,' said Peabody, 'he never killed a
bear ?'

'I cannot undertake to do that,' I said ; 'but I do not
believe he ever shot one, nor do I think he ever had the
opportunity of doing so.'

'Will you swear he never frightened one to death ?
because that's the way I am told he got the name of Bear.
I'll tell you how it was. He was one day out huntin' on
that everlastin' big swamp, back of Red River, and the
day was dark and cloudy, and he lost his way ; so down
he puts his rifle, and up he climbs a great big dead pine
tree as tall as a factory chimney, to see which course to
steer. Well, when he got to the top, and surveyed the
country all round, and see'd where he was, just as he
turned to descend, he thought he heerd a noise in the tree,

and seeing that it was hollow, what does he do but let
himself down into it like a sweep ; but, as he got near the
butt, the size of the hollow increased, so he couldn't
brace himself no longer, either by his hands or feet, and
he slipped right down to the bottom chewallop, and what
should he find there but two young cubs. Well, he gev
himself up for lost. He knew he couldn't crawl up again ;
and he knew if the old bear came arter him there would
be no room to fight her, and he would be chawed up like
a piece of baccy. Well, while he was thinkin' the matter
over, all at once he heard an awful grunt, and the place
grew dismal dark, for the bear was coming down, raving,
roaring, distracted mad, starn foremost, as bears always
do. What does *he* do, when he sees the fix he was in, but
stand below, and, as the bear was about touchin' bottom
with her hind legs, he seizes hold of her by the fur of her
thighs with his hands, gives a tremendous, great, long,
enduring yell, like a panther, and then seizes the tail in
his teeth, and bit away like a shark. Up runs the bear
as fast as she could, dragging Ellice after her, who, when
he got to the top, gave another nip and another yell, and
then slid down the tree arter the bear, got hold of his gun,
and just as he levelled on her, down she dropt dead from
fright ; so he just skinned her, and made tracks for the
Fort. Ever arter that they called him " Bear Ellice ;"
fact, I assure you.'

' Why, Peabody,' said the Senator, ' that's Colonel
Crockett's story ; why, surely, you know better than that.'

' Well,' replied the other, ' so I always thought it was
the Colonel that performed that are feat, and when I was
at the diggins to Frazer's River, I told that story one
night, as Colonel Crockett's, but there wer a Scotchman
there, a great, tall, raw-boned critter, as hard as a racer
and as lank as a greyhound, and Scotch like (for they

boast of having done every clever thing since the flood),
he swore it was their great factor and hunter, Ellice, that
did it. I bet twenty dollars with him on it, and we left
it to the company to decide, and as there was only seven
of us in camp, and five were Scotchmen, they gev it
against me, in course, and I paid down the money, and
did the thing genteel. Well, plague take the money, I
don't care for that, but I am proper glad to hear it was
Crockett arter all, for the credit of our great nation. If
ever I meet that are great, gaunt Scotchman again, I'll
take the money out of his pocket, or the valy out of his
hide! see if I don't.'

' Well, well,' said the Senator, ' if that don't beat all,
it's a pity ; how hard it is to believe what you hear, ain't
it, let your authority be ever so good ? Perhaps, after
all, the thing never happened to either, and was what we
call " made out of whole cloth." But that monopoly was
a foolish thing, and well-nigh cost you the country, for
had it not been for the discovery of gold at Frazer's River,
it is probable the whole territory would have passed by
possession and squatting into our hands.' ' How is it,' I
said, ' you talk so little about the gold fields?' ' Because,' he replied, ' as I before observed, I consider them
merely " as the means to an end." I have been speaking
of that which depends on industry and enterprise, of permanent intrinsic resources, of a commanding position, of a
commercial depôt, that, with our knowledge of the globe,
can never be rivalled. The gold deposits will attract the
population necessary to settle the country, and nurture
and mature its commerce ; but it has a value far beyond
" the diggings " that will enrich it for ages after the gold
fields have been exhausted. I do not undervalue the immense auriferous deposits of British Columbia. You
must trust to them to stimulate emigration, but you must

c

look to the country itself to retain the population thus attracted. The diggers must be fed, and their expenditure
will support the farmer and the fisherman, until extended
commerce will require and repay the united efforts of all.
In a few years the whole face of the country will be
changed, and communities and cities will start into existence as if by magic. The enterprise, science, and energy
of the West, will require and command the labour of the
East, and Vancouver will be the centre where the products
of both hemispheres will be exchanged.'

'What do you make the distance,' I said, 'from Liverpool to Vancouver's Island, *via* Halifax, for much of
what you say must depend upon that?' 'I estimate,' he
said, ' the entire distance at about 5,600 miles—

	MILES.
Liverpool to Halifax, say	2,466
From Halifax to Quebec	600
Thence to Lake Huron, is	500
Thence to the head of Lake Superior	534
Thence, *via* Red River and diggings to the mouth of Frazer's River, on the Pacific	1,500
	5600

That is, the passage to Halifax will occupy nine days,
and the journey thence to Vancouver's Island, six days—
in all, fifteen days to the Pacific from Liverpool. Why,
stranger, I was once fifty-five days in a sailing-vessel,
making the voyage from England to Boston. You will
remember the route, with the exception of the Atlantic, is
wholly through British America, while the shortest one,
now in use, through Panama, is 8,200 miles, being 2,600
miles longer than by the Canadian route. From Vancouver's Island to Canton, the distance is 6,900 miles, and to
Sydney, 8,200. Thus, the saving in distance is such that
the mails can be conveyed to Australia in ten days less
than by Panama, while the journey to Pekin can be per-

formed in thirty days. But enough has been said; you have the shortest possible route, and the most practicable, through your own territory, from one ocean to the other, the finest harbours in the world (Halifax and Es-quimault), abundance of coal at the termini, and the most direct communication with all the eastern world. With the exception of the sea voyages, you can proceed from London to the Himalaya mountains on the borders of China, through British possessions. And now, what do you say to the route to bed?' 'Good night, and good-bye,' I said; 'I have to thank you for a very agreeable and instructive evening, and am sorry we must part so soon. I embark for Southampton to-morrow; here is my address; I shall be happy to see you there.'

'Thank you,' he replied; 'we shall find ourselves there next week, and hope to have the pleasure of meeting you again.'

'Stranger,' said Mr. Peabody, as he shook me by the hand, 'you were not born yesterday, I guess. I was only sparrin', and had the gloves on. If I hit you, it was only a poke given in fun. Good night;' and as he emptied his glass, he added, 'Here's to our next meeting, when-ever and wherever that may be.'

No. II.

WALKS, TALKS, AND CHALKS.

THE older I grow the less reliance I place on circum-
stantial, or what lawyers call presumptive evidence. This,
we are told, is founded upon the connexion which human
experience demonstrates usually to exist between certain
facts and circumstances and certain other events. When
the one occurs, the others are presumed to accompany
them, almost as a matter of course. The probability is so
strong in some cases, that they say it creates a moral
conviction. In my opinion, this ought not to be called a
presumption of law, but a piece of presumption in lawyers.
Nothing can be more unsafe or uncertain than this mode
of drawing conclusions from probabilities; for my experience accords with that of Rochefoucault, who maintains
that 'what is probable seldom happens.'

Indeed, it appears to me sometimes as if everybody and
everything in the world was perverse. Few things turn
out as you expect. No one does what he is desired to
do; even if he complies with an order he fails to execute
it in the manner and at the time prescribed. Our best-
laid plans are frustrated, and our fondest hopes destroyed;
'The race is not always to the swift, nor the battle to the
strong.' If you wish to exhibit a child to advantage it is
sure to misbehave; if you are anxious to show the walking or trotting powers of a horse, he obstinately refuses

to use either pace, but persists in breaking into a canter;
if he has speed, he either won't exert himself, or he bolts,
and you lose both your patience and your money; if you
have a good church living, your son will not take holy
orders; if you have an entailed estate, your wife most
provokingly presents you with daughters only. Without
any reasonable cause you dislike the heir presumptive,
and your life is consumed in vain regrets that your property
must not only pass away from your family, but go to the
very person above all others in the world whom you do
not wish to be your successor. The rector of your parish,
whom you fondly hoped would be an ally, a confidential
adviser, and a welcome guest, is a thorn in your side that
you can neither extract nor endure. He is either a
Puseyite, who opens the gate, rubs out his Master's marks,
lets his sheep escape and mix with the flock in the next
pasture, and is not honest enough to follow them; or he
is an ultra Evangelical, who despises all ecclesiastical
authority, until he becomes a Bishop, when he preaches
from every text but charity and humility. As a landed
proprietor, you sometimes think his sermon is personal,
and is meant for you; and the congregation seem to be of
the same opinion, for when he alludes to Ahab coveting
his neighbour's vineyard, all eyes are turned upon you.
If, after consulting the moon and the barometer, you give
a fête champetre, as soon as the company assembles a
gale of wind arises, prostrates your tents, and the rain
falls in torrents, driving your dripping guests into the
house; the piano is appealed to as a last resource, and
some wicked friend sings, in mockery of your affliction—

'There's nae luck about the house.'

Nor are you less perverse yourself. If you have to rise
early for a journey you are sure to feel so uncommonly
sleepy that morning, that you would give all the world

for another nap ; if you have a duty to perform, it becomes
irksome, not because it is difficult, but because it must be
done ; it is therefore postponed until the latest moment,
and then something occurs that prevents its being attended
to at all.   Indeed, the events of life, like dreams, appear
in the words of the old proverb, ' to go by con*tra*ries.'

I have been led into this train of reflection by what
occurred in the smoking-room at Cork.   It was natural
to suppose that our conversation, as travellers, would
have turned upon the place we were in, or the country in
which it was situated ; but instead of that, we transported
ourselves more than five thousand miles away, and dis-
coursed upon Vancouver's Island and the Interoceanic
Railway.   It is always so.   At sea we never talk of the
ship, unless it be to ascertain our progress ; and when we
arrive at the port of our destination, the past, and not the
present, occupies our attention.   The reason we are so
little improved by our travels is, we allow our thoughts
to be diverted from the object we had in view when we
left home.   Experience ought to make us wiser ; and I
shall endeavour hereafter not to fall into a similar error.
I have neither the station nor the ability to lead conversation, but I shall strive for the future to turn it to
topics connected with the country in which I am sojourn-
ing.   But what avail good resolutions ?

As I have already said, I had just taken a season ticket
on the line between Southampton and London, and had
no sooner determined on that mode of amusement, than
unforeseen circumstances for a time diverted me from my
plan, and induced me to cross the Channel to Ireland.

It is not very easy to know one's own mind, but we no
sooner arrive at a conclusion than the wind veers, and
we change our course.   The South Western Company
have got my money, and I have my ticket in my pocket.

When shall I use it? Time alone can answer—I cannot.

On the morning after my accidental meeting with the Americans, as related in the last chapter, my friend Cary called to say that unforeseen difficulties having arisen to prevent the completion of the business on which he had come to Ireland, he could not possibly return for several days, and he begged me to remain till he was ready to embark.

'Zackly,' said Mr. Peabody, who just then entered the coffee-room—'Zackly, stranger: hold on by your eyelids and belay where you be. Senator and I are going right slick off to Killarney, like a streak of greased lightning, and will be back agin 'bout the latter eend of the week, as sure as rates. S'posen you go with us. It will help you to pass the time, and that's better nor being caged here like a toad, that's grow'd over when it's asleep with bark, and gets coffined in a pine tree. Let's have some "*walks, talks*, and *chalks*" about the Lakes. Senator can talk "Proverbs of Solomon" to you, for he is well up in the Book of Wisdom, and the Irish are the boys for "Lamentations." It's no wonder they had a famine, when the country raises nothen' but grievances, and that's a crop that grows spontenaciously here. It covers the mountains and bogs, and the hills, and the valleys; it pysons the lawns, and it overruns the parks. It spiles the gravel walks, and it grows in the pavement of the streets. It's like that cussed weed charlock, if you kill one root of it, fifty come to the funeral, and a hundred more put in a claim to the soil. If you go for to weed it, the Devil himself couldn't pull it out without tearing up the wheat along with it. But that's neither here nor there. It's their business—not ourn; and my rule is, to let every feller skin his own foxes. If an Irishman will fill his

knapsack with grievances, he has a right to do so ; he has
to carry it, and not me. I am looking arter fun, not
grievances. You are all packed up. S'posen you jine
Senator and me ? We have both travelled a considerable
sum. I'll swop many nannygoats with you, and give you
boot when you tell the best one. Waiter, put the gentleman's plunder and fixins into the car ;' and before I had
time to reflect, I was off.

        ' Quomecunque rapit tempestas, deferor hospes.'

'Perhaps,' I thought, ' it is all for the best ; as I have
had no opportunity of forming expectations I cannot be
disappointed.'

After we had proceeded a short distance, Peabody
suddenly stood up on the car, and addressing the driver,
said, ' Hallo ! where under the blessed light of the living
sun are you a-going to, you scaly son of a sea-sarpint ?
Didn't I tell you to drive to the Railway ?'

' Sure, yer honner, isn't it to the rael road I am going
with yer honner, and his lordship from England there,'
pointing to me. ' Well, let her went then,' said the
Yankee, ' for I am wrathy, and if I lose the train, the
devil a cent will you get out of my pocket, if you take me
up by the heels and shake me for an hour. Go ahead,'
and he gave a yell that brought to their feet a dozen men
in a field, who were lazily contemplating from the ground
the *incredible* amount of work they had done that morning.
The horse started under its influence into a gallop, which
nearly jerked us off the car, and the driver cast a terrified
glance at the performer, to ascertain whether or not he
had the devil for a passenger, for neither he nor any one
else who had not ascended the head waters of the Mississippi ever before heard such an unearthly shriek. Then,
suddenly, seizing the reins, Peabody stopped the horse,
and said, ' Come now, a joke is a joke, and I have no

objection to one when I fire it off myself, but I ain't a target for every fellow to prac*tise* on, I tell *you*. Now, do you know where you are going, you skulpin, you?'

'Is it do I know where I am going to?'

'Come now, no shuffling, but be straight up and down, like a cow's tail. Say yes or no?'

'Well, I do, yer honner.'

'Where to?'

'To Killarney. Sure I heard yer honner say you was going to Killarney.'

'Yes, but I didn't tell you to go there. I told you to drive to the railway.'

'And so you are on the rael way, yer honner; and the rael way it is for gentlemen like you to travel where you can have the whole carriage to yourselves, and see all the country, instead of being shut up like a convict going to Spike Island, in that coffin of a box on the line, where you can't see nothen for the smoke and the dust, and can't get out to walk up the hills, and stretch your legs, let alone have a pipe. Sure it's myself that knows the country entirely, every inch of it, far and near; all that you can see, let alone what is out of sight, and the demesnes, and them that they belong to, forby them that was the real owners before the confishcations. Didn't I drive the American Ambassador and his niece, God bless 'em both; and didn't they bestow their money on the poor as free as hail. "Pat," says his lordship to me (tho' my name is Larry, for furriners always think an Irishman's name is Pat), "take that trifle, my boy," putting a piece of goold into my hand, that had an aigle on it, wid its wings spread out as if it was making for its own nest at Killarney—"take that, Pat, and drink to the health of the Americans, the friends of old Ireland."'

All this, and more, was addressed to Mr. Peabody,

whom the quick-witted driver soon perceived, from his pronunciation and manner, to be an American; nor was it thrown away upon him; it reconciled him to the trick that had been played upon him, about the railway station. 'But,' said he, before he assented to this change of route, 'how can that horse take so many of us?'

'Take so many of yez, is it? Bedad, he'd take the whole of ye, and two more in the well besides, and be proud to do it, too. He is worth both of Mike Callaghan's nags, who travelled the whole distance with only one leg atween the two.' 'How was that?' said the Yankee. 'Why, he rode one of them hisself, and as he didn't set sideways like a gall, in coorse *there was only one leg atween them.*' 'Stranger,' said Peabody, 'you may take my hat. Score me down for that; you have airned it, and I will stand treat. Drive on!'

It is needless to say that the animal, as Pat knew full well, was unequal to the work, and that we had to hire relays on the road, to complete our journey.

It is not my intention to narrate the incidents on the way, or to speak of the country through which we passed. Guide-books and 'Tours' innumerable have exhausted the subject. Nor shall I attempt to describe the far-famed Lakes, and their varied scenery, at once so sublime and beautiful. Indeed, had I the inclination, I am free to confess I have not the power to do so. I had seen Killarney before on several occasions, and every time came away more and more impressed with its singular beauty. No description I have ever read conveys an adequate idea of the exquisite scenery, and no place I am acquainted with in any part of the world can at all be compared with it. The American lakes are in general too tame and isolated, and those of Canada too large. There is nothing like Killarney; of its kind. It is unique. The

English lakes, lovely though they undoubtedly are, are on a different scale ; and much of the interest attached to the Scotch is poetical and adventitious.   Killarney is as dissimilar as it is superior to them all.   And now that it is so accessible, and the hotel accommodation is so good, it argues either great prejudice or want of taste in English tourists to leave it unvisited.

The Senator expressed the same high opinion of these Irish lakes, but appeared to think that those in the White Mountains of New Hampshire might well bear a comparison with them, and regretted that they were so remote, and so little known. ' I have seen the lakes to which you refer,' I said ; ' but I must beg leave to differ with you when you put them on an equality with these.   The White Mountains are so lofty (for they are the highest range north and east of the Mississippi), that they dwarf, as it were, the lakes they enclose, which seem mere basins, while the evergreen pines and firs (for there is but little variety in the forest trees) are sombre and melancholy, and a sense of loneliness and isolation comes over you that is almost appalling.   Here there is every variety, as well as great luxuriance of foliage—the elm, the ash, the gigantic holly, and the arbutus, are beautifully intermingled, while the mountains not only vary very much in size, but, what is of still more importance, do not overpower the scene.   Everything here is in keeping, and in due proportion, and I may add, in its right place.   The wild, barren, and rocky Gap of Dunloe, instead of protruding into the foreground, is so situated as not only not to disfigure the scene but to prepare you by contrast for the magnificent and gorgeous panorama which so suddenly arrests and enchants you as you emerge from the gorge.   The scenery of the New Hampshire Mountain Lakes is grand, but not pleasing ; and the locality is so apart from the world, that you feel as if you were the first and only man that had ever looked upon it. They have no tone, no light and shade, no mellowness; all is bright, sunny, and dazzling. The outline, though waving and graceful, is too distinct and too sharply defined, while the atmosphere is so dry, and the sky so high and clear, that it presents one unvarying aspect: you can take it all in at one view, and carry away with you a distinct impression of it. But Killarney, from the peculiarity of its climate, displays every variety of expression. The errant fleecy clouds, the passing shower, the translucent mist, and the deep black thunder-cloud, the oft-recurring, often-varying light and shade, and the smiles and tears of nature, must be seen to be appreciated; they defy alike the pencil and the pen. The lake of the White Mountains, like every other in America, has no associations connected with it, and no extrinsic interest. Poetry has clothed it with no charms; History has refused it a name, and excluded it from its pages. The primeval shades of the mountains chill you, and the unbroken silence of its solitude fills you with awe. Killarney, on the other hand, has its ruins of noble structures, its traces of the hand of cultivated man, its memories, its legends, and traditions. Learning and piety have had their abode here in remote ages, and heroes and warriors repose in death in the strongholds and fastnesses that proclaim their power and valour. It is a fairy land, and the marvellous mirage reproduces their departed spirits in shadowy forms, as they return at long intervals to revisit the spot that, living, they loved so well. The monks rise from their graves, and in long and solemn processions devoutly enter the ruined temples, the walls of which were once vocal with their music; and the spectral O'Donoghue emerges with his charger from the lake, and

madly courses through the mountains, in mimic rehearsal
of the chase—a ruling passion strong in death.'

'Well, stranger,' said Peabody, 'what's all that when
it's fried? Do you mean to say the dead walk here?'

'I mean to say,' I replied, 'that there are many persons who have seen what I have related, fully believe in
the reality, and are ready to swear to it.'

'Do you believe it?'

'I saw a procession of monks once myself pass over a
bridge erected at the instant, and enter the ruins of the
abbey on the Island of Innisfallen, when both bridge and
priests suddenly disappeared from view; this was about
ten years ago.'

'Stranger,' said he, 'travellers see onaccountable things
sometimes; but, in a general way, these wonders happen
far from hum. Now, I once saw a strange thing, and only
once, *near* hum,' and he sang, to the tune of 'Oh, Susan-
nah,' the following stanza, with an indescribably droll
expression :—

> 'I took a walk one moonlight night,
>   When ebbery ting was still,
> I thought I saw dead Susan dere,
>   A coming down de hill.
> De buckwheat cake was in her mouth,
>   De tear was in her eye;
> Says I, "My lub, I'm from de South,
>   Susannah, don't you cry."'

'So you don't think the lake of the White Mountains
equal to Killarney, eh? Did you go through the notch?'
'I did.' 'And ain't that equal to the Gap of Dunloe?'
'I think not.' 'Well, did you see that are great lake
with a 'tarnal long Indian name to it that no created critter can pronounce without halting and drawing breath,
it's so full of a's, and i's, and o's, and u's, that if stretched
out straight it would reach clean across the water? Be-

cause, if you did, in course you saw the hot, biling spring
in the bank, at the foot of the falls, where trout a yard
long jump right in, alive and kicking, and cook themselves
without any touss or trouble; did you see that?' 'No,
I did not.' 'Neither did I,' said he, with an uproarious
laugh, 'nor ere a Green or White Mountain boy that ever
lived neither; but I thought *you* might, for there are folks
in England who think they know more about our everlastin' great nation, and have heard and seen more of it than
any Yankee that ever trod shoe-leather. Why, one of
your British Keounsals to Boston vows he has seen the
great sea-sarpint there, with his own blessed eyes, and his
wife says she will ditto the statement with her affidavy!
As for comparin' the two lakes, the American and the
Irish, and saying which is the handsumest, I won't undertake the task : p'raps you are right, and p'raps you ain't,
may be kinder sorter so, and may be kinder sorter not so.
But what's the odds? Beauty is a very fine thing; but
you can't live on it! A handsum gall and a handsum
view are pretty to look at (though of the two give me the
gall) and if you had nothen' else to do but to look, you
could afford to stare as hard as an owl. But in this here
practical world of ourn, the mouth requires to be attended
to as well as the eyes, and kicks up an awful bobbery if
it's neglected. Now, this place is all very well in its way,
but *it don't pay.* The wood is scrubby and not fit to cut
for timber; and if it was, though there is plenty of water
there is no fall for a saw mill—no powerful privilege of
any kind. There are many other places I would sooner
spekelate in to set up saw, grist, or factory mills. There
is a 'nation sight of good localities in this country for the
cotton fabric business, and I have been prospecting near
Galway, now that the Atlantic steamers come to Ireland.
But it won't do to establish manufactories in this country,

the people are too divided. Factories and factions, like
fire and water, are antagonistic principles: put the fire
onder the water and it biles right up, foams, frets, and
runs over, and if you shut it up, it explodes, scalds, and
kills everybody; put the water on the fire, and it first
squenches, and then puts it dead out. There is no such
country in the world, if the people had only sense enough
to know it. But they can't see, and if you give 'em tele-
scopes they either look through the big eend, and reduce
great things to trifles, or they put the little eend to their
eyes, and magnify mole-hills into mountains. It takes a
great many different kinds of folk to make a world, and as
every country is a little world in itself, it must have all sorts
of people in it too. Italy has only Italians, Spain, Spaniards,
Portugal, Portuguese, and so on, and the y are all Romanists; and see what a mess they make of it in their manufactures, commerce, and government! They are behind all
creation, they are just what creation was made out of—
chaos! They are all one way of thinking. You must have
many men of many minds to go ahead. Now, England and
the United States produce every sort and kind of opinion:
Catholics, Greeks, Church (high and low), Presbyterians
(Kirk, Antiburghers, Free Church, and Seceders), Me-
thodists (Primitive and Episcopal), Unitarians, Baptists
(of all shades of colour and dye), Independents, Quakers,
Moravians, Universalists, Lutherans, and ever so many
more dittoes, too numerous to mention in a catalogue, so
we must call 'em etcetera. Well, you see what is the
consequence? Why, they all get along their own road,
and no one asks the other where he is going, and p'raps he
couldn't tell him if he did.

'No man wants to know another man's creed, any more
than he does his name. He has got his own conscience,
his own purse, and his own luggage to look arter; it is as

much as he can cleverly do. Each one minds his own
business, and never mislests another. Now, here you
see, it is another guess kind of matter. There are only
two sorts, as a body might say—Celt and Sassenach, or,
Catholic and Protestant—and Protestant here means
only Church and Presbyterians, who make common cause
against the other. Well, what's the result? These two
great bodies, you see, can't agree in nothen. If you go
for to talk of schools, they keep apart, like the two for-
rard wheels of a stage coach, five feet exactly. If they
come to elections, it's the same thing; if they meet, they
fight; all, too, for the sake of religion; and if they assemble in a jury-box, it's six of one and half a dozen of
the other. Killing comes natural, half the places in Ireland begins with kill; there is Killboy (for all Irishmen
are called boys), and what is more onmanly, there is Kill-
bride; Killbaron, after the landlords; Kilbarrack, after
the English soldiers; Killcrew, for the navy; Kilbritain,
for the English proprietors; Killcool, for deliberate
murder, and Kilmore, if that ain't enough. Stranger,
one sect, whatever it is, won't do, for then the clergy are
apt to get fat and sarcy; and only two sorts is worse, for
they fight as they do here. But you must have all sorts
and kinds, so that no two will agree to quarrel with another. Sectarian spirit is either too strong or too weak
here; if it is too strong, it should be diluted by mixing
other kinds; if it is too weak, the English should send
them more ingredients to strengthen it, and make it rael
jam. You have seen the Mississippi where the Ohio
joins it? Well, the two streams keep apart, and you
can trace the separate waters of different colours, ever so
far down; they don't mix. And you have seen the
Gulf-stream. Well, you may talk of ile and water not
mixing, and there is no wonder in that, because their

natures are different; but the Gulf-stream won't unite
with the ocean; it keeps to itself for thousands of miles,
and this is a natural curiosity, for they are both water,
and even storms, tempestical hurricanes, and currents
won't mingle them. Now, that's the case here—the Celt
and the Sassenach elements won't mix; and yet, both
call themselves Christians, and both, like the two streams
in the Mississippi, have different colours—one orange, and
one green. It fairly beats the bugs. They want other
currents to neutralize them. What's your ideas? What's
the reason, while we are one people in the States, the
English one people, and the Scotch united also, the Irish
are *two* people? As you are used to expoundin', Ly,
expound that, will you? for it passes me.'

'Mr. Peabody,' said the Senator (who seemed a little
disconcerted at the allusion to his functions as an Elder),
'let me remind you, again, that when you speak of religion in the flippant and irreverent manner you have just
now done, you exhibit a want of good taste and good
sense. It is not suitable to refer to it in a conversation
like the present, so I must decline to pursue the topic.
As regards the fatal affrays, and agrarian outrages that
sometimes take place here, recollect that they are often
magnified for party purposes; and as the British public
have an appetite for horrors, every case is paraded in the
newspapers with a minuteness of detail that is calculated
to pander to this diseased taste. The number of homi-
cides in Ireland falls short of what occurs in the United
States. I am informed on the best authority, that, on an
average, there occurs one a day in the city of New
York.' 'What do you call the best authority?' asked his
friend.

' The Bishop of the Diocese.'

'Well, I don't,' said Peabody. 'I call the police

records the only reliable accounts. Recollect bishops must paint——'

'Pray, abstain from that style of conversation,' said the Senator. 'What you say about our being one people, is true of us as a whole, but not locally so. The French and their descendants, at New Orleans, as you know, keep apart, and live in different sections of the city. So they do in Canada and other places, because they are, in fact, two people, with two different languages, and two different creeds, sympathies, and customs, and *one is a conquered people.* They are gradually becoming absorbed, because they are on all sides surrounded by the Americans; but the process of absorption is not yet complete.

'This is the case with the Irish (who are also a *conquered people*) with the exception of their having less tendency to amalgamation, because they are surrounded—not by the English—but *by the sea.* In addition to this, the old penal laws and disability acts of former times, which were equally unjust and impolitic, erected impassable barriers between the two races. Such distinctions in our country cannot long be maintained, for there are no old grievances for demagogues to agitate upon. There are no confiscated estates there before their eyes to remind the descendants of the former owners that their patrimony is in the hands of the spoiler; no ruins to attest the ravages of the conqueror; no mouldering cathedrals to recal to mind the piety and misfortunes of their ancient clergy; and, above all, no tithes to pay to a church which they disown and dislike. So there is a reason for the state of things we see here, though no justification; for it matters little whether a grievance is well founded or not among the commonalty of mankind so long as they think it a grievance. I regard the ancient language as the greatest difficulty to be encountered here. It contains

the records of all their traditions. To impose your laws
and institutions goes but little way towards changing the
feelings of a people; indeed, it estranges as often as it conciliates them. Impose your language, and the conquest
is complete.'

'Zactly,' said Peabody. 'It reminds me of an Eye-
talian I once knew at Utica, called Antonio, who, when
he had learned a little English, married a Scotch gall,
that could only speak Gaelic. I used to split my sides a
larfing to hear the gibberish they talked; a droll time
they had of it, I tell you, and their signals was as onin-
telligible as their talk. Well, some years afterwards,
who should I meet but Antonio, in the market at Boston.
So says I, "Antonio," says I, "how do you and your
Scotch wife get on?" "Well," says he, "so well as we
did, and more better now, except scoldy, then she talk
Gaelic so faster as ever, and I speak Italian, and we no
understandy one 'nother no more. Then she first cry,
then laugh, and we shake hands, and talk slow, and come
good-natured." You are right, Ly, you must larn a gall's
language, or she must larn yourn, afore you can make love.
When I was a boy at night-school, I used to find larnen
came easier by kissing over a book than by crying over it
by a long chalk.'

'What nonsense you talk, Peabody!' said the Senator.
'It's not the fault of the Government now,' he continued,
'though folks are always ready to blame Government for
everything that goes wrong, but it's the fault of circumstances. Time, railways, and the general civilization of
mankind are gradually making the change. The Danes,
the Romans, the Normans, and so on, are all amalga-
mated in England now, and form one race—the better
for the mixture—who have one language, the richer and
better for the mixture also. Ireland has hitherto been

out of the world, steam has now brought it within it, and
it can't help feeling the influence of extended commerce
and free intercourse with the people of other countries.
Railways have completely altered the character and habits
of our backwoodsmen. They have brought them to our
cities, and taken our citizens to them, and they are acquainted with all that is going on in the United States
and elsewhere. Steamers have civilised the whole population of the Mississippi, who were in fact a few years
ago, what they called themselves, " half hunters, half
alligator, with a cross of the devil." There is now no such
place in the Union as Vixburg was twenty or thirty years
ago. The Church has superseded the gambling-house, and
Lynchers and Regulators have given place to the duly
constituted officers of the law. We owe to steam more
than we are aware of. It has made us what we are, and,
with the blessing of God, will elevate and advance us still
more. The same process is going on in Ireland, though more
slowly, from the causes I have mentioned. Still the improvement is so great, that I, who have not been here for
ten years, hardly know the country. The famine was an
awful scourge, but Providence ordained that it should
furnish a useful lesson. It taught the people that Protestants had kind hearts, and generous impulses, and it
promoted a better feeling between the two sects. A
common danger produced a common sympathy, in which
brotherly love can alone take root.'

'Yes,' said Peabody, 'but when a common danger is
over, common instincts spring right up again, like grass
after it is mowed, and are as strong as ever. My brother
Jabez had an awful instance of that onst, that frightened
him out of a year's growth, indeed it stopped it altogether
he was so allfired skeer'd. He is six feet two, now, in
his shoes, and if it hadn't a been for that are shock to

his narvous system, I do raily think he would have stood seven in his stocking feet. Was you ever in Indianny, stranger?'

'Yes, I have hunted buffalo there.'

'Well, then, Jabez lived there once afore the flood.'

There was something so comical in this expression that I could not resist laughing outright at it. He joined in it most good-humouredly, and then proceeded—'You are welcome to your laugh, stranger; but, by gosh, if you had been there, you would have found it no laughing matter, I can tell you. Well, Jabez bought a location from Government, built a shanty on it, in the upper part of that territory, and cleared some two or three acres of land, close on the borders of the prairie, intending to hold on for a year or two, till settlements advanced up to him, and then sell out and realize. He was all alone, some miles from our brother Zeke, who had squatted on those diggins some five or six miles farther down, and moved his family from Kentucky. Well, one night he went to sleep as usual, and dreamed he was drownin' in the Mississippi; and when he woke up, he found he was near about all under water, for the flood had come on all of a suddent, and he had been fool enough to build on too low a level. He hadn't a minute to spare, the flood was rising so fast, so there was nothing for it but to cut and run quick-stick while he could. So he outs at the door like wink, and, as luck would have it, his old hoss, Bunker, had come home, as you say, "in a common danger, for common sympathy." He slips the rope-halter on him in a jiffy, and off, full chisel, to cross the prairie to brother Zeke's. But, bless your heart, when he got to the plain it was all kivered with water for miles every which way he could see. The only thing discarnible was, here and there, the tops of a clump of cypress trees

a-stickin' out, like chimbleys in a fog, and they wern't
overly distinct neither, for the sky was cloudy and broken.
Well, on, and on, and on they went, he and the old hoss;
and the water rose higher, and higher, and higher. It
was fust trot, then walk, then crawl, then wade, then
stumble, then stagger, then swim. Well, old Bunker
began to breathe so quick, and sneeze so often and so
short, he thought he'd just slip off his back and hold on
by his tail; but that was heavy work for the hoss, to tow
him arter that fashion. He felt sartified it was gone
goose with both of 'em, and was a-thinkin' they had
better part company, and try to fish for it on their own
separate hooks, when he 'spied a log a-driftin' by; so he
lets go of the tail and climbs on to that; and, as the
current was setting down towards Zeke's, he began to
feel at last as if he could hold on that way till break of
day, when, all at once, somethin' got up at t'other eend
of the log, and what should it be but a tarnation painter!
(panther). There was a pair of eyes, like two balls of
fire, making the water boil a'most, a-starin' right straight
at him, and he a-trying to look as much like a sea-devil
as he could—both on 'em feeling as if one darn't and
t'other was afraid—both guessing they had trouble enough
of their own without fightin'—and both wishing the other
would make his bow and retire without loss of honour on
either side. At last, brother Jabez seed a little island,
as he thought, a-looming up in the dark waters; but it
warn't an island—it was only an Indian mound, or ground-
house, as they call it, where their dead used to be buried.
The moment he seed it, he slipped off the eend of the
drift-stick to swim for it, when down goes t'other eend
of the log, like a tilt, and off slips the painter, chewallop,
into the water, and they swam, side by side, to the land.
Well, when they arrived there, what should he see but

the old hoss (who had got to land before him), four or
five deer, two buffalo bulls, a bear, a coon or two, and a
possum, all standin', tremblin', and shakin', but as peaceable as if they war in the ark. When day broke, Jabez
seed the water was a-fallin' fast, and the mound gettin'
bigger and bigger, so he ups upon old hoss and takes another swim, to be out of the way afore breakfast-time
came on, and lots was drawn which of the crew was to go
for it to feed the rest. Well, the current helped them,
and he and old Bunker soon reached Zeke's, when he and
his brother loaded their rifles and started off in the canoe
for the island, or mound. The painter was helpin' himself to the coon when they arrived, and the two bulls were
standin' sentry over the bear, who was grinnin' horrible
at 'em. The *common danger* was over, you see, and the
common instincts broke loose again. Jabez had no pity
for his half-drowned companions neither, and pinked the
deer as if he had never seen them before.

'That was pretty much the case, I guess, here, too,
arter the famine was over. Both were oncommon peaceable during the plague—orange and green were turned
wrong side out for the time; but, you see, they wear
them now as they used to did, and the colours are as
flaunting and fresh as ever.'

''That's a very good story,' said the Senator, ' and it is
a very true one, for I knew your brother well, and have
often heard him tell it; but it does not apply. If men
were of different species, instead of different races or
tribes, or were beasts of prey, the analogy would hold
good; but the comparison is both unjust and degrading.
The circumstances to which I have alluded have kept the
two races apart; but there are other and no less powerful
influences now in operation of an opposite tendency that
cannot fail to produce the most beneficial results. In

addition to those I have already enumerated, I may
mention that emigration has relieved the country of a
superabundant population that pressed heavily upon its
resources, and by the withdrawal of so much unemployed
labour, has ameliorated the condition of those that are
left. There is now sufficient occupation for all, and increased wages have both stimulated and rewarded the
industry of the poor. The Incumbered Estates Court
has worked wonders for the advancement of agriculture,
by opening to cultivation lands that were closed to improvement by absentee landlords and bankrupt proprietors ;
while railways have afforded access to markets, furnished profitable fields for the investment of capital, and
facilities for intercourse among the people, without which
there can be no interchange of opinions, and no enlarge-
ment of ideas. Thirty years ago, a journey from the
west coast of Ireland to London occupied, under the most
favourable circumstances, as much time as a mail packet
of the present day does in crossing the Atlantic. Now a
line of steamers is established at Galway to compete with
the Cunard vessels at Liverpool for London passengers to
the States. This one fact alone contains more information, and suggests more reflection, than all the statistical
tables of the Boards of Agriculture and Trade combined.
It shows that Ireland is commercially, geographically, and
politically in the right place, and has the right men to
stimulate and direct its energies in the right direction.'

'Ly, you talk like a book,' said Peabody. 'That's a
fact. I can't state a thing as clear as you can, but I can
tell when you state it right, and when you don't. Many
a judge would decide wrong if a case wern't well argued ;
and that's about the only use a lawyer is. I am glad to
hear you say Pat is improving, for he is a light-hearted,
whole-souled critter, and full of fun. They are droll

fellows. Lord! I have often larfed at the way an Irish
help we had at Barnstable once fished me for a glass of
whisky. One morning he says to me : " Oh, your honour,"
says he, " I had great drame last night entirely—I dramed
I was in Rome, tho' how I got there is more than I can
tell ; but there I was, sure enough, and as in duty bound,
what does I do but go and see the Pope. Well, it was
a long journey, and it was late when I got there—too
late for the likes of me ; and when I got to the palace I
saw priests, and bishops, and cardinals, and all the great
dignitaries of the Church a coming out, and says one of
them to me, 'How are you, Pat Moloney,' said he, 'and
that spalpeen your father, bad luck to him, how is he ?'
It startled me to hear my own name so suddent, that it
came mighty nigh waking me up, it did. Sais I, 'Your
reverence, how in the world did you know that Pat
Moloney was my name, let alone that of my father?'
'Why, you blackguard,' says he, 'I knew you since you
was knee high to a goose, and I knew your mother afore
you was born.' 'It's good right your honour has then to
know me,' sais I, 'let alone my father.' 'Bad manners
to you,' sais he, 'sure this is no place to be joking in at
all at all ; what is it you are after doing here at this
time o' night?' 'To see his Holiness the Pope,' sais I.
'That's right,' says he, 'pass on, but leave your impudence with your hat and shoes at the door.' Well, I was
shown into a mighty fine room where his Holiness was,
and down I went on my knees. 'Rise up, Pat Moloney,'
sais his Holiness, 'you are a broth of a boy to come all
the way from Ireland to do your duty to me ; and it's
dutiful children ye are, every mother's son of ye. What
will ye have to drink, Pat ?' (The greater a man is, the
more of a rael gintleman he is, your honour, and the more
condescending)—'What will you have to drink, Pat ?'

D

'A glass of whisky, your Holiness,' sais I, 'if it's all the same to you.' 'Shall it be hot or cold?' sais he. 'Hot,' sais I, 'if it's all the same, and gives no trouble.' 'Hot it shall be,' sais he, 'but as I have dismissed all my servants for the night, I'll just step down below for the tay-kettle,' and wid that he left the room and was gone for a long time, and just as he came to the door again, he knocked so loud the noise woke me up, and, by Japers! I missed my whisky, entirely. Bedad, if I had only had the sense to say, 'Nate, your Holiness,' I'd a had my whisky, sure enough, and never known it warn't all true, instead of a drame." I knew what he wanted, so I poured him out a glass.

'"Won't it do as well now, Pat?" says I.

'"Indeed, it will, your honour," says he, 'and my drame will come true after all; I thought it would, for it was mighty nateral at the time, all but the whisky."

'Droll boys—ain't they?'

'Well,' said the Senator, 'there is something very peculiar in Irish humour—it is unlike that of any other people under the sun. At times it is very pointed; at others it is irresistibly droll, from a certain incongruity or confusion of ideas. I am not certain, however, whether a good deal of it is not traditional. I am not very fond of telling stories myself; for though you may know them to be *original*, still they may not be *new*. I am satisfied the same thing has often been said in different ages, and by people in different countries, who were not aware a similar idea had occurred to, and been expressed by others. I have heard repartees and smart sayings related here, as having been uttered by well known wits, that I have myself heard in America, and often long before they were per-petrated here. If you relate a story of that kind, you are met by the observation, "Oh, that was said by Sydney

Smith, or Theodore Hook, or some other wit of the day."

' For instance, there is the story of the man, who, on his death-bed, recommended his son to be honest, as he knew it was the best policy, *having tried both courses.* Now, it is certain that has been told in Scotland, in England, America, and Spain. To tell it, gives you the reputation of being too familiar with Joe Miller.

' Discoveries are of the same kind : many men gain credit for what was known ages ago. Harvey has the credit of being the first who discovered the circulation of the blood, and his remains are at present sought out, for the purpose of erecting a monument to his memory. But that it was known to the ancients is very certain. Longinus'——

' I knew him,' said Peabody. ' I was present at his trial, and saw him hanged at New Orleans—I did, upon my soul. He was a nigger, and one of the most noted pirates on the coast of Cuby. He made more blood circulate, I guess, than any man I ever heard tell of; he was of opinion dead men tell no tales, so he always murdered the crew of every vessel he captured ; he cut the throats of all his prisoners, and then threw their bodies overboard. I shall never forget a rise I took out of Mrs. Beecher Stowe about Longinus. I met her once at New York, just before she came over here, to make fools of whimpering gals and spoony Lords about Uncle Tom. Just as if such things could be true ! Why, stranger, does it stand to reason, and convene to common sense, now, if a real good workin' nigger, and a trusty one too, is worth a thousand dollars, his master would be such a born fool and natural idiot as to go and flog him to death, and lose both him and his money, any more than he would ill-use a super-superior horse ! Why it has impossibility

stamped on the face of it, as plain as her Royal Highness
the Queen's head is stamped on a twenty-shilling piece that
they call a sovereign. I hate such cant—I hate them
that talk such rigmaroles, and I despise the fools that
believe them and turn up the whites of their eyes, like
dying calves, and say: " Oh, how horrid ! how shocking !
what a pity it is such a bitter thing as slavery should bear
such sweet fruit as sugar," and then call for another lump
to put in their tea, to show their sincerity. It makes my
dander rise, I tell you. Well, Aunt Stowe was collecting horrors, like Madame Tussaud, when I met her. So,
thinks I, if I don't stuff you like a goose, it's a pity ; and
I'll season it with inions, and pepper, and sage, and what
not, till it has the right flavour. Here goes, says I to
myself, for fetters, handcuffs, chains, whips, pollywog
water for drink, and stinkin' dried fish for food—enough,
if put under glass cases, to decorate the chimbley-place of
Buxton, Shaftesbury, and Sutherland, and fill Exeter
Hall, too.

  ' "I hope," said she, "you are an Abolitionist, Mr.
Peabody, as I said to the Duchess."

  ' "To the backbone," sais I ; " it's the great Eastern ticket
now for the Presidential Chair. New England never had
but two Presidents, and them were the two Adams, father
and son. The younger one, Quincey, first started the 'Man-
cipation Ticket, to go ahead against the Southerners. One
of his eyes was weak, and if he touched it, it was like starting a spring in digging a well, out gushed the tears in
a stream ! Whenever he talked of niggers at public meetings, he'd rub his right eye with his nosewiper, and it
would weep by the hour ! People used to say, ' What a
dear man ! what a feeling man that is ! what a *kind,
soft heart* he has,' while he thought *how soft their horns
was !* He acted it beautiful, but it takes time to work

up a ticket with us, you know. Charles Sumner matured it, though he got an awful cowhiding in Congress for coming it too strong; but you will put the cap sheaf on it, see if you don't. Arter your book called 'The Key to Uncle Tom' is out, we shall be able to carry a President from the Eastern states, that's a fact."

' " Oh, Mr. Peabody," she said, " oh, fie! now, don't your heart bleed (as the Duchess said to me) for the poor niggers?"

' " No, marm," sais I, " I am happy to say it don't. Bleeding at the lungs is bad enough; it's like goin' up-stream with a high pressure boiler: you don't know the minute it will burst and blow you into dead man's land. But bleedin' at the heart, marm, is sudden death any which way you fix it."

' " Oh, dear," she said, " Mr. Peabody, what a droll man you be; but our people down east are so clever, as the Duchess observed to me, ain't they? You feel for them, as the Countess of Ben Nevis told me she did, don't you?"

' " Countess of Ben Nevis," said I; " only think of a lord being called Ben? like Ben Franklin, the printer! But I suppose there are vulgar lords as well as vulgar Yankees?"

' " Pooh!" she said; " Ben Nevis is the name of a Scotch mountain; I am sure you know that, and the title is taken from that classical spot."

' " Well then," sais I, " Joe Davis' County, in Illinoi, which I used to think a disgrace to our great national map, is not so bad arter all, for it's *classical*. Oh, Lord! oh, Lord! just fancy the Countess of Joe Davis," sais I; and I almost rolled off the chair a larfing, for I hate folks bragging everlastingly of nobility, that only invite 'em to have something to talk of, and that look at

them through the big eend of an opera-glass, to make
'em seem smaller than they be. Who the Duchess was
she quoted so often, to astonish my weak nerves, I don't
know, and don't care, for I 'spose I shouldn't be one mite
or morsel the wiser if I did hear her name. But one thing
I do know, and that is, all the nobility don't think like
her, for there was a top-sawyer one lately had up for throwing sticks at Aunt Sally, who was a nigger as black as the
ace of spades or the devil's hind leg. The magistrate said
Aunt Harriet and Aunt Sally were both American ladies,
and bosom friends, and any insult might provoke a war with
the States. "Still," said Aunty, drawin' herself up a bit,
as if the joke stung a tender spot, "still, Mr. Peabody,
you feel for the poor negro, don't you?" "Well," sais I,
"marm, to be serious, between you and me, I must say,
though it's only in confidence" (and I looked round as if
I was anxious no one should hear me), "I am not altogether certified I do feel for people that are unable to feel
for themselves." "Do you think, sir," said she, still
perckin' up, as proud as a hen with one chick, "do you
suppose, sir, a negro, when tied up and flogged, dn't feel
as acutely as we should? Do you deny he has the same
flesh and blood as we have? or that he is as sensi*tive* to
the torture of the lash as we should be?" "Well, marm,"
sais I, looking very grave and very wise (for all fellers
that say little, and look solemn, are set down, in a general way, as wise), "as to the same flesh and blood, I won't
say, though I should doubt it, for they tell me sharks
(and they ain't overly nice in their tastes), when a boat is
upset, always prefer whites, not liking the flavour of
blacks; so I won't dispute that point with you; but this
I will maintain, they hain't the same colour, nor the
same feelings we have." "Of course they hain't the same
colour, but 'nimium ne *cread collary*,'" (though what

that means when the husk is took off and the nut cracked I don't know), "how do you make out they have not the same feelings we have?" "Why," sais I, "you have heerd tell of Longinus, haven't you?" "In course I have," sais she, "he was a great man in the court of Zenobia." "He was a great man, and a great villain," says I, "and no mistake, for he was the wickedest, fiercest, most cruel pirate ever seen. He wasn't tried in the court at Zenobia, for that's an inland town of Texas, but at New Orleans. I was present at the trial, and saw him hanged, and the way the crowd yelled was a caution to sinners. If they had had their way they would have thought hanging too good for him, I can tell you, for once a nigger gets the taste of blood he is more like a wolf or a tiger than a human being. Well, there was one Jeduthan Flag, a Connecticut pediar, there, who bought the body of the sheriff on spekelation, and hired a doctor to take his hide off, and he dressed it with alum and lime, cut it up into narrow pieces, and made razor-strops of it." "Pray what has the dead negro to do with sensibility and pain?" said she. "Well, I was a-going to tell you," sais I; "I bought one of the strops, and I have got it now. I gave fifty dollars for it. Would you believe it, the leather is near half an inch thick. It is like pig-skin, that they use to cover saddles with, soft and pliable, and oily too, just like that, and has little wee holes in it, like as if a needle had made them; it's the grandest strop I ever had in my life. Now, if a nigger's hide is as thick as that, how in the natur' of things can he feel a whip? Why, it don't stand to reason and the natur' of leather that they can any more than a *rhinoceros*." "Mr. Peabody," said she, "is that a fact?" "True as any story you have got in your book," says I, "and that's noticeable, I assure you." "Well, I never heard anything so horrible," sais she.

" Oh, Mr. Peabody, how slavery hardens the heart, how
debasing, how demoralizing it is! What will become of
our great nation, when we not only buy and sell negroes,
but make a traffic of their skins! I like an authentic
story. I am delighted to be able to publish this horror-
ing tale to the world What a sensation it will create!
May I make use of your name?" " Certainly," sais I,
" say Amos Peabody told you, and refer them to me for
further particulars." I left her making a memorandum;
and what I told her I'll swear to, and that is, that it is as
true as any story she has in her novel.

' The fact is, stranger, slavery is a cussed thing, and
there is no two ways about it. It is a black page in our
history; but how to tear it out without loosening all the
other sheets is the great difficulty we have to encounter.
We all deplore it with grief and mortification. But what
in the world is the use of a woman a racing all over the
world like a ravin' distracted bed-bug, a screeching and
screaming out as loud as if she was whipped herself? *It
ain't them that yell the loudest that feel the most.* I had
almost forgot the story of Longinus, till you mentioned
his name, Ly.'

' You are a strange fellow,' said the Senator; ' the
moment you hear people talking seriously, you immediately turn the conversation to some nonsense or another,
that has no connexion with it. As I was a saying, sir,' he
continued, ' when our friend here interrupted me, even
many modern discoveries, although original, are not new,
and were well known to the ancients. The circulation of
the blood is one; it is clear, from a line quoted by Longinus from an ancient poet, that the circulation of the
blood was then a well-established fact. I cannot repeat
the line, for my Greek is rusty, and we have not the book
here; but refer to it when you are at leisure, and you will

be convinced I am correct. But in humour also, as I have already said, the coincidence is very striking. Without undervaluing Irish humour, I am inclined to think something is to be attributed to traditional fun, and something to a people whose perceptions are quick, whose characteristic is cunning, and whose habits of thought are so much alike. That cunning has much to do with it is quite clear from the fact that the lower orders are very much more ready and droll than the upper classes. It is also remarkable that they are far more humorous at home than in America, which perhaps is also in part attributable to the circumstance of their being more industrious there, and in consequence more matter-of-fact. Their whole character becomes changed there. Here they are idle, there they are the best labourers we have, more persevering and enduring than the English, and more honest in their work than the Scotch. The Americans form the mass, and they are compelled, by the force of circumstances, to mingle with them; here they form the mass, and every inducement is held out to them to prevent others from mixing with them. I do not blame their clergy for encouraging them to remain a separate people, because I believe they sincerely think it the safest way to keep them from the contamination of heresy. It is but common justice to them to attribute this to an honest, though mistaken, conviction. But what do you say to your English patriots, who, being aware of the predisposition of the people, encourage them in it, for the purpose of securing their votes, who set tenants against their landlords, Catholics against Protestants, and the whole population against the Government! who create grievances for the purpose of being chosen to redress them, and use the power conferred by their confidence for their own advancement. " Bunkum," as we

D 3

call it, or political humbug, as you term it, though the
same thing has a very different effect here from what it
has in America. No man is deceived by it there; it is
used by every party, and understood by all. It is incense
offered to the majesty of the multitude, who very justly
suspect every public man, and disregard their reasoning,
but who compel them to bow down and worship them,
and at last choose that side that best suits their interest.
In the United States, there is no principle involved in
party struggles, because all men are equal and have
similar rights. It is men, not measures. Here there is
a most important one at stake, and that is the preservation
of the monarchical element in a mixed constitutional
government, where, from the various orders of social and
political structures, men are not equal. There, deception,
bad as it essentially and morally is, works no serious
injury, for it merely substitutes one party for another;
and it is of little consequence to the country which pre-
dominates. Here it is of vital importance, for if demagogues succeed, the balance of the constitution is in
danger, and a democracy may supersede the monarchy.
That noblemen, and gentlemen of property and station,
can lend themselves to such a fraudulent system of politics, and condescend to play such a dangerous game, is to
me wholly unaccountable. I can understand the conduct of a man like Bright. He is desirous, as we say,
to come out of the crowd. He has no position in the
country, and is anxious to make one. A social one, he
knows, is impossible; a political one is within his grasp,
especially as he has the manufacturers with him, and
is identified with their money and masses. Though
deficient in constitutional knowledge, he is a very good
declaimer. His business is to demolish, and a strong
though unskilful workman is equal to that sort of work.

I can understand *him*. He is not a dangerous, though a mischievous man. He is better suited for Congress than your Parliament. But there is one lesson he would learn there that might be of use to him, and that is, that although a Quaker, and not expected to fight, he would be held accountable for his words, and find his broad-brimmed hat no protection for intemperate language. Your dangerous man is your titled radical representative of an Irish constituency. There never was a people so cajoled, fooled, deceived, and betrayed, as the Irish. It is time they turned their attention to the material, and not the political condition of their country; and everything I see induces me to augur well of their future.'

'Oh, it does, does it?' said Peabody. 'Well, I'd rather see it than hear tell of it by a long chalk. I wish they'd hire me to write their history since Cromwell's time; for I'd make my forten by it. If I had the contract. I'd do it in three lines. Their lords lived abroad and screwed their agents; the agents screwed the tenants; the tenants screwed the poor, and all combined to screw the Government. The gentry lived in houses they didn't repair, on farms they didn't cultivate, and estates they couldn't transfer. The trader didn't import, for he wasn't paid for what he sold. The labourer didn't work, for he didn't earn his grub at it. The lord blamed the disturbed state of the country for not living in it; the agent blamed him for high rents and absenteeism; the farmer blamed both for extortioners, and the peasantry cussed the whole biling of them; while lawyers, like flies, swarmed where there was corruption, and increased the taint they fed on. When the patient is in a bad way, there is always a quack who has a nostrum; and political quacks rose up by the score, who had each an infallible remedy. One tried repeal of the union; another, tenant-

right; and a third, rebellion. Parliament tried its hand
at it, and spent millions in jobs. But I agree with you,
the Incumbered Estates Act, steam, and (what you have
forgotten to mention) temperance, have effected, and will
work wonders; and it's their own fault now, if the Irish
don't go ahead. Cardinal Wiseman missed a figure
when he was here, I tell you. He might have saved this
country, if he'd have taken the right course, and know'd
as much of representatives, Ly, as you and I do. He
may be a Cardinal, but hang me if he's a *wise man*. I
wish I had his chance and his power, I'd a said, "Pat,
my boy, if anybody goes for to talk politics to you, up
fist, and knock him down, and I'll absolve you on the
principle of self-defence. Patriots, as they call themselves, are no friends of yours, or old Ireland either.
They have honey on their lips, but pyson in their tongues.
What is it to you whether Tory, or Whig, or Radical is
uppermost, any more than whether democrats or repub-
licans are ins or outs in the States? The object of law
is to protect life and property; and so long as it does
that, and don't interfere with your liberty and religion,
that's all the call you have to it. Mind your own
business, and live in charity with your neighbours. Be
sober, industrious, and peaceable. Respect yourselves,
and others will respect you; *but eschew politics as you
would the devil.* It is better to be a free agent, than a
tool at any time. Obey the law, but never look to
Government for patronage. They will feed you on
promises till you are unfit for anything, and then give you
something not worth having. They are like torpedoes,
they paralyse everybody they touch. Avoid secret societies, work diligently, be honest and grateful to your
employers, and God will prosper you in all your under-
takings. But if you choose to serve the Devil, do so; he

is a good paymaster, and rewards his servants. *The wages of sin is death,* and if you earn it, I hope you will get it." Now, Ly, if that ain't poetry, it's truth ; and if it ain't Irish, it's plain English. It's the rael ticket, and no mistake. What the plague is the sense of harping for ever on old grievances—it's the tune the Old Cow died of. They are like spilt milk, and we all know it's no use to cry over that. If the Cardinal would go in up to the handle for that, he'd do more good than all the patriots, hung or unhung, ever did or will do for Ireland, from July to etarnity.'

'Well done, Peabody,' said the Senator. 'I never heard you utter so much sense before ; it's a pity you would not always talk that way.'

'Well, I don't think so,' said Peabody ; 'there is a time for all things in natur'. When sense is trumps, why I can lead off with an ace, if I like, for I am not the fool you take me to be ; but when fun is the word, well then I'm ready to cut in and take a hand. Laughing wasn't given us for nothin', or we shouldn't have been made so everlastin' ticklish as we are. Courtin' would be stupid work if it wasn't for romping. But here is the postman. Now, do you look solemncholy, Ly, and important, and say you have got a despatch from the President of the United States. It sounds well afore the waiters ; and I'll see if there is ere a letter from my sister Deliverance, for she always writes me a long one, under pretence of giving me news from hum, and eends with a postscript containing a commission for me to send her something worth a hundred dollars.'

In the package of letters, I found one from my friend Cary, announcing the completion of his business, and requesting my immediate return to Cork. I was there-fore obliged to take leave of my companions, and set out

at once on my journey.   They expressed great regret at
not being able to accompany me, in consequence of expecting a party of friends from New York, to arrive the
next day ; but they assured me that they would not fail
to renew their acquaintance with me on some future
occasion at Southampton.

The bell rang, the guard blew a shrill blast from his
whistle, the train started, and in a few minutes Killarney
faded in the distance.

No. III.

HOMEWARD BOUND.

THE facetious driver of the car, who called the main road to Killarney the 'rael way,' conducted us thither through Macroom, Inchigeelagh, and Gougane Barra. I returned by the railway to Cork, not merely to save time, but to vary the scene. It is not my intention to describe the country through which we passed. Men and things are my topics; but I cannot help mentioning a peculiar feature of Irish scenery that has never failed to attract my admiration as constituting its extraordinary beauty. I allude to the number and extent of its rivers and lakes. Few countries of its size in the world are so well watered as Ireland, and the deep verdure of the landscape is at once relieved and heightened by the silvery light of its innumerable streams.

The Emerald Isle is an appellation more literal than poetical, and founded on fact rather than fiction. It is no wonder that the Irish have an enthusiastic admiration of their country; but there are other causes besides its beauty and fertility that attach them to it, which makes their nationality a very different thing from that of either the Scotch, the English, or the French. It is a far deeper and stronger, as well as a more lasting feeling. It embraces not merely their country, but their race and their religion. A Scotchman is clannish, proud of the achievements of his ancestors, and fond of his native land. But he is fonder of money and distinction than of either. He emigrates with more of hope than regret, and fully relies on his industry and economy to enable him to found a new home in a new world; he anticipates revisiting his kindred at some future day—a design in which ostentatious success is often mingled with affection. A prophet, however, has no honour in his own country, and he is willing to exchange it for another, where the obscurity of his origin may be hidden under a name that will pass without scrutiny as remotely connected with some illustrious family. The Duke of Argyll has more *distant* relatives than he is aware of, both in America and Australia, and the house of Buccleugh can never be extinct while there are so many presumptive heirs, *in partibus exteris.*

Where the region of Fable ends that of Truth begins, and the Elliots and Dundases are no pretenders. Their name is Legion, and their pedigree is acknowledged in every branch of every public department in the empire. He who leaves Scotland seldom returns. The inclination may exist, but an opportunity for its indulgence rarely occurs. An Englishman goes abroad because he is fond of adventure; he thinks he has a right to a living somewhere, and is not particular as to the locality in which it is to be sought. Wherever he is he grumbles, not because he is disappointed, but because it is natural to him to find fault. He is dissatisfied at home, and is never contented anywhere else. Nothing pleases him in his own country, and when abroad he abuses every place but England; he has neither the civility of an Irishman nor the servility of a Scotchman—the industry of the one nor the acuteness of the other, while economy is a word he could never comprehend. The consequence is, he is not so popular or so successful as either. A Frenchman is never happy out of France; not that he is so attached to it or its institutions, or that colonial life does not afford an easier subsistence and greater facility for accumulating a fortune, but because he misses the café, the theatre, the guinguette, the spectacles, and the cheap and frivolous amusements, without which existence appears to him to be intolerable. If he migrates to another country, it necessarily involves continuous industry, which is as foreign to his habits as his inclination; if to a tropical climate it compels him to be domestic, and makes his house a prison, where if he remains he dies of *ennui*, and if he effects his escape he perishes from fever. He must talk, sing, dance, or die; he has a tradition, which he fully believes, that every other country but his own is inhabited by barbarians, and that Frenchmen are the only gentlemen in the world; although he has neither the manners nor the principles of one, he takes it for granted he must everywhere be received as such. He likes France, therefore, not so much for itself as that it is inhabited by those whose tastes are similar to his own, and who are the only people who know how to live. He is a philosopher; he is not ambitious of wealth, but of enjoying life. He—

> ' Wants but little here below,
> Nor wants that little long.'

And, therefore, his great study is to make the most of that modicum. No colony of Frenchmen has ever succeeded.

Poor Pat leaves his country because poverty compels him to do so. He is attached to the soil on which he lives, and that scantily supported his forefathers. Its legends and traditions appeal to his heart. He is attached to his countrymen, with whom he has so many sympathies, a common language, a common poverty, and a common religion; and although he has been taught from his birth to believe that he is a bondsman, he is ever willing to exchange the freedom of a republic for the imaginary chain of a slave at home. America disappoints him; he is surprised to find that he must work for his living even there, and that priests who defied the law in Ireland are compelled to be circumspect by a higher power than law—the force of public opinion. He could beg in peace and in rags at home, but among the free, enlightened, and most liberal Yankees a beggar is treated as a vagrant, while rags are ridiculed as an emblem of idleness, and not pitied as an evidence of want. To work or to starve, is the inexorable law of republicanism. His religion is essentially aristocratic, and there is nothing congenial to it in democracy that reduces a priest to the common level of vulgar equality with his flock. He despises a President who receives people sitting in his shirt sleeves and smoking a cigar, and a Governor who drives to the State-house on the top of a coach or buss, and carries a change of clothes in his pocket-handkerchief. There is some fun at home in pulling down the political edifice; there is noise, dirt, disturbance, and danger enough to make the work exciting; but there is nothing but hard toil and patient drudgery in building it up again in the States. When the work is finished it is but an upstart after all; it has no ancestral or historical associations; it is vulgarly new. Senators armed with revolvers and bowie knives inspire him with disgust and contempt, while those who both cant and spit, when declaiming on independence and slavery, he regards as beings even below himself, if the pictures drawn of him by his friends the patriots and agitators be at all true to nature. The illicit distiller looks back with regret on the excitement of his lawless occupation at home, in the prosecution of which he had the sympathy of the whole population, who deluded the police and the soldiery with false information, or defended him with arms at the risk of their own lives. He is surprised to find that freedom which he had always sought in sedition and rebellion, or in the midnight forays of Ribbonism, when actually possessed means, after all, nothing more than a choice of occupation and an obedience to those laws, which, while they protect him in his rights, protect the community also ; and that when justice is either too slow or too weak to reach an offender, the people institute a court themselves and appoint a gentleman to preside, under the title of *Judge Lynch*, who, by the aid of elective officers, styled regulators, calls out the *posse comitatus* of the county when occasion requires, and seizing the criminal, tries him summarily, and executes him on the spot.

It is no wonder that an exile of this description, who flies from Ireland to avoid an untimely end, gives vent to his disappointment in the pathetic remark, so characteristic of the Irish :—' By Jingo ! this is no counthry for a jontleman to live in.' There is some truth in the observation as he expresses it, but none whatever in its application. It is eminently the poor man's home. If he is willing to work, he can find employment, and labour is well remunerated. By industry and economy he can rise to a position of ease and comfort, perhaps of affluence. There he must be contented to rest. The higher orders are wanting in America ; and that which money cannot purchase is neither known nor valued. Time, however, works great changes in the Irish, whether in the United States or the Colonies. They are the few among the many. They cannot long maintain their distinctive character; they become gradually absorbed, and are soon incorporated with the mass of the people. They adopt the dress, the habits, and the feelings of the Americans. Their clergy taught them to disregard a Protestant sovereign; the Americans, in their turn, teach them to disregard their priests. One half of their lives is spent in learning what

is wrong, and the other in unlearning it. Renunciation
is soon followed by recantation, and the Queen and the
Pope both lose their subjects.   By this process, the
emigrants are protected from themselves and their own
violence ; they individually obtain that freedom which,
collectively, they never allow to each other. A Roman
Catholic who becomes a Protestant in Ireland is considered as a man who deserts his colours, and he is pur-
sued and punished by the whole community. In America
he is neither hailed as a convert by one side, nor insulted
as a pervert by the other.   The event is regarded by the
former with unconcern, and by the latter as an occurrence
rather to be regretted than resented. Public opinion
tolerates and protects every sect, but has no sympathy
with any.   Franklin thought them all right, and Jefferson
pronounced them all wrong ; the natural result is general
indifference.   Religion is left to shift for itself, the supply
is regulated by the demand, and competition has lowered
its value by adopting an inferior material, and coarse
workmanship.   Fashion invents new patterns, and each
succeeding season announces some attractive novelty.
The original emigrant retains with some difficulty the
creed he received from his priest ; his faith is less lively,
but still he is a believer.   It is different with his descendants, who often exercise their own judgment, and choose
for themselves.   But, though he adheres to his church,
his habits are altered and improved : he becomes industrious, and his condition is ameliorated.   His kind-
hearted and affectionate feelings are not merely preserved,
but enhanced by distance.   He works hard to save, and
he saves to import his relatives to the comfortable home
he has provided for them in the West.   The Irish poor
are rich in love—in love for their parents, their children,
their friends, and their countrymen.   No one is so

destitute, but that he will give of his last loaf and divide
his last sixpence with one poorer or more destitute than
he is, and, when all is gone, he mingles benedictions on
others with prayers for himself. Poor Pat! Your
virtues are all your own, while your faults are engrafted
upon you by others. Your impulses are good, but your
training has been vicious. Providence has bestowed upon
you a beautiful and fertile country, and a climate the
most agreeable and salubrious in the world. You are in
possession of the same civil and religious liberty as the
English, and the union of the two countries insures to
you any amount of capital that may be required to
develop the resources of Ireland. Receive with cordiality
those who are willing to assist you, as well because it is
their duty, as because it is their interest to do so. You
yourselves oppose the only obstacles to your own prosperity.

While preparing for my departure to England, I
witnessed one of those sad scenes that, alas! are of
constant occurrence in Ireland—an assemblage of emigrants embarking on board a steamer, to be conveyed to
the clipper ship, 'Cariboo,' bound to Quebec. It was a
touching spectacle. Old and young were taking leave of
their relatives and friends to seek their fortunes in a
distant land ; and the mutual grief of the parties, as they
bade each other a long and final farewell, was most heart-
rending. Entreaties were exchanged amid tears, embraces, and blessings on the one hand, to be remembered
in the prayers of those who were about to embark ; and on
the other earnest vows never to forget them, and to
provide funds as soon as possible to enable them to reach
their new home. Again and again they renewed their
adieux, and at last were only separated by the bystanders, and the stern voice of command from the
steamer. Long after the ship got under weigh, hats and

handkerchiefs were waved by the passengers and their bereaved friends on shore, until they faded from the view of each other in the distance. Both the emigrants and their attendants appeared to have come from the wilds of the west coast of Ireland. They were an uncouth and uncivilized people, many of whom were ignorant of English, and spoke only their native language, and most of them were dressed in a garb now but rarely seen, even at Cork. They were all poor, and in appearance far below the average run of Irish emigrants, while their chests and boxes were of the most primitive and rustic kind I ever beheld. It was long ere the sorrowing friends who had accompanied them to the quay withdrew their anxious gaze from the river, and began to think of their return homeward. Little was said; it was a silent and mournful group; their hearts seemed too full for utterance. So many ties had been suddenly rent asunder; so many recollections rapidly passed through their minds; and so little knowledge of the distant country to which the exiles were bound existed among the mourners, that the world appeared to them a dark, dreary waste, without one ray of hope to lighten it. The priest had blessed them, it is true, but, alas! he was no prophet; he had often blessed the dead, as well as the living; still it was a consolation to know that his holy benedictions followed them. But the sea—the awful, unknown, bottomless sea—was to be passed, and storms, hurricanes, and mountain waves waylaid them in their course, and who could say whether they would survive all these trials and reach their destination. Their minds were agitated by doubts and fears; they could think of but one thing at a time, and that was their desolation and their sorrow. Short and inaudible prayers were uttered from the depths of their hearts for the beloved seafarers, and for patience and endurance for themselves. All at present was blank, but hope might come with the morning to illumine their darkness, and to vivify a faith which, though it slumbered, was strong even unto death. 'God,' said the priest, in words they had often heard, but never fully and deeply felt before, 'God knows all, ordains all, and is merciful to all.'

It was a spectacle never to be forgotten. I have not the nerves to witness human misery without deep emotion, and I shall avoid a scene like this for the future. A stranger, at best, can give but little consolation, and his presence is often irksome to those whose only relief is in an unrestrained utterance of the sorrows of their hearts. There were others, however, unconnected with the exiles, who viewed their departure in a different light, and envied their good fortune, in being able to leave poverty and wretchedness behind them, and to exchange the land of buttermilk and potatoes for that of substantial abundance.

A small band that had just landed from a river steamer struck up a merry tune, 'Cheer, boys, cheer,' which was followed by 'Garryowen,' and 'There's a good time coming.' The music, as it was kindly intended, diverted the attention of the idlers, whom the bustle and excitement of the embarkation had collected on the quay. Conspicuous among them was a tall, powerful, unshorn countryman, carrying a stout shillelagh under his arm, and having a rollicking, devil-may-care sort of air that gave you an idea of a very droll but dangerous fellow. His habiliments bespoke an utter disregard of the becomings. His hat had survived the greater part of its rim and its crown, and bore evident marks of rough usage and hard blows. It looked as if it had been thrown, rather than placed on his head, and had nearly missed its hold, hanging jauntily on one side, as if regardless of its safety. His coat reached nearly to his

heels, and exhibited many rents and fractures, that had
carried away much of the original materials; a loose,
sailor-like, black tie displayed a strong, muscular neck;
while soap-coloured breeches, unfastened at the knees, long
grey stockings, and a pair of coarse, strong brogues,
completed his costume. He was one of those peripatetic,
rustic philosophers, so often met with a few years ago in
Ireland, whose philanthropy was inexhaustible. He
went about doing good, assisting a friend to fight at a
fair, doing honour to the dead, by carousing at his wake,
and howling and drinking at his funeral. Work was not
his vocation : he considered it only fit for a 'nagur' or a
Scotchman (for both of whom he had a supreme contempt),
and not at all suited to the superior dignity of a Galway
boy. Still he was most scrupulous in the fulfilment
of an oath, for having sworn not to drink whisky again,
as long as he remained on earth, he climbed into a
tree, and got drunk there, to keep his vow to the letter.
Addressing himself to me, whom he had previously
scanned and measured with his eye, he said, 'It's a noble
counthry entirely, yer honour, that the boys are goin' to.
They tell me Canady is a beautiful island, where land
can be had for the asking, let alone the whisky, no rent
to pay, and no agents (bad luck to them) to grind up the
poor along with the corn. I hope it will be my turn next.
Did yer honour iver see that counthry ?'
  ' Yes,' said I ; ' I know it well.'
  ' Then, it's glad I am to fall in wid yer honour.
Maybe you'd be after knowing one Phelim M'Carty,
there, a brother of mine, by his father's side, but not by
his mother's? You'd know him by the loss of an eye.
He took two of them into the fair at Ballinasloe, and only
fetched one home wid him. Bad luck to the boy that
did him that turn. It was more by accident than any

thing else he hit him that blow; for sorra a man could stand before Phelim; and a dacent lad he was too; and great at book-larnin'. Did yer honour ever see him in yer thravels?'

'No,' I, said 'I never saw him. Canada is a large country, larger than England, Ireland, and Scotland put together, and it would have been mere accident if I had seen him.'

'Bedad, I didn't think of that, yer honour; so it is; and maybe if you had seen him you couldn't have known his name was Phelim M'Carty, unless he told you himself. It's mighty well he is doing too, for he gets four pounds a month wages, and is after having me out, to do for me also.'

'The reason he is doing well there,' I said, 'is because he is obliged to work. If he had been willing to labour, he could have done equally well at home, for this is as good a country as Canada; and if a man is industrious and prudent, he can earn an honest livelihood anywhere.'

'It's chape talkin',' he replied, 'but the work is not to be had; and when a poor man gets it, it's not worth havin'; the pay won't keep body and soul together. They won't give us a chance at all, at all, here.'

'Well, my friend,' I said, 'if you were to make your appearance in that dress in Canada, you would stand a poor chance to get employment, I assure you. Why, now, don't you cut off a piece of the tail of that long coat of yours, and mend the rest with it?' A deep flush suffused his cheek at that question, as if he would like to resent it; but suddenly assuming an arch look, he said, 'Did yer honour ever hear of Corney O'Brien's pig?'

'Never,' I replied; 'but what has that to do with mending the coat?'

'Yer honour will see it has a good dale to do with it,

E

when you hear about that self-same pig. He was a knowing craythur,' he continued, casting a significant glance at me, 'and there is many a larned pig don't know as much as he did, after all. Well, he knew if he hadn't a penny in his mouth, the devil a bit would the keeper let him go through the pike. So what does he do, but watch for a chance to slip through unbeknownst to him. He walked about unconcarned, as if he was only looking for a bit of a thistle to eat, or a root of grass to grub up; but for all that, he kept one eye on the bar and the other on the keeper the while, and when it was opened, he dashed through in spite of him, but, faix! he left his tail behind, for the keeper shut the gate to so quick, it cut it short off, to the stump. Well, the craythur was so ashamed of the short dock, he never could look an honest pig in the face ever afterwards. It would be just the same with me, as Corney's pig, yer honour. If I was to cut the tail of my cut off, I should never be able to look a dacent man in the face afterwards,' and he walked away with the triumphant air of a man who has silenced his adversary.

'Ah,' said I, to my friend Cary, 'emigration is the only cure for such a fellow as that. *Here,* he is either proud of that badge of poverty, or indifferent to it. In Canada he would be ashamed of it, and could not wear it. *Here,* his countrymen see no harm in it, *there* they would see nothing but degradation and national disgrace in it.'

'Cœlum non animum mutant,' &c. &c., is not applicable to Irish emigrants. A change of country involves an entire change in the man. But it is now time for us to proceed to Queenstown, and embark for England.

Cork has something more to boast of than its noble harbour and its splendid scenery. It is the birthplace of more eminent men than any other city in Ireland. It has had the honour of producing Crofton Croker, Murphy, Dr. Maginn, Father Prout (Mahony), and Sheridan Knowles, besides many others distinguished as painters and sculptors, such as Barry, Maclise, and Hogan. It is but a faint expression of my feelings to say that I left Cork with great regret. We impose needless obligations on ourselves, and then obey them as if they were inevitable. I intended to remain only a short time, and I returned home, for no better reason than because I had so decided.

In an hour after witnessing the embarkation of the emigrants we were on board the Peninsular and Oriental Company's steamer, the 'Madras,' and under weigh for Southampton. This beautiful ship was on a trial trip, and the Directors kindly offered us a passage home in her. I have more than once made a voyage in the noble vessels of this Company, in other parts of the world, and they well merit the high character they have for speed, comfort, and safety. The Cunard line belongs to a firm, and the Directors are the owners, who derive all the advantage resulting from their management, a stimulant far beyond salaries or commissions. Their own capital is at stake, as well as their character. They are neither subject to the caprice nor the penuriousness of shareholders, nor are they tempted into extravagance under the idea that the expenditure, as well as the risk, falls principally upon others. The net gain, and the whole loss, is distributed amongst the members of the firm. It is therefore, like all partnership concerns, better managed than when the authority is deputed to others. In the one case it is the interest of all to exercise a minute and careful supervision over the affairs; in the other, the larger the expenditure the greater the remuneration received by the agents. This Transatlantic line is therefore an exceptional case, and cannot be compared to those of a joint stock character. But of all the other Ocean Steam Associations, that of the Peninsular and Oriental Steam Company is by far the best managed, and the most successful. It has a great advantage in having grown up by degrees to its present magnitude, whereby the experience of the managers grew with it, while others, originally undertaken upon a large scale by persons not conversant with such affairs, broke down, to the loss and mortification of the subscribers, and the great disappointment of the public. This is a circumstance wholly overlooked by the Government, by which large sums of money have been recklessly thrown away. The tender of the Australian Steam Company for the conveyance of the mails to Melbourne, though exceeding that of the Peninsular and Oriental line for the same service, by £40,000 per annum, was accepted by Government, under the absurd idea of distributing their contracts among different parties, in order to prevent any association from becoming too powerful. The result, as predicted by those acquainted with the subject, was complete failure, and after an immense loss resort was ultimately had to this association, who perform the work most admirably. Steamers are built, and run at an enormous expense, and although the postal subsidy may seem large, and the passenger and freight traffic very great (which are obvious to all, and easily calculated), the outlay is so continuous and enormous, the staff so numerous and costly, the losses (when they occur) so large, and the deterioration in the value of the property so rapid that nothing can insure success but the most careful and judicious management, combined with a thorough knowledge of the business in all its various branches. Hence the failure of many French and American companies including those known by the name of the 'Collins Line of Steamers,' and a similar fate awaits others that are now struggling with hopeless difficulties.

Infinite credit is due by the travelling public to this association, and by the proprietors to their Directors, for furnishing a line of steamers equalled only by those of Cunard, superior even to them in number, and in all respects far beyond those of every other nation in the world. Safe in foul weather, commodious and agreeable in fine, they have smoothed and shortened the route to the East, and by affording easy access to those distant possessions have strengthened our hold upon them, both politically and commercially. System, order, regularity, due subordination, and economy pervade every department of their vast establishment, while no money is spared in procuring the strongest and best vessels, the ablest and most efficient officers, and in providing good accommodation and liberal fare for the passengers. I like a steamer, and only wish the present voyage was longer than from Cork to Southampton. What a glorious thing is the sea, the vast, the boundless sea! How bracing and refreshing the breeze! How the spirits are exhilarated by speed, and how proudly you walk the deck, in conscious strength of having subdued the ocean and made it subservient to your will. The flapping sail and the listless calm, the dull and monotonous rolling of the inert and helpless ship, the drowsy, dreamy days of time that stood still, the anxious survey of the sky for indications of the awakening breeze, the baffled hope, the oppressive feeling of despondency at head winds and adverse seas that overpowered us of old, are recollections of the past that only seem to increase the pleasure derived from a power that bears us on with unabated, unaltered speed, regardless alike of currents or adverse gales. How superior is it to a railway

train: you have room to move and to walk about, you
inhale with delight the fresh air, and you soon become
known to all your fellow-travellers. You relish your
meals, and have an increased appetite for them (if you
are a good sailor, if not, you had better stay at home and
read the travels of others). You have time to eat, your
progress is not delayed by the operation, and you can sit
and sip your wine at your leisure ; and enjoy the varied
conversation of your companions. How different is all
this from the rush into a refreshment room, where stale
pastry, coarse meat, detestable coffee, thick soup, and bad
tea are served and swallowed in haste, amidst a standing,
elbowing, noisy crowd. The hour, too, after a light supper
is most enjoyable ; your companions are generally men of
the world, and from all parts of the globe, and the conversation is equally various and amusing. Every man is
a walking, talking book of travels, having the advantage
over a printed one of possessing the ability to explain
what is obscure, to abridge what is diffuse, or enlarge
what is too brief. There is less reserve than in general
society, and individual character is more developed. It
affords a good study of human nature. When the bell
rings for the extinguishment of lights, instead of spreading out a railway wrapper and reclining your head against
the corner of the carriage, you get into your snug, comfortable berth, and are rocked to sleep by the lullaby of
the billows. Oh ! commend me to an ocean steamer, and
let those who prefer railways have their monopoly of
smoke, dust, noise, tremulous carriages, and sulky, supercilious companions.

As soon as I had disposed of my traps in my state-
room, and mounted the deck, I recognised an old supernumerary officer of the Company with whom I had made
a voyage or two in the Mediterranean. Captain Rivers

is a well-known character, and has been so long in the
service that he is generally styled 'Commodore.' He
was not attired in the uniform of the Company, as he
was not on duty, but in the usual undress sea suit of a
seaman, and a jolly, thoroughgoing sailor he was! Short,
thick set, rather inclined to corpulency, and bearing a
full, florid, good-humoured countenance: who that had
ever seen him could forget the Commodore!

'Ah, my good friend,' he said, as he shook me heartily
by the hand, 'I am glad to see you, I thought you were
in the Pacific.' After a while our conversation naturally
turned on the past, and the incidents of our voyages in
the Mediterranean. 'Did you ever meet that Yankee
lady again,' he said, 'who came from Malta with us, Mrs.
Balcom? A pleasant little woman that: she was the only
American lady I ever met that laughed heartily: they are
generally so formal, precise, and cold. Their smiles are
like winter sunbeams on ice, bright enough to dazzle your
eyes, while your feet are freezing. A Yankee lady is
like a badly boiled potato, floury outside, but with *a bone at
the heart*. Give me an English girl after all; when they
do love they love you in earnest. I won't say there are not
matches made for money here as elsewhere; but in a general way they don't begin with the "everlasting dollar."'

'No,' I said, 'they may not originate in it, but how
often mere love matches end in "dolor."' It was a bad
pun; I never perpetrated a good one in my life, and I am
glad of it, for there is little beyond knack in making
them. Good or bad, however, the Commodore did not
take it, though, like every one else who don't perceive the
point, he looked rather abroad, smiled, and said, 'Oh,
yes, that is very true.'

'But to get back to my story,' he continued. 'I
thought Mrs. Balcom would have died at a story I told

her of a German lady's delicate health, who made a trip with me from Marseilles to Alexander—did I ever tell you that story?'

'Not that I recollect.'

'Well, one morning I overheard the stewardess inquiring kindly after her health: she answered her very despondingly: "Oh, ver bad. All ze night I was more bad zan avair; ze head, ze back, ze limbs, zo bad I cannot tell."

'"Would you like to have some breakfast, madam?"

'"Don't know—ver sick wiz de sea mal—what ave you?"

'"Get you anything nice, madam."

'"Ave you ze beefsteak?"

'"Yes, madam."

'"I take ze beefsteak. Ave you ze mutton-chop, ze potate, ze tomate, wiz ze coffé and hot cake?"

'"Oh, yes. Is there anything else you would like to have, madam?"

'"Ah, mon Dieu, I cannot tell. I ver indispose. Stop, mamselle; bring me after dat ze lobstair, cowcumber, and ze oil. Tell I you I ver bad apetize?" And she tucked them in one after the other in great style. Lord! how Mrs. Balcom laughed at that story; and then she went, and got out her writing-desk, and made me say it over and over, word by word, until she had it all correct. She said she was paid to write letters about what she could pick up in her travels for newspapers, and it helped to defray her expenses—a queer idea, ain't it? "Well, ma'am," says I, "if you want queer anecdotes, I can tell you them by the dozen, for in course I have seen a great many people in my day, and heard all sorts of things, as you may suppose from my having been so long in the service. Why, bless your heart, ma'am," says I, "I took *three-fourths* of the English and French army to the Crimea in that noble ship the Simla."

' " Oh," said Colonel Van Ransellier, an American friend of hers, " come now, Commodore, you are going that rather too rapid. I won't say you lie, because that ain't polite, but you talk uncommonly like me, when I lie. Do you mean to say that you actually took three-fourths of the allied army to the Crimea in that are ship ?"

' " I do."

' " All at onest ?"

' " No, not all at once, because that would be going rather too rapid, as you say ; but I did it in three trips, though. What do you think of that ?"

' " Well, I'll tell you what I think of it," said he. " Did you ever see the celebrated American Circus Company, belonging to Squire Cushing, that's performing to London ?"

' " Yes, I have."

' " Well, so far so good. Did you ever see the man that climbed up a pole, and stood on his head on it ?"

' " I have."

' " Well, I told a down-easter, from the State of Maine, I had seen it done, and he replied he did not doubt it, for he had done more nor that himself."

' " What, says I.

' " Why, says he, I climbed up the pole the same as he did, only I guess it was an everlasting sight longer one, and then I stood on my head on it.

' " Well, says I, what then ?

' " Why, says he, stranger, I don't suppose you'll believe it ; but I'll tell you what I did. When I was standin' on my head on the top of that are pole, I jist raised myself up a little with my arms, opened my jaws, put my teeth to it, and pulled it right up out of the

E 3

ground, and then jumped down, with one end of it in my mouth.

' " Well, says I, I don't believe it, and that's flat.

' " I shouldn't wonder, said he, if you didn't. But I have told it so often, I believe it myself—I actually do.

' " Now, Commodore," said the Colonel, " I guess you have told that ere story so often, you begin to believe it yourself, like that Kentuckian chap. What will you bet you did it ?"

' " A hundred dollars," says I.

' " I'll bet you two hundred," said he, " you didn't."

' " Done !" said I, and we staked the money and appointed our umpire. " Now," says I, " I took the Fourth Foot one voyage, the Fourth Dragoons the second voyage, and the Fourth French Chasseurs d'Afrique the third voyage ; and that is the *three-fourths of the army* in three voyages. What do you say to that, Colonel ?" said I.

' " Sold !" said he, " every mite and morsel of me, and well sold, too—that's a super-superior catch. Write that story down, and sign it, and put the P. and O. ship's name, the Simla, down, too, lest I should forget it, and let the umpire write on it that he decided it against me, and sign his name and title in full. Let it appear an ondeniable fact, that's all I ask. I don't grudge the money, it's only fifty pounds, and I'll make as many hundreds out of it when I get home."

' Lord ! I shall never forget the day I was commanded to prepare to take the first regiment. A lieutenant in the navy came on board with the order : and they are gentlemen that recognise no officer afloat but themselves, and think they have a monopoly of all the seamanship and knowledge of navigation in the world. So when he comes on board, said he : " I want to see Mr. Rivers." My first officer, who saw he was giving himself airs, and had no mind to stand it, said : "There is no Mr. Rivers here, sir ; you have come to the wrong ship."

' "Isn't this the Simla ?"

' "It is."

' "Who commands her ?"

' "Captain Rivers."

' "Well, tell Mr. Rivers I want to see him."

' "I tell you, sir, there is no Mr. Rivers here."

' "Well, tell him that commands her, then, that Lieutenant Jenkins, of Her Majesty's ship the Blunderbuss, is the bearer of an order from the Admiral."

'So what does he do but call the second officer, and says he, "Tell Captain Rivers a Mr. Jenkins is here with an order from the flag-ship." The lieutenant was very angry; but other people have short memories as well as navy officers. When he delivered the order, he complained to me of my officer for rudeness, and I called him and rebuked him for it. Says I, "If this gentleman forgets what is due to others, you should never forget what is due to yourself." I must say, though, that the Admiral always treated me with great condescension and kindness; and a thorough sailor he was, too, which was more than could be said of some others I knew in the fleet. Steam has played the deuce with our sailors; they are not what they used to be in my younger days. Still, they are far before the French in every way, although machinery has put them more on a level with us than I like. I am sorry you have been away this summer. You should have seen the *fête* at Cherbourg. Ah ! sir, that was a beautiful sight. We had glorious weather for it; and, I think, we must have astonished the French.'

'You mean,' I said, ' that Cherbourg astonished you; didn't it ?'

'Not at all,' he said. 'There is a superb dockyard

there, and a beautiful harbour, with an entrance at each end of it, well protected by powerful batteries. But what of all that? Any harbour can be well fortified; but this place is constructed on old principles, and the improvement in modern artillery, and the recent invention of new projectiles, render it far less formidable than you would suppose. The fleet can be shelled by Whitworth's guns, and burned in the dockyard. But what I was alluding to was the spectacle. Why, sir, it was an English exhibition in a French harbour. Just imagine a fleet of five hundred yachts, belonging to English country gentlemen. Beautiful craft, well fitted, well manned, and appointed in the most perfect manner, and all decorated with every variety of flag, with just wind enough to wave them to advantage. It was a beautiful sight. Then there were three of our splendid ships, the Pera, the Salsette, and the Benares, three of the finest ships afloat—not belonging to Government, but to a company of merchants—not selected as show-vessels, but taken promiscuously from a fleet of more than fifty, merely because they were supernumerary at the time—and this company only one of the many great ocean steam companies of England. Then there was the Etna, belonging to the Cunard fleet, as large as a seventy-four gun ship; besides numerous other smaller private steamers. To these were added the British squadron of men-of-war; and, above all, the royal yachts of Her Majesty, fitting emblems of the Queen of a maritime nation like Great Britain. Depend upon it, that spectacle must have struck the French as an evidence of the strength, spirit, and resources of Great Britain. What *they* had to show consisted of Government works, some ugly forts, a breakwater, and a dockyard. Their line-of-battle ships were so constructed as to render their lower guns useless, even

in moderate weather; and their sailors neither knew how
to man the yards or to cheer, how to salute their friends
or daunt their enemies. There is nothing equal, sir, to
the cheer of the British sailor. It does my heart good
to hear it. Cherbourg is a good skulking place: it's the
worst thing in the world to make a navy depend for its
safety on a fortified harbour. They are used to being
blockaded, and Cherbourg shows they expect to be
chased home again. It is a great tribute to our navy,
but it is a depressing thing to theirs. Fight or sink, do
or die, is our motto. Cut and run, if they get the worst
of it, is theirs. If they had no place to run to they would
fight better. Sebastopol and Cronstadt were the graves
of the Russian navy, and Cherbourg will prove the same
for that of the French. The badger and the fox, when
they "earth," confess they are not equal to a stand-up
fight. The bulldog shows his teeth, but never his tail.
It would have done you good to see the members of the
House of Commons that went there in the Pera, and to
listen to their collective wisdom about things they knew
as much of as a cat does of a punt. The salvos startled
Roebuck out of a year's growth (indeed Bright says he
never will grow any more), and *Wis*count Williams was
outrageous at the amount of powder wasted in the salutes,
and vowed he would move for a return of the cost. Sir
Charles Napier was for blockading the harbour, to
prevent the French ships from getting out, and an old
Tory Admiral, to keep them from getting in. "There
you are," said Bernal Osborne, "both of you at the old
story of 'ins and outs;' can't you leave your party
politics at home?" "Or change them," said Roebuck,
"as you did your name, from Bernales to Bernal, and
then add on Osborne, as the Irishman does an outer coat,
to conceal the holes in the inner one. But the Jew will

peep out after all. What a national love you have of torturing a fellow you do not like." "Not so much as Dizzy has," he said, good-naturedly. "By jingo," said an Irish member, "I wish you and your friends Roths-child and Solomons would only commit treason; we'd confishcate your property and pay off the national debt wid it entirely." "I dare say you do," said Spooner; "the Irish are used to treasons and confiscations, and always will while the Maynooth"——"Order, order," said Roebuck. "You may well say order, order," replied the Irishman, "after you have fired your own shot. It's the way you did with poor Butt: after you had been the paid agent for the Canadian rebels for years, you charged Butt with having been the advocate of an Indian prince. By the powers of Moll Kelly, if"——"Come, come," said Lindsay, "no personalities and no politics, for, as an Irish friend of mine said of some articles in the *Times* (two of the writers of its editorials being Bob Lowe and Dasent), ' *These things are more Lowe than Dasent.*' I move that we nominate a committee of management and supply." Oh, dear, it was great fun. They couldn't agree upon anything, and first moved resolutions, and then amendments, and gave notice to rescind, and then debated it all over again, finally adjourned, and then resumed the discussion at night. Well, the committee of management mismanaged everything. When the boat went ashore it got aground and remained there; when it returned to the ship it remained there also; those that landed could not get off, and those that wanted to land had no means of reaching the place. One-half of them did not get into the docks, and those that did either were kept waiting to enter, or were shown out by a different gate to that they came in by. It was a droll affair. They seemed to have a monopoly of shindies, as the

Governor of Malta has of his capers. You know they grow on the ramparts there, and people used to help themselves to what they wanted, till a notice was put up to prevent them, which ran thus—"*No person, except the Governor, is allowed to cut capers on these ramparts.*"

'If they had left things to us they would have been as comfortable as the day was long; but they took the direction themselves, and were as uncomfortable as people of different opinions well could be. But how can you expect politicians to agree, except in disagreeing?' Here he suddenly broke off the conversation, saying, 'Here is old Tom Skinner, who sailed with me in the Simla. He is a character, that fellow,' and, allowing me to pass on, accosted a queer-looking seaman that was going aft to the wheel. 'Is that you, Tom Skinner?' said he. 'How are you?'

'Pretty well in bodily health, sir,' said the sailor; 'but the Lord fetcheth it out of me in corns.'

'Are you married yet, Tom?'

'Well, I be.'

'And how do you get on?'

'Well, I can't say it's a woman lost or a man thrown away; it's much of a muchness, sir. She tried it on at first, saving your presence, sir, by going to bed missus and getting up master; but I soon fetched her up with a round turn, and made her coil up the slack. She knows her course now, sir, and answers the helm beautiful.'

Here the dinner-bell rang, and we went below.

Whoever has been at sea, as I have, in the old sailing-packets, can hardly believe the great improvement that has been effected in the arrangements of ocean steamers for the comfort of passengers. The saloon is as different a thing from the cabin of former days as can well be imagined. Well lighted and ventilated, spacious and ad-

mirably adapted, either for the purposes of a dining or
sitting room, it has all the convenience that a vessel is
capable of affording, while the means and mode of cooking, and the number and training of the waiters, are
such as to leave passengers no ground to complain of
their dinner, or the manner in which it is served. They
are literally floating hotels.   On referring to this subject,
in a conversation with the Commodore, he said, ' This, sir,
arises from our having a fore and also an after cabin.
Each has its separate price, and is provided accordingly.
Those who pay the full fare have the best accommodation ;
those who are in the forward cabin, and whose passage-
money is less, are supplied in proportion to what they pay.
It is not like a Yankee hotel, where there are *turkey*
boarders, and *corn-beef* boarders, I have often laughed
at a story told me by the Governor's aide-de-camp at
Gibraltar, who was a passenger of mine some four or five
years ago.   He said he was once travelling in Connecticut, and arrived at an inn, where the members of the
Legislature boarded and dined together.   A queer col-
lection of sages they must have been from his description,
consisting of farmers, lawyers, ship-builders, lumbermen,
land speculators, and so forth.   The landlord kept a
capital table, on which was every delicacy of the season.
Well, a primitive old fellow, a representative of a rural
district, who knew more of personal than political economy,
and had been used to coarse fare at home, did not much
like the expense, and wanted to be served at a lower rate
than the others ; so he applied to the landlord to reduce
the fare.   " I don't want your venison," he said ; " your
turkeys, your canvas-back ducks, or your salmon ; let
those have them that like them, and can afford them ;
corned-beef is good enough for me.   If you will give me
that, it is all I want, therefore you must reduce the board

to me accordingly." The master of the house, who was a bit of a wag, agreed to this, and promised to keep silence on the subject of the bargain. He knew very well it was the secret, and not the arrangement, that would punish Master Skinflint; accordingly he left things to take their course. Well, the servants, who were ignorant of the private compact, offered him in turn every dish on the table. "Bring me corned beef," was the invariable order. At length this singular and oft-repeated answer attracted the attention of everybody at the table, and the waiters, seeing them enjoy the joke, continually plied and tempted him with every other dish in succession before they obeyed the demand for corned-beef. At last the member for Squashville lost all patience, and roared out in a voice of thunder to the servant, " Confound your ugly picture, don't you know I am a *corned-beef boarder* and not a *turkey boarder ?*" It grew into a by-word that ; and every shabby fellow at an hotel now is called a "corned-beef boarder ;" so you see the *turkey passengers* are here, and the *corned-beef gentlemen* forward. Neither of them have any reason to complain. Everything is done liberally here ; and this I must say, I prefer this service to that of the navy ; the officers are better paid, better found, and better treated in every respect.'

After dinner I lighted my cigar, and paced up and down the deck, which being flush fore and aft made an extended promenade. While thus enjoying my Havannah, the first officer, Straglash, whom I had also known in the Mediterranean, offered me a chair in his cabin, which opened directly on the deck. He was a tall, fine-looking fellow, active, intelligent, and every inch a sailor ; but his face was tinged with that colour that bespeaks exposure to a tropical climate, and exhibited traces of the fearful liver complaint, which seldom fails to await a lengthened service in the East. He appeared to be a general favourite among the Directors, who had promised him the command of the next new ship that was to be added to the fleet. There are two most excellent regulations in this service—one is, that every officer must, before entrance, have previously served four years at sea in a sailing vessel, and be able to produce testimonials as to competency; and the other is, that there is a regular scale of promotion. The first insures the safety of the passengers and the ship, and the other, the continued services of efficient officers. I accepted Straglash's offer of a seat with great pleasure, and we soon fell into conversation upon the subject of the service he was engaged in, and the character and speed of the new steamers the company had recently built. 'They are capital ships, sir,' he said. 'You see, our Directors are practical men, while their head resident engineer, and local manager, are first-rate people.

'There is a vast difference in their way of doing things from that of the Government. You may have heard of the loss of the " Transit," an Admiralty ship. Well, sir, we sold her to the Government, and what do you think they did with her? Why, they took her into dock and put the masts of a line-of-battle ship into her, and when they went to take her out she was top-heavy, fell over, and smashed in the roof of a warehouse. Our sailors used to laugh, and say that she knocked over a church. Sir Charles Block, who made this little mistake, ought to be a good man, too, sir, for I believe he has crossed the Channel two or three times, and I am not sure he didn't once go as far as Corfu.' 'Then you don't approve,' I said, 'of the First Lord of the Admiralty being a civilian.' 'Well,' he said, 'I won't say that either. Perhaps there ought to be one civilian at the Board; but he should be a practical man himself, if not a ship-owner, and ought to confine himself to the business part of the department. Navy officers, of course, know more about building, fitting, and sailing a ship than others; but they live so much at sea they don't know enough of the business part of it, which ought to be left to landsmen. The two branches should be kept separate. Leave nautical matters to nautical men, but financial and similar matters to civilians. What does a country gentleman know of lengthening a vessel by cutting her in two, or razeeing a line-of-battle ship? If you converse with him about a *paddle* he thinks you are talking of a horse's pace, and calls it bad action; or of a *screw*, he applies the remark to an old seasoned, but unsound animal, and tells you he prefers him to others for work. In short, he is all abroad. And what does an admiral know of mechanics' wages, duties, or work, or of contracts for building, for furnishing materials, or supplies? It is only when they step out of their own respective lines they go wrong. Both do this occasionally, and both get into a mess.' 'Excuse me,' I said, 'for interrupting you, but who is that gentleman talking to the Commodore; he looks to me like a clergyman?' 'So he is,' said Straglash; 'he is the Rector of Dockport; his name is Merrit, but he is better known as *Old England;* he can never remain contented at home for any length of time, and is always calling upon others to do his work for him; so they gave him that nickname, because "England expects every man to do *his* duty." "Ah," said he to me one day, "Straglash, how I should like to be chaplain to this ship! It is just the parish to suit me exactly—150 feet long, 60 feet wide—no marrying, no christening, no catechising children, no dissenting ministers to drift across your hawser, no running about to visit the sick as they are all in one ward, and no superintending schools and quarrelling about the books to be

used in them. It's just the place where I could be useful,
and not be exhausted with labour. My work is now so
hard I am obliged to keep constantly travelling to recruit
my strength. How I could devote all my energies to my
duty, and perform it quickly and quietly! It is a great
matter to be quit of wardens, church-rates, and vestry
meetings. I should like to be a chaplain amazingly. I
wonder the company don't manage to have one." He is
a very amusing man, sir; it's worth your while to talk to
him, for he is full of anecdote, and takes original views of
everything. He is always taking a rise out of the old
Commodore, when he meets him, and I have no doubt he
is poking fun at him now. You know Captain Rivers
has been at sea ever since he was a little boy, and has
been in the service of this Company from its commence-
ment; of course, he has met a vast number of people in
his day, and perhaps he has a larger acquaintance than
almost any man afloat. Lately his memory is affected by
age, and he thinks he knows everybody. England and I
were talking the other day about the Russian navy, when
the Commodore joined in the conversation. So, says the
parson (giving me a wink at the time), " Rivers, did you
ever meet in your travels, Captain Cut-em-off-tail?"
" Cut-em-off-tail—Cut-em-off-tail," said the Commodore,
" let me see." And he put his hand to his forehead.
" Oh, yes," he said, " I know him; he commanded a fort
in the White Sea, when I was there in the *Freebooter*,
from Hull—oh, of course, I know him well—a jolly fellow he was too, but a devil to drink brandy." " You are
mistaken," said Old England, " he is in the navy."
" You are right," replied the Commodore, " he commanded a three-decker at Sebastopol. I thought I recollected his name—no, I don't know him personally, but
I have often heard of him. Their names are so queer,
they confuse a fellow." '

Resuming our former topic, ' What is the reason,' I said,
'the Admiralty has such difficulty in manning the navy,
while you retain your men from year to year, and find it
so easy to get additional hands when you require them ?'
' There are many reasons,' he replied, ' but the Admiralty
is either ignorant of them, or won't believe them. The
main cause is that the men are not well used, either by
the country, or on board ship, and the consequence is,
the service is unpopular. When a war occurs, every inducement is held out to sailors to enter, and as soon as it
is over, they are paid off, and turned adrift to shift for
themselves. They are discharged in such numbers, the
labour market is glutted ; they can't readily find employment, and there is much suffering. Many of them quit
the country in disgust, and all resolve to have nothing
further to do with the navy, which, while it almost dis-
qualifies them from entering merchant ships (for there is
a feeling against employing men-of-war sailors), recog-
nises no claim for consideration on account of past services in the hour of need. There are other reasons also.
They are often away on distant voyages, separated from
their families and friends, for a very long period, and not
allowed those indulgences on shore that 'they obtain in
the mercantile marine. No man will bear this from
choice, nor will he voluntarily submit to the strict discipline of a man-of-war, unless great pecuniary advantages
are held out to him. Jack is not the thoughtless fellow
he used to be, and he can distinguish between necessary
and arbitrary discipline as well as his superiors. Hence,
the difficulty some officers find in obtaining a crew, while
others can man their ships with comparative ease. The
character of every captain in the navy is generally known
at all the great seaport towns in the kingdom ; and if any
one is a tyrant, he cannot complete a crew without obtain-

ing drafts from other ships. When a case of this kind
occurs, it ought to be the duty of the admiral on the
station to inquire into it; and if, where sailors are not
scarce, men decline to enter a particular ship, and their
refusal can be traced satisfactorily to this cause, that
circumstance ought to disqualify the captain from being
further employed. It would be a long story to enter into
details, but there are many other reasons of a similar
character to those I have mentioned. One thing is
certain, if men were as well paid, found, and treated in
the navy as in merchant ships, and received similar indulgence when in port, they would sooner enter it than the
other, *for the work is far lighter.* If they refuse, then
some one or more, or all of these conditions do not exist.
Don't look for remote causes, take obvious ones. If the
service is unpopular, there is a reason for it. Ask the
sailor himself why he declines, and he will assign some of
the objections I have mentioned ; but the last man to examine on the subject is an officer. If the shoe pinches,
the sufferer can point to the tender spot better than any
one else. Don't treat a sailor like a horse, and try with
a hammer where the nail pricks him, but ask him to put
his finger on it, and then draw it out. It is in vain to
pump a ship, unless you stop the leak, or she will fill
again immediately.

'It reminds me of a trick I once saw played upon a
couple of Irishmen in Boston Harbour, when I was there
in the " Europa " mail steamer. Two emigrants went on
board of a fishing schooner that was lying there, and applied
for work. They were told there was nothing for them
to do, and were entreated to go away. But they wouldn't
take no for an answer, and the men on board, finding they
couldn't get rid of them, set them to work, and told them
if they would pump the vessel dry they would give them

a dollar apiece, but that they would have to keep at it incessantly, or they couldn't do it. Well, the Irishmen commenced in earnest, and worked away with all their might; and the sailors leaving them to finish their job, landed and went into the town. Three or four hours afterwards, the Captain came on board and found the poor fellows almost dead with fatigue, and inquired of them what they were at. When they informed him of the bargain they had made, he almost laughed himself into fits. The vessel, it seems, had a false floor, and between the bottom and that, the space was filled with water, by means of holes near the keel, to give a continued supply to the fish that were brought alive in that manner to the market. Of course it flowed in as fast as they drew it; and they would have had to pump Boston harbour dry before they could free the vessel. It was the greatest case of sell, I think, I ever saw.

'That is pretty much the case with the inquiry the Board of Admiralty make about manning the navy. They must go to the bottom of the thing. They must ascertain the cause of the repugnance sailors entertain to the service; and having discovered and removed that, they will have more volunteers than they require, and every ship will have a picked crew. Competitive examination may be a good thing, sir, but believe me, common sense is far better.' But, rising abruptly, he said: 'Here we are, sir, at " The Needles;" excuse me if you please; we must have our eyes out here. It won't do to have the same old story of collision.' Each well-known object, as we passed it, afforded a subject for remark; but continuous conversation (as is always the case towards the termination of a voyage) was at an end.

I safely landed at Southampton. To-morrow I hope to avail myself of my Season Ticket.

No. IV.

'A TRAIN OF THOUGHT, AND THOUGHTS IN A TRAIN.'

HERE I am at last at Southampton, after my Irish trip; but unlike most tourists, I am not content. I have travelled so much of late years, that restlessness, like the policeman, admonishes me to ' move on.' I shall now use my Season Ticket, going up to London one day and returning the next. It will give me what I require—change of scene and amusement. I cannot yet settle down to any occupation; but this daily routine will soon become wearisome, and when I am tired of it I shall be content to be stationary. I do not call it travelling; it does not deserve to be dignified with such a name. It is taking a daily drive with new companions; it is a mere change of place and associates. Travelling is a far more comprehensive term, and is undertaken for very different objects, and very different reasons. Some go abroad, not to gain information, but because others go, and they consider it disgraceful not to have seen as much as their neighbours. In like manner, few people read ' Paradise Lost,' for any other reason than that they feel ashamed to confess their ignorance and want of appreciation of the poem. Men do not like to be considered heretics, and are therefore compelled to conform to the received opinion, instead of confessing the difficulty they have had in wading through the beauties of Milton. If they dared to do so, they would say they infinitely preferred Hudibras; but alas! they have not courage to speak the truth. To people of this description, 'The Grand Tour' is a 'customs duty,' that must be paid, like the Income or Property Tax. It is an incident of station. There is nothing in the prospect, but heat or cold, fatigue or disappointment, extortion or robbery; bad inns, bad beds, and worse attendance; bad roads, bad wines, and a long catalogue of various sufferings, haunt them like uneasy dreams. But they have no option; go they must, or be set down as nobodies, or thrown out in conversation. It won't do now-a-days to say 'England is good enough for me.' It may, indeed, be good enough for you, but *you are not good enough for it*, unless you have been abroad. The schoolmaster has gone there, so you must follow him.

When people marry, fashion ordains that they should make a wedding tour. Some go to Ireland (it is a pity more do not follow their example), and some to Paris; while others feel that a trip up the Rhine is more desirable, because they can then understand Albert Smith, and ascertain whether the German they have learned at school at all resembles what is spoken by the inhabitants. If these newly married persons really love each other, they can have but little inclination for sight-seeing; and if they don't, both matrimony and its inevitable tour must be great bores.

In my opinion, custom has ordained it rather as a penance than a pleasure, for it has in general mercifully limited its duration to a month. There is a prescribed course that must be followed. Folly presides at the arrangements, and regulates the ceremony. There is a well-dressed mob in the church, and a badly-dressed one at the door; there is a crowd of bridesmaids, and another of groomsmen, while two or three clergymen assist the

F

overtasked bishop in a laborious service that extends to the extraordinary length of fifteen minutes. The bells ring a merry peal, so loud and so joyous, one can scarcely believe they could ever toll. There are heaps of ornaments, instead of simplicity, and heaps of dresses and their concomitants, in defiance of the injunction against ' outward adorning or plaiting the hair, and of wearing of gold, and putting on of apparel.' There are also lots of gossip among young spinsters, and of envy among those of a certain age. The bride is loudly praised and flattered ; but it is sometimes whispered she is sacrificing herself to a stupid old millionaire, or, what is no less deplorable, parting with her own large fortune, to regild a tarnished coronet. The *déjeuner* follows, with its dull speeches, some of which draw tears, and others blushes ; and then comes the inevitable tour. There are new trunks, new dressing-cases, and new equipages. Everything is new—they ought to be so, for they are to last a long time. It is a pity the bridegroom is not new also. He is a good deal worn ; but, then, he is well got up, and looks as fresh as ever. The happy pair are united at last, tears and kisses are mingled.

Mixtures are apt to be cloudy or discoloured, and the current of true love does not always run smooth—at least poets say so, and they, like painters, are always true to nature, when they copy it. The experience of others is of little value, and we all hope to be exceptions to general rules. Smack go the whips, and away fly the horses—the happy couple commence their wedding tour. They will not receive company for some time, so we shall not intrude further upon them.

This is the fashion—and fashion must be obeyed : the high and the low, the rich and the poor conform to it. Even the American negro apes his betters. When I was at the National Hotel at Baltimore, Jackson, the black butler (General Jackson, as he was called), was married with much pomp and ceremony to Miss Venus Cato—both were slaves. The wedding feast was liberally provided by the landlord, and the lodgers all attended to do honour to the faithful servants. At its close, a carriage drove to the door, and, to my astonishment, conveyed away the smiling and happy bride. 'Why, General,' I said, 'what is the meaning of all this? Why don't you accompany your wife?' 'Massa,' he said, 'you know de quality all take de *tower* when dey is married; so as I can't be spared (for as me and massa keeps dis hotel, we must attend to our business; dat ar a fac), I tought I'd send Miss Wenus by herself to take her tower, an enjoy herself. I wouldn't 'prive her of dat pleasure for nothen in de world. I scorn a mean action as I does a white servant.'

Perhaps, after all, there is some sense in wedding tours. At first, the attention of the happy pair is drawn from each other by change of scene, and afterwards by the duties of life. It lets them down easily. It is a dissolving view, that imperceptibly discloses a stern reality.

Then there is travelling on business. This is work, and not pleasure. The horse does the same; he performs his daily stage, and returns to his stall at night; but neither he nor his driver are much the wiser for the journey—it must be done, and what is compulsory is always irksome. There is, also, an absconding trip by the night express train to the Continent, which promises so much immunity, that a return ticket is unnecessary. Men who live too fast, are apt to take sudden journeys, and travel post haste. It is an Israelitish exodus. The Egyptians are plundered before the flight, and left to mourn the spoils that were obtained from them under

F 2

false pretences. The sea is placed between the fugitives and their pursuers. The air of France is more suited to *complaints of the chest*, than that of England. It is vulgar economy to avoid incurring debts, true wisdom consists in evading their payment. Many a debtor is whitewashed by a sojourn on the other side of the Channel. When he lands, he has a receipt in full for all past liabilities. Several French towns are honoured by this class of travellers; and their conduct and character are such as to give foreigners a very exalted opinion of ' Milord Anglais.' Their expatriation is a strong proof of their paternal affection, for the reason generally assigned for their exile is, that they may obtain a suitable education for their children. They avoid the society of those they knew at home, for recognition invariably brings painful remembrances; but they are hospitable and considerate to their young and rich countrymen who visit them, and show them practically the danger of gambling, by first winning their money, and then console them, by pointing out how fortunate they have been in not falling into the clutches of foreign professional sharpers. In return for all these delicate but most useful attentions, the only favour (and that is a very small one) which they condescend to ask or receive is, to have a bill cashed on their banker, C. Stuart, Esq., No. 1 Cockspur-street. The travellers are well pleased to accommodate their hospitable English friends in such trifling matters; it is the only compensation they can make for their kindness, and for the visit they have rendered so agreeable. What could they have done without these residents, for they were unable to understand the natives, and the French never speak English? The money is paid and received, as a matter of course, and when the bill is presented, the enlightened tourist finds that C. Stuart is the bronze statue

of Charles the First, which obstructs and disfigures
Charing Cross; that a bankrupt king makes an indifferent
banker, and that worldly wisdom can be acquired in
London as easily, and far more cheaply, than either at
Nice or Boulogne.

Yankee travellers are not so easily taken in. As they
say of themselves, with great complacency, 'they have
cut their eye teeth.' 'You might as well try to catch a
weasel asleep as to find them napping.' 'You can't draw
the wool over their eyes.' 'They were not born yesterday.' 'They are wide awake.'

These and many other elegant phrases of the same
description indicate at once their superiority over Britishers and their contempt for them.

These English absentees and Yankee bagmen, are the
scum of Great Britain and America, that floats on the
surface of the Continent. They are avoided by the *élite*
of both countries, and must not be considered as types of
either nation. The former go abroad to avoid the payment of debts; the latter to incur expenditure they cannot
afford, and both bring discredit on their countrymen.
These Yankee tourists thoroughly enjoy the trip to
Europe. They set apart as large a sum of money for the
purpose as is compatible with safety, and when that is
expended they return to America. It is a matter of indifference whether this happens in three or in six months.
Money is no object, credit is capital—as long as one lasts
the other abounds. If they cannot afford the expense,
some one else can. John Bull will 'do, or die;' Jonathan will 'do, or break.' That is the difference between
a high and a low tone of principle. To die in the pursuit
of any object is sheer folly. To fail, and then to try
again, is worldly wisdom. A good bankrupt law is a
great blessing; there is no sponge like a judicial one.

It effaces all scores; it gives a clean slate to recommence
addition and multiplication; it prevents total annihilation.
Instead of utterly ruining one merchant, it diffuses the
loss over a great multitude of traders and manufacturers
who have no reason to complain, because allowance is
made for bad debts in their prices. The world is merely
a large mutual insurance association, which sustains individual losses, and pays the amount out of the premiums
represented by their gains. To pay a dividend is more
honourable than to repudiate a debt. The importer can
afford to fail, while the loss falls on the ' soft-horned '
manufacturer, who resides at Manchester, Belfast, or
Glasgow. The Americans, therefore, spend freely. A
hotel-keeper, at Liverpool, once told me he regarded
them with unbounded admiration; he said they were
model travellers, for they never examined the items of a
bill—they merely looked at the *end of it* to ascertain
what Joseph Hume used to call ' the tottle of the hull,'
and then, in the most gentlemanlike manner, gave a
cheque for the amount. They go in pursuit of pleasure,
and, cost what it may, they are determined to enjoy themselves. It is a great relief to get out of a country that
labours under the infliction of a Maine Liquor Law. It
is irksome to keep up the appearance of morality in deference to a public opinion which will tolerate an offence,
but has no sympathy with detection. Once on the ocean,
the jurisdiction of the People's Court ceases, and the un-
willing slave of custom asserts his freedom. He drinks,
he gambles, and becomes a *fast man*. He does not
remain long in England; for though he considers himself
equal to the oldest peer of the realm, his claim is unfortunately not recognised, and he quits the country in disgust. Before he leaves it, however, as he is a sight-seer,
if there is a levee, he attends it, and is enabled on his

return to boast of the honour of knowing the Queen.
His patron, the Minister, is dressed like a butler, and
sometimes mistaken for one, while he, as his *protégé*, assuming that the rule which dispenses in the case of Re-
publicans with a court suit, is an evidence of royal
submission to presidential orders, dresses himself accordingly, and resembles a shopman in holiday attire. A
snob is always an object of aversion, but a Yankee snob
is detestable. He has no pretension to be presented, for
even in his own country he is not one of the ' upper ten
thousand ;' but his ambassador dares not refuse him an
introduction, for he has influence if not position, and in
revenge will proclaim him, on his return home, throughout the length and breadth of America, to be an aristocrat.
He has more privileges than an Englishman in this
respect ; but, alas! they are more political than social ;
he can intrude into the presence of royalty, but he cannot
force himself into society. He, therefore, goes to France,
where Yankee pronunciation passes for good English,
where people are too accustomed to boasting, to be dis-
gusted at his exaggeration, where monarchical principles
have no root, and where everybody will agree with him
in abusing the English. Society is freer and looser there,
than either in Great Britain or the United States.
People live in hotels and dine in public, as in America.
They have social liberty, though not political ; and in his
own country he has neither. He has not the first, because
the form of Puritanism, which has survived the spirit,
exacts implicit uniformity in appearance ; nor has he
political freedom, because he must either belong to one
or the other of two factions, or be squeezed to death by
their pressure. Whatever intervenes between scissors is
cut in two. France, therefore, presents every attraction
that he values. Wine, wit, and women—what a trio!

Wine he can taste and appreciate, most probably he has dealt in it, and made money in the traffic. Wit when badly translated (for he is a poor French scholar), degenerates into a pun which he can comprehend, or is converted into humour, for which he has a decided turn, and he enjoys it uncommonly. French women enchant him. They have not the *mauvaise honte* of the English, or the coldness of the American ladies. They can converse in a way to charm him, and as love is the end and aim of their lives, if they do not warm under its influence, they are so well versed in theatricals they can act their part most admirably. Paris is only a portion, but not the whole of Europe. Time flies, but money makes wings to itself, and flies faster. If he is to see more than that great city, he must be up and doing. He is off for the Rhine, or Italy. Luggage is inconvenient. Two carpet bags tied together, and united by a strap to a hat box, are all he requires for his expeditious journey. You may meet him with others of his countrymen in one of the river steamers; you cannot mistake him, for he is distinguishable from every other passenger. He is a tall, spare man, with a narrow chest, a long neck, and a gait that is a singular mixture of a strut and a slouch. His complexion is sallow, his cheeks hollow, his eyes bright, but sunken, and his hands small, thin, and terminating in long, taper consumptive-looking fingers, of a colour that exhibits the effects of a contempt for gloves or soap. His hat is unbrushed and rests on the back of his head, his hair is long, lank, and uncared for, while his face is shaggy, and his beard untrimmed.

An Englishman has an open countenance, guarded by great reserve of manner; his is the reverse. It is not ingenuous or frank; but he converses freely, and is ready to talk with any one he meets. He is devoted to Bacchus and backy. He prepares, in honour of the first as many compounds as an apothecary, and burns incense continually to the second. He expectorates incessantly (I use that expression, because I do not like the common term) to the annoyance and evident danger of every one around him. Bragging never fatigues him; but as this is generally a matter of comparison he makes it more odious by disparaging everything out of his own country. A friend of mine lately steamed up the Thames with one of these gentry when he was in this agreeable mood. When they arrived off Woolwich he pointed to a line-of-battle ship anchored there, and said, 'What do you call *that?*' 'That is the Dreadnought,' was the reply, 'an old man-of-war, but now used as a receiving ship.' 'Ah,' he said, 'we raise cabbages in the States as big as that *thing.*'

Proceeding farther up the river they came opposite to the Leviathan, which was just ready to be launched, when he put a similar question as to her. 'What do you call *that?*' 'That,' said my friend, 'is a great iron kettle we are building to boil the Yankee cabbages in.' 'Stranger,' he replied, with a loud laugh, 'I guess you wern't born in the woods, to be scared by an owl, was you? Well, that ere ship is as big as all out doors, that's a fact.'

Of the quality of land he is a good judge; but he is indifferent to the beauties of nature; he ascends the Rhine that he may have the opportunity of boasting of a larger American river. The scenery, he says, is not worth looking at, it is so inferior to that of the Hudson. So he takes off his hat, and extracts from it a pack of cards, seats himself in the first vacant place, and commences playing with some vagrant countryman a game at *écarté,* which is enlightened by sundry expressions of triumph or disappointment, that are as unintelligible to you as to the Germans. You meet him again at Rome, where you see him coolly walk up to one of his countrymen, and taking his cigar out of his mouth, light his own by it, remarking, at the same time, that ' he knew he was an American as soon as he saw him,' a discovery which, no doubt, many others had made before him. When he returns to his native land his friends are able to appreciate

'How much a donkey that has been to Rome
Excels a donkey that is kept at home.'

Then there is the scientific traveller, who writes unreadable books which are illustrated, not with sketches, but unpronounceable words of Greek compounds, with Latin epithets—a sort of plated ware with silver handles. He is to be found in the mountains or the ravines. He is armed with a hammer, and carries a bag filled with fragments of rocks that are enough to load a donkey. He is silent, distrait, and neglectful of his person. The police have an eye to him, as a man either weak in intellect, or assuming the appearance of a geologist, to disarm suspicion, while he is intriguing to overthrow the Government.

There is also the connoisseur traveller, who criticises pictures, statues, and architectural buildings in a way to astonish alike the learned and the uninitiated. Publishers tell him his books will not sell, but he knows better, prints them at his own expense, and loses money. The only consolation he has is, that he is in advance of the age, and posterity will do him justice.

But of all travellers, perhaps, the John Murray class is the most numerous. They buy his hand-book, that enumerates the churches, hotels, theatres, and museums they have to glance at ; and, when they return, they are just as wise as if they had studied these manuals and remained at home. The character of the people, their laws and insti-

tutions, their system of education and government, their
taxes, resources, domestic trade, foreign commerce, and
everything that is worth knowing, are all omitted. They
cannot all be comprised in a five-shilling volume, and it
cannot succeed if it is too diffuse. It is the idler's manual:
a continental Bradshaw, with letter-press, a distance table
with a list of prices and fares, and a catalogue of things
to be seen if you have time and inclination. Such travelling, however, is not without its use: if it does not furnish
much information, it supplies topics of conversation when
tourists return home.

The English see more of their own country now than
they did before the introduction of railways. They are
also more communicative. This is particularly the case
on the Southampton line, where there is always a fair
sprinkling of persons who have just returned from abroad,
and who freely enter into conversation with their neighbours. Just before I took my departure for London the
Pera arrived from Alexandria and Malta, bringing a large
number of passengers, some of whom were from Australia and others from India. Most of them retained the
dress of their respective countries, and the whole formed
singularly picturesque groups. Here a man moved
about, with an air of independence and self-reliance,
that marked the settler in the bush, who required nothing
that he could not do for himself; and there another was
assisted ashore, by black attendants, without whose aid at
every turn he seemed utterly helpless. Maltese dogs,
Arab horses, paroquets, cockatoos, cum multis aliis, were
landed in great numbers. They appeared to have been
put on board in the vain hope that, like the homœopathic
system, one cause of nausea would neutralize another—
that a singing in the head could be cured by the screams
of birds—and that the vermin of a ship could be expelled

by introducing animals and birds whose bodies were covered with them.

A farmer, who stood by me on the quay, after gazing in wonder at the singular appearance of these people, their attendants, and living animals, addressing himself to me, said, 'That vessel, sir, is a sort of Noah's Ark; for it contains birds, beasts, and all sorts of queer things. As soon as it touches the shore how they rush out, as if delighted to see the land again. There are some things about the ark I never could understand. Can you tell me, why in the world Noah took on board a rat, a weasel, and a turnip-fly, which were sure to destroy his corn, and his green crops? I'm thinking they must have got in unbeknownst to him, afore the ark was finished, for he never could have taken them in on purpose. The old gentleman, you see, was six hundred years of age at that time, and it is natural to suppose that his eyesight was none of the best, especially as glasses hadn't been invented then. I suppose the rats sneaked into the sacks of corn, afore they was put on board, and that the egg of the turnip-fly was concealed in the seed, for Swedes and turnip-flies naturally go together. The best way I knows on to secure the crop, is to take the seed and roll it over '—

Here this disquisition was cut short by the rapid passage of a hand-truck, which, striking his legs from under him, rolled *him* over on it, and carried him off, (minus his hat,) sprawling and roaring, to the infinite amusement of the bystanders. 'Take that drunken man off the quay,' shouted the warehouse keeper, 'or he will fall into the dock.' Picking up the poor fellow's hat, I followed the truck; and having released him from his unpleasant situation, restored it to him, and then proceeding with my friend Cary to the train, set out for London. Recurring to this ludicrous scene, after we had comfortably seated ourselves in the carriage, I remarked, that the man was as stupid a clodhopper as I ever saw, but that he was not intoxicated, and added, he was 'as sober as a judge.' 'That is rather an equivocal standard,' replied Cary. 'I once heard Lord Broadlands, who was a fast man, ask dear old Mr. Justice Mellow, of convivial memory, if there was any truth in that old saying, "As sober as a judge?" It was a good hit, and we all laughed heartily at it. "It is perfectly true," replied the Judge, "as most of those old saws are." They are characteristic, at least; for sobriety is the attribute of a judge, as inebriety is of a nobleman. Thus we say, "As sober as a judge," and "*As drunk as a lord.*" Mellow was the readiest man I ever knew; he went on to say, "I know there are men too fond of the *bar* to *sit* on the *bench*, and that there are peers who richly deserve a *drop*. The first are unworthy of elevation; the last seldom get what is their due."'

'Talking of sobriety,' I said, 'how fares teetotalism now? for I have been so long out of England, I am hardly aware what progress it has made. In the States, the attempt to enforce the Maine Liquor Law has increased drunkenness to an alarming degree. At first, the legislature prohibited the issue of licences for the sale of fermented liquors, but this was evaded in every possible way. The striped pig was a very amusing dodge. A man advertised that he was possessed of a singular pig, which was striped like a zebra, and that it was to be exhibited under canvas, at a certain price daily. Crowds pressed forward to behold this wonderful animal, but every one who entered the tent in which it was shown, expressed his indignation at having been cheated by the substitution of a common hog, that had been shaved and painted in longitudinal stripes. The keeper feigned great regret at the disappointment and want of taste of the spectators, and begged them to accept a glass of rum and a biscuit, as some compensation for the deception. It was soon whispered about, that it was an acute evasion. The money was paid for a *sight*, in order to obtain a *taste;* it was the admission ticket that was sold, and not the liquor. "The law," he said, "did not prevent a man from being liberal to his friends."

'Another evasion was, to import from the adjoining state, where this rigid law did not prevail, a coffin, containing a tightly-fitting tin box, filled with brandy. When emptied of its contents it was supplied with a corpse, the victim of the poison it had previously concealed. To prevent these tricks, all persons were prohibited by penal enactments from selling spirituous liquors, unless a professional order was obtained, prescribing it as a medicine. The mere production of the order was declared to be a protection; but the Act was silent on the subject of the qualification, or the sex of the practitioner, so every man prescribed for his neighbour, and nurses ordered it into every house they attended. In short, the law was so loosely worded and so badly amended, that as soon as one hole was soldered up, another appeared, and it was never "liquor-tight." In my opinion it increased the evil it was designed to remedy, by adding to it fraud and hypocrisy. You may induce a man to be temperate by appealing to his reason, or his sense of right and wrong, but you can never compel him to be so by legal enactments, or pecuniary penalties. If the fine is too large, it creates a sympathy for the offender, and it is paid by subscription; if too small, it is added to the price of the illicit spirits. If its enforcement violates personal liberty too much, and calls in the aid of inquisitorial powers, the executive officer subjects himself to personal outrage, and his property to serious depredations. In several cases, I have known a temperance hall to be blown up with gunpowder, and in others, maroons to be exploded in the premises of the Clerk of the Licences. Wherever tried, such laws have always failed to effect the object for which they were enacted. Low duties, or free trade, are the only effectual checks on smuggling, and, in like manner, example and persuasion can alone repress intemperance.'

'I entirely agree with you,' said a gentleman who sat opposite to me, 'as to the inefficacy of the American prohibitory laws, and of the hypocrisy engendered by compelling people to take pledges to abstain from the use of fermented liquors. When I was canvassing the borough of Sewermouth, during the last general election, many of my constituents inquired of me whether I was in favour of the introduction of the Maine Liquor Law into this country, and upon my stating my objection to it, they positively refused to vote for me. At last I came to a publican, whose support I felt certain I should obtain. "Ah, my friend," I said, "I feel as if I had a natural claim to your cordial assistance. Every member of the Temperance Society in Sewermouth has declined to vote for me, because I will not consent to the introduction of the Maine Liquor Law; my opinion is, that it is incompatible with the liberty of the subject. If you think proper to retail beer or spirits, you have a right as an Englishman to do so," and so forth, in the usual electioneering declamatory manner. "Stop, sir," said the publican, "if you please; I will have nothing said in this house against members of Temperance Societies; they are the best customers I have. When one of them slips in here on the sly, he throws his ha'pence on the counter, and says, Give me a glass of gin, which he snatches up, without stopping to see if the glass is quite full, lays his head back, and tosses it off like winky, and then passing his hand over his mouth, this way," (and he suited the action to the word), " and giving his lips a dry wipe, he goes to the door, looks cautiously up and down the street, to ascertain that nobody is observing him, and then walks off as innocent as a lamb, feeling good all over, and looking at peace with himself and the world, like a righteous man that is setting a good example to all his neighbours, for conscience sake. But your open audageous dram drinkers, sir, set all decency at defiance, and pride themselves on their independence. When they come here, they swagger in, as if they felt they had a right to drink whatever they could pay for, and wished all the world to know they would exercise that privilege, in spite of all the temperance societies in the kingdom. I hate them; I detest them, sir; they are noisy, blustering, impudent rascals. Instead of quietly taking their nip, and walking off about their business, they sit down and jaw all day—there is no getting rid of them—they disgrace themselves and bring discredit on me and my business. Don't say anything against the members of temperance societies, if you please, sir, for they conduct themselves like gentlemen, and I am proud to have such quiet, decent customers ; they pays as they goes, and runs up no scores. Next to them, sir, I respects servants ; they are both civil and liberal, and act on the principle of ' live and let live.' Like teetotallers, they study the decencies of life ; they get what they want, and don't stay long. In general they comes on business, and merely takes a glass of som'at when they are fatigued. Butlers to quality are always real gentlemen, and half the time are better dressed and better mannered than their masters. The busses and the carriers stop here, and in

course servants must come for their parcels. Butlers and
cooks have lots of hampers to send away, and very seldom
receives any in return; a losing business I should suppose, too, sir,"—(and he gave me a wink, which, to render it
quite intelligible, was accompanied with a twitch of the
corner of his mouth, and a nod of the head.) "You'd
naturally think, sir, it was a trade leading to bankruptcy,
with a third-class certificate, without protection. An export commerce, without an import of the raw material,
looks as if the balance of trade was again them, as those
upstarts, Cobden and Bright say, don't it?" "May it not
be," I replied, "that the export is paid for in hard cash?"
"I didn't think of that," he said, with another arch look;
"but you know I never inquires into other folks' affairs—
I have enough to do to attend to my own. I don't belong
to the teetotal club, sir, tho' I have a great respect for
it; but I do belong to the 'Anti-poke-your-nose-into-
other-people's-business Society,' and I find it a safe and
profitable consarn. When those parcels of the butler and
cook are brought here, as these people have a great deal
to do at home, and under servants read addresses, which
leads to gossip, I puts on the directions for them, and
forwards them. I said these two officials, butlers and
cooks, were genteel and honourable people, sir, and so
they are; and so are ladies' maids too—I loves them, the
dear little creatures, for they is so refined and fashionable—how they perk up their pretty mouths when they
speak, don't they? and mince their words as fine as if a
big one would choke them, or crack their tender young
jaws. They have little secrets of their own, too, and
they knows they can trust me, tho' I am a single man, so
I says nothing further; indeed missises have secrets sometimes as well as they have, at least so their ladies tells
me. *The truth is, sir, this world is a great secret, if we*

could only find it out. Upper servants of nobility and
gentry behaves well to me, I must say. Instead of making me give them presents, or commissions, they scorns
such conduct, and makes *me* handsome acknowledgments. It's only tradesmen they taxes, such as butchers,
bakers, fishmongers, and grocers. They makes them
pay a 'nad walorem duty,' as they calls it ; and what
government could be carried on without taxes? Why
debts, sir, would soon be repugiated, if supplies was
stopped. Their custom ain't much, to be sure, for they
have better liquor at home nor I have ; but their friendship is valuable as patrons, and they recommends my
house to all their visiters, and any little forwardin of exports abroad that I does for them is liberally relumarated.
They sends all their company's carriages here, with an
order that their horses should have their corn wet instead
of dry, which means beer and gin for the coachman, and
only hay for their cattle. It is better for both. Dry oats
is apt to swell in the stomach of animals that travel fast,
and produce inflammation ; but hay and water is cooling,
while liquor gives a quick eye and a steady hand to the
gentleman what drives. 'Stout,' says the butler from
the Hall up there, to me the other day, when he and his
friend from the Castle dined here, with me, 'Stout,' says
he, 'I can't bear your wine, you ain't a judge of the
article ; beer and spirits is more in your line, so I took
the liberty to send here some old port, wintage '25, that I
ordered yesterday, as a sample to try afore laying in for
our governor.' When we was discoursing it arter dinner,
sais he, 'Stout, I respect *you.* You are a man of great
talents, far greater talents than are a Meux or Hanbury,
or any other compounder of hops and cocklicus Indigus,
that sits in Parliament, and objects to the courts of marriage and divorce taking jurisdiction over adultery in beer,

and that wants to take duty off paper, (readin being out
of their line,) but won't let farmers malt their own barley.
They are *bruin* by nature, and *bruin* by occupation. You
see, Mr. Stout, (as our governor says, and werry properly
too,) we levels down to where we be, but we don't fill the
walleys up to us.   It stops the water courses you see, and
breeds a flood ; and when the floods come, if you
haven't any high hills to fly to why you are done for, and
the fishes get your precious bodies.   Now that's the way
with them brewers I named ; they sing out for free trade,
but buys up all the public-houses, and them and their
friends won't licence any that won't sell their beer ; they
are hypocrites and Pharisees that treat publicans that
way.   Your health, Mr. Stout,' says he, ' how do you
like the flavour of that wine ? it's of the wintage '25, so
marked in the governor's cellar—ahem ! I mean in the
wine merchant's.   It ain't to be sneezed at, is it ?'—Then
he held up his glass to the light, ' See,' says he, ' it
has the *bee* in it.' ' The devil it has,' says I ; ' how in
the world did it get in there ? let me get a teaspoon, and
take it out.'   He nearly laughed himself on to the floor
at that ; he was like a horse that has the staggers ; he
shook his head, reeled about, and quaked all over.
When he recovered, says he, ' Stout, you are a capital
actor, that's the best thing I ever heard. As I was
saying, I respect you : eyes to see, but don't see ; hears
to 'ear, but don't 'ear ; fingers to pick and pry, but don't
pry into what you ain't wanted to know ; a tongue to
speak, but that don't speak ill of your neighbour ; a
memory to remember what is important to retain, but that
can forget what ain't convenient to recollect. It's a
perfect character, for none are so blind as them as
won't see, so deaf as what won't hear, or so ignorant as
won't know what ain't their business to know.'   Well,

sir, I likes coachmen also; they are discreet, prudent people; they calls to see if there is anything come from the saddler's; and when they inquire if *that* parcel is arrived, I am to understand it is one that was expected, and called for before, and I am to entreat them (only as acquaintances, and not as customers) to take a glass, which they does reluctantly, and tells me to blow up the carrier 'when I see him, for not obeying their orders. That glass is to be charged; they have their reasons for what they says and does: they knows who is who in the shop, and they wants it to be seen they came on business on that occasion, and not for pleasure.

'" Footmen likewise have, or expect something by the carrier, or they want to ascertain addresses, or to inquire after all sorts of persons and things. They complain bitterly that instead of a list being given them, they are sent several times to my house, when once would answer; in short, they talk of leaving their places on that account. All these are respectable customers, sir; they never stay long, or make a noise, for they knows what's what, and are up to the time o' day.

'" Willage servants I despise; they are ignorant, underbred varmin. What is parquisites of office in the upper class is no better than prigging with them; one is what they calls superfluities, the other is low pilfering and nothing else. They toss up their heads, particularly females, as if they had been used to high life, and say they won't live with people who ' throw up and lock up.' ' What do you mean by that?' I said; ' I never heard the expression before.'—' Why, sir,' said the eccentric publican, ' it is where a tradesman's wife is her own housekeeper, and locks up her pantry, and has the ashes sifted, and the cinders thrown back into the fire again. They say they want to live where the gentlemen wear

powder, and where their missises are 'carriage people.'
I forwards no parcels for the like of them ; they ain't safe
customers. I leave them to charwomen, who carries
messages from their loviers, and takes money from one,
and money worth from the other. Them women, sir, are
regular smugglers; they have long cloaks, large aprons,
and big pockets; they introduces sweethearts and gin,
and smuggles out groceries and provisions; and when
they ain't a running of goods, they act as coast-guards ;
they stands sentry for them, and gives the signals that the
coast is clear for them as are in to get out, and them as
are waiting for a chance to slip in on the sly : they are a
bad lot, sir, the whole on 'em ; I am afraid of them, and
I never want to see them here, for they are very tonguey
sometimes, and it don't do for the like of me to have a
noise in my house. I had to turn two of them out this
morning.

'"They met here quite accidentally, and says one of
them to me quite loud, on purpose to be overheard,
'Mr. Stout, who is that? she is one of the "has-beens."
'I'd have you to know,' said the other, 'that the "has-
beens" are better nor the "never-wases" all the world
over,' and she flew at her like a tiger. Liquor, you see,
sir, acts different on different people. Some it sets a
laughin, and others a cryin; some it brightens up, and
others it makes as stupid as owls. Melancholy, highstrikes, kissing, quarrelling, singing, swearing, and every
sort of thing is found in drinking, when enough grows
into too much, and the cup runs over. Women never do
nothing in moderation. A little does them good, but
when they goes beyond that it is ruination. No, sir, take
'em all in all, as far as my experience goes, I give the
preference, by all odds, to the members of temperance
societies. They use liquor without abusing it. It never

excites them, for they never talk over it; and it is
astonishing how much a man can stand, if he will only
hold his tongue. I'll vote for you, sir; but don't say
nothing against temperance society people in my house, if
you please." '

Such was the whimsical account my fellow-traveller
gave of his reception by the publican, when canvassing
him for his vote; and he added that he thought teetotalism, in any shape, when not founded on religious
principles, was illusory; and that if attempted to be
enforced by penalties, it would be successfully resisted or
evaded. A relapse in the case of a drunkard he considered fatal. 'It is hard,' he observed, 'to wean a calf
that has taken to sucking a second time.'

'I never hear anecdotes of drinking,' said another passenger, 'that I do not think of one that was told me of a poor
clergyman in Lincolnshire. He had received, for the first
time in his life, an invitation to dine with his bishop. It
was at once a great honour, a great event, and a great
bore. He was flattered and frightened: flattered by
being considered worthy of dining with those who dressed
in purple and fine linen, and fared sumptuously every day:
and frightened at his own ignorance of the usages of
episcopal palaces. Not having a servant of his own, he
took his parish clerk with him to attend him, and desired
him privately to ascertain from the other servants any
particulars of etiquette he was to observe as a guest, and
also what he was to do himself. Soon after the dinner
was served, the bishop, who was a kind and condescending,
though formal, man, asked the poor rector to do him the
honour to drink wine with him. To be selected for this
special mark of favour (for he was the first whom his
lordship had asked to drink with him) was most gratifying
to his feelings. It was a distinction never to be forgotten.

He bowed low and quaffed his wine, that warmed a heart
already glowing with pride and gratitude.   He had, however, no sooner replaced his glass upon the table, than his
humble attendant, the clerk, stepped up behind him, and,
leaning over his shoulder, carefully wiped his mouth with
a napkin.   His first thought was that all this ceremony
was unnecessary, and that this luxury was effeminate, to
say the least of it.   It was the first time in his life his
mouth had ever been wiped by another since that kind
office had been performed for him by his mother or his
nurse when he was a child.   The singularity of the
incident attracted much observation and amusement.
The archdeacon followed the example of the host, rather
to ascertain the meaning of this extraordinary whim of the
parson than to do him honour or indulge his own desire
for another glass.   They mutually bowed and drank
their wine, when the clerk again stepped forward, and
again wiped the rector's mouth with great gravity.
Another and another tried the same experiment with the
same result, but with increased merriment.   The poor old
gentleman was confused by this extraordinary attention of
the company, and the still more inexplicable conduct of
his attendant.   When the entertainment was over, and he
had retired to his room, he summoned the clerk, and
requested an explanation of the singular ceremony.

'" It's quite right, sir," said the artless man ; " I inquired of the servants at his lordship's what I was to do,
and how I was to behave myself, and they told me to
stand near the sideboard, out of their way, and to keep
my eye on your reverence, and when any gentleman
asked you to drink wine, my duty was to wipe your
reverence's mouth with the napkin, and then return to my
place, and that if you called me, they would attend to
your wishes ; but that I was on no account to stir from

my post." "You are a born fool, a stupid blockhead," said the rector; "couldn't you see that that form was not observed to any one else at table?" "I did, sir, and when I said so to the butler, he told me it was always done to every gentleman who had the honour of dining at the palace for the first time, and was meant as a great mark of favour to a stranger. He told me that every other clergyman present had been, on his first visit, honoured in the same way." The poor old parson was overwhelmed with shame; and what is worse, he has never been able to boast, as he otherwise would have been most proud to do, " of once having had the honour of dining with the Bishop of Lincoln." '

I have often observed that when a person tells a good story, it seems to recall to the recollections of others one of a similar nature, until the conversation becomes anecdotal. This story of the poor rector and the bishop reminded me of one told by an old admiral, since deceased. In his early days he went to sea as a midshipman, with poor Captain Hawser, of the Vesuvius. Hawser was a tremendous fellow for grog; worse even than Old Charley, and that is saying a good deal. Well, when they arrived in the West Indies, this indulgence soon brought on a fever, and Hawser nearly lost his life, or (as they say at sea) ' the number of his mess.' The doctor totally inhibited the use of rum or brandy, but told him that when he found himself in a cold climate, he might take them moderately; and the farther north he went, the more freely he might indulge. Shortly after they returned to England, the Vesuvius was ordered to the Baltic; and as soon as they sailed for their destination, Hawser resumed the grog, so long discontinued. He daily asked to have it increased in strength, as they proceeded on their way, and when they reached the Baltic it was considerably more than *half-and-half.* The further he sailed, the stronger it became, until, at last, there was scarcely any water in the composition. The invariable order was given to the steward, ' farther north,' which meant ' mix it stiffer still.' One day he sternly commanded him to make it ' farther north.' ' I can't, sir,' he replied ; ' *you have been due north for three days.* It is no longer grog ; it is clear rum.' ' The force of nature could no farther go.' There is a limit to libations, even when ' far north ;' and *delirium tremens* terminated the career of one of the kindest, bravest, and noblest fellows in the navy.

Those who cannot afford good wine, are apt to substitute rum, or brandy and water in its place ; and if taken in small quantities, it is not only unobjectionable, but wholesome. But it is a dangerous habit, and one that is difficult to keep under proper control. I have often laughed at a conversation I once heard between two old country squires, who were lamenting the dissipation of a young friend of theirs. ' Ah,' said one, shaking his head, and speaking most dolefully, ' they tell me the poor fellow has taken to drinking spirits.' ' Yes,' replied his friend, with a still more rueful countenance, 'yes; but that is not the worst of it,' and he lowered his voice as if it was something very horrible, ' *he puts the water in first*, sir ; what dreadful depravity ! !' ' I don't understand,' said the first mourner, ' how that alters the case.' ' Don't you ?' said the other. ' Why no one can tell how much spirits he puts into the tumbler. Concealment, sir, is a sure sign of guilt. It's the last stage ; it shows he has sense enough to be ashamed, and yet wants resolution to act prudently. It's the drunkard's dodge. I consider a person, sir, who does that a dishonest fellow. He gets drunk under false pretences : he is a lost man. To drink brandy and water, sir, is low, very low ; but *to put the water in first is the devil.*'

G

'That story you told us just now,' I said, addressing
the gentleman who related to us the remarks of the publican upon teetotallers and others who frequented his house,
'is a capital one, but it is also a melancholy sketch. The
condition of servants is one that cannot be viewed otherwise than with great regret, if not with apprehension.
Servitude is, at best, a state of humiliation, and we cannot
wonder that it leads to a certain degree of disaffection.
To view it philosophically it is, after all, a mere contract.
On the one side a stipulated sum is paid for certain services, and on the other there is a promise faithfully to
obey and execute all lawful orders in consideration of the
wages thus agreed upon. We pay our money, and we
expect the equivalent But although the terms are
settled to the satisfaction of both parties, the master and
the servant mutually desire to derive the utmost advantage from the bargain. The former wants the entire
time and devotion of the servant, while the latter strives
to limit his services, as far as he can, to such a moderate
and reasonable discharge of his duties as he finds most
compatible with his own ease and comfort. Both look to
the terms of the contract, and severally interpret its clauses
in their own favour. From the artificial state of society
in which we live, we are both led to stand on our rights.
As there is no favour conferred on either side, so there is
no gratitude. If we are kind to our servants, they regard
our liberality as a just tribute to their merits; while on
their part, if they do their duty tolerably well, they think
they have earned their wages, and are under no sort of
obligation to us. Personal attachment seems altogether
out of the question. I was very much struck with the
observation of the hotel-keeper at Paris, where Orsini
lived when he made the attempt on the life of the Emperor Napoleon. He was asked whether he had any

suspicion that Gomez (who acted as his valet) was what he represented himself to be—Orsini's servant. He replied that he had his doubts; for he had kept an hotel for thirty years, and in all that time had never heard a servant but Gomez who spoke well of his master! It struck him as a very suspicious circumstance. Can this be true? If it be, what a satire it is upon poor human nature!'

Much of the disappointment we experience in the conduct of servants, is our own fault; we are afraid to speak the truth; we dread an action for slander, if we venture to state what we know to be true, without being quite in a position to prove our assertions. We give them characters to which they are not entitled; we pity them, and, concealing their defects, say all we can in their favour. We enable them to bring other employers to grief, as they have brought us. Their former masters assisted them in deceiving us, and we aid them in imposing on others. What right have we, then, to complain? We bring inconvenience and trouble upon ourselves, by our negligence or want of firmness and candour. The remedy is not wholly in our own hands, but we can protect ourselves to a great extent if we please. Knowing how little reliance is in general to be placed upon written characters, let us, if possible, have an interview with the last employer. He will probably *tell* us much that he will not venture to *write*, and, at all events, is open to cross-questioning. And when a servant either leaves our employment, or is discharged, let us give him (as far as the law will permit plain speaking) the character he deserves, whether for good or for evil. The faithful, painstaking domestic will then derive all the advantage resulting from good conduct; and the disobedient, negligent, or dishonest one, will be punished in not having an

opportunity afforded him of annoying another master.
Let us thus teach them the value of character, by showing
them we consider it indispensable; and compel them to
be circumspect, by depriving them of the means of deception. Strict discipline insures obedience, while kind and
considerate treatment ought to produce attachment; and
a combination of *both* cannot fail to make a good and
faithful servant.

'Tickets, if you please, gentlemen,' are the last words
we hear. They remind us that we have reached Waterloo station, and that our journey is now terminated.

No. V.

JOHN BULL AND HIS DIGGINS.

In travelling over a country, it is desirable to pause a while on the hills, and look back on the lowlands through which we have passed. We are thus enabled to embrace in one view all that we have seen in the various stages of our journey, and to judge of it as a whole, to compare it with other portions of the globe of similar extent, beauty, and fertility, and pronounce on its comparative merits. In like manner, when we return home from foreign travel, it is desirable to bring our native land into contrast with other countries, and our people with the inhabitants of other empires. Without such contemplation, travelling is of but little value. It may amuse and occupy us, but it can make us neither wiser nor better men. One scene replaces another, on the principle of dissolving views, and the last is alone remembered of them all, not because it is more striking, or more effective, but *because it is the last.* Whoever has twice left home to wander among foreign nations, if he has given himself time, on his return, for meditation, must recollect that the second tour has corrected some of his first impressions, and modified many more. The first visit satisfies his curiosity, the second matures his judgment.

In subjecting England to this 'competitive examination,' I find it is entitled to rank first among the nations of the earth.

Whence arises this pre-eminence ? Ask those who dwell
in it, and every man will assign a different cause.   One
will tell you it proceeds from its climate ; another from
its insular, geographical, and political position ; a third
from its free institutions, and Protestant religion ; and a
fourth from its soil, inexhaustible mineral resources, and
extensive fisheries.   This one attributes it to the race
that inhabit it, and that to its extended colonies, and
countless thousands of subjects in its distant possessions,
while most ascribe it to the intelligence and skill of its
artisans in all mechanical arts.   But the true reason is to
be found in a wonderful combination of all these causes,
with others equally characteristic.

The English people are as remarkable as their country ;
they have many traits of character in common with the
inhabitants of other portions of the globe, but they have
some that are peculiar to themselves.   Among the former,
they have that presumptuous vanity which is so inherent
in human nature, that it should be added to the generic
definition of man, which describes him as an animal that
is ‘bipes implumis, et risibilis.’   They form a very high
estimate of their own worth, and a very low one of that
of others.   As the Americans say of them, ‘it would be a
losing concern to purchase them at their own price, and
sell them for what they would bring in the market.’
Their contempt for foreigners is returned with interest.
Even the Chinese consider them as barbarians and heathen.
They claim for themselves the highest place in civilization,
the most illustrious ancestry, and the monopoly of all
wisdom.   Descended from the brother of the Sun and
Moon, it is no wonder they call their country the ‘Celestial
Empire,’ and carefully exclude strangers from a territory
reserved for the Children of Light.   All the rest of the
world dwell in ‘outer darkness,’ in which there is no tea

to imbibe, no porcelain to hold this divine beverage, and no opium to inspire dreams of Paradise. The little foreigners know they are charged with having acquired stealthily when trading at Canton, the citizens of which, according to their account, imparted to them the art of printing, of making pottery, of manufacturing silk, of carving ivory and stone, and the knowledge of many other things. But, above all, they say that they taught the English to cultivate the soil, so as to produce the greatest crops from the smallest possible extent of ground, and also the mode of preparing exquisite dishes from rats, dogs, cats, snakes, slugs, locusts, lizards, birds' nests, and innumerable other delicate materials. They consider them, however, as deficient in taste, in not properly appreciating these dainties, and as bungling imitators of all that they attempt to copy or adopt. They laugh at their pedigrees as modern assumptions, and their decorations as glittering tinsel, regarding the griffins, lions, unicorns, and dragons on their armorial bearings as plagiarisms from their ancient religion. It is therefore natural that they should look down upon the English with profound contempt.

In like manner the French consider themselves as models of gallantry, as the first in refinement and taste, and as excelling in 'the court, the camp, the grove.' The English they style a nation of shopkeepers. London they regard as a gloomy and dirty manufacturing town, but Paris as the very centre of civilization, intelligence, and fashion. The Germans they denominate 'learned pigs;' they ridicule their propensity to drink beer, their devotion to tobacco, the formal and frigid etiquette of their nobles, and the slavish and stolid submission of the lower orders. The name of Russia is associated in their minds with frozen lakes and polar bears, with drunken nobles and Siberian exiles, or with serfs, bristles, cordage, tallow, black bread, and rancid oil. They shrug their shoulders when they talk of their army, with which they became acquainted at Moscow, and during the occupation of Paris, and have many anecdotes, which they relate with much spirit, of officers with splendid uniforms, but no shirts or stockings, and soldiers who repeatedly left Paris in darkness by drinking up the oil of the street lamps. They admit that they are brave, otherwise it would have been disgraceful to be beaten by them; but they ascribe their power to brute force, directed by great science and practical skill. They excuse their own failure at Moscow, by asserting that it arose from the superior intelligence and gallantry of the French soldier, who, while he thinks *for* himself, never thinks *of* himself, and therefore preferred death to retreat. They are loud in their disparagement of the Americans, and say they are a bad edition of the English, neither cooks nor gentlemen, knowing neither how to eat, drink, or live like Christians, and mistaking rudeness for frankness, cunning for talent, scurrilous abuse for the liberty of the press, and the ownership of slaves as compatible with free institutions. Frenchmen talk loudly of their honour, and lay their hands on their hearts while asserting their preference of death to the loss of it, and yet observe treaties no longer than it suits their convenience, or their *parole* as prisoners when they can find an opportunity to escape. Their motives are not what they assign, and, therefore, they doubt the sincerity of all other nations. They call England 'Perfide Angleterre.' Their religion is a destiny; their mission universal dominion; their freedom is the liberty to say and do what they are ordered; might makes right in their eyes. They become frantic on the subject of the slave trade, which they abhor, and will never consent to traffic in human beings; they only purchase their labour, and merely reserve to themselves the power to enforce the right of perpetual servitude. In short, France is the finest country in the world, and they are superior to all other nations. Their army has never suffered a defeat, except when it was vastly outnumbered, or their generals bribed, as was the case at Waterloo.

The Americans, also, have been well trained in the bragging art, both by the English and French. They are as aristocratic as the nobility of the one, and as republican as the Socialists of the other. They assert that all men are free and equal. This is an abstract proposition; but, like all general rules, it has exceptions. It means *all white men*. Their minister refused to sit beside the 'Nigger' Ambassador from Hayti at the Lord Mayor's table—he did not recognise him as a brother! He said it was an insult to a country which considered blacks as inferior beings, and held them as slaves, and referred to Buxton, Wilberforce, and Shaftesbury, as authorities, as all three were stated to have declined matrimonial alliances for their daughters with African princes. They boast that they are white (an exultation no European understands); that they are free, which none but themselves comprehend; and that they are descended from a nation which they insult and affect to despise. Similarity of name with them means consanguinity; they boast that they are descended from the best families in Great Britain, and have 'good blood.' They can, therefore, afford to ape humility and talk of equality, because being on a level with the English nobility they can condescend to admit others to their society without the risk of derogating from their own importance. 'The English have whipped all the world, and they have whipped the English.' Their superiority is unquestionable. They have the largest rivers, the highest hills, the widest prairies, the richest soil, the fastest horses, the prettiest galls, the best revolvers, cutest lawyers, *peowerfullest* preachers, and smartest generals, that are to be found on the face of the airth; also clippers that beat all natur, steamers that streak it off like iled lightning, and men that are half horse and half alligator, with a touch of the devil, and a cross of the airthquake.

Is it any wonder they are 'the greatest nation in all creation?' If you have any doubt as to this fact, ask their minister "to the Court of St. James', Victoria," and he will tell you—'I rather guess it's a fact—stick a pin through it, for it's noticeable.'

John Bull has this vanity in an eminent degree. He is convinced, beyond all doubt, that he is the greatest man in the world. He takes it for granted every one knows it; and if it is not admitted, he attributes the denial either to ignorance or prejudice. He does not assert his superiority so loudly as the Yankee; but he feels and looks it. He is a supercilious gentleman, and regards the rest of mankind with a condescending and patronizing air. He is rich, and measures the respectability of foreigners by their wealth, and as this standard is in his favour, he considers them as a 'beggarly crew.' He is a bluff, ruddy-faced, resolute, good-hearted fellow, and inclined to corpulency, which is no wonder, for he feeds heartily, and drinks strong wine and heavy beer. Like many animals, he is not to be approached with safety while hungry; he is liberal in his charities, but he won't subscribe till after a public dinner and some very fulsome speeches, in which his generosity, his tender disposition, his wealth, and his benevolence, are duly extolled. He is a practical man, and will pay for services rendered, but he grumbles at the expense of erecting monuments to commemorate them.

He says, if he wishes to see a national tribute to the glory of the British arms, he would rather go to France, where, in the enumeration of their victories over various nations, the name of England is omitted. He says he is content with that, for it is an admission far outweighing any assertion of his, however well grounded. He is hospitable, and keeps a liberal table; but is not above letting you know the merits and high prices of his wines, to which he draws your attention, lest your want of taste might prevent your fully appreciating your good fortune in being asked to partake of them. He does not always boast loudly; he sometimes affects to speak disparagingly of what pertains to himself—he considers it more delicate. His stately mansion in the country he calls 'his little place in Meekshire,' his town house 'his *pied à terre*,' and so on.

'And the Devil he laughed, for his darling sin
    Is the pride that apes humility.'

He looks upon the Scotch, the Irish, and the colonists with an air of great superiority. He is fond of telling you Doctor Johnson's definition of oats, 'food for horses in England and men in Scotland,' and 'that their best road is the one that leads to England.' He delights also in repeating the observation of one of his admirals, relative to Ireland, 'that the only cure for the discontent of that country, is to scuttle it for forty-eight hours, to destroy the vermin.' He declines to be introduced to any one from Australia, because he knows he is a returned convict. If he meets a man from Canada, he asks him if it is a penal colony. He is himself full of provincialisms, calling 'H-eve the mother of us h-all,' and talking of his 'orses and ounds;' and yet, his ear is so sensitive, the

Irish brogue and Scotch accent distress him, on account
of their vulgarity. But his nationality is insufferable.
He has an idea that one Englishman is equal, in war, to
three Frenchmen; and has the vanity to believe that a
navy in name is superior to one in fact; that his maritime
supremacy is indisputable, and has been so often proved
that farther evidence is unnecessary. He is of opinion
that a mere notice that 'spring guns and man traps are
set on his premises,' will as effectually protect his property
as if they were really placed there. He grumbles, therefore, at the estimates for a service which has the double
duty to perform, of protecting the sea-board of the British
Isles and the commerce of the colonies. Although he
regards the French as fools, he does not think they can
be so utterly devoid of sense as to invade a country that
has never been visited by an enemy since the landing of
William the Conqueror.

If you suggest the possibility of an attack, he boasts
that though a landing may be effected, not one of the
hostile force would ever return to their native country;
an idea which is supported by the fact, that none of the
Normans ever did so, except for the purpose of bringing
over their wives and children. He maintains that those
who make guns, must, as a matter of course, know how
to use them; that hedges are better fortifications than
batteries, and foxhunters more to be depended upon than
dragoons. He regards the Treasury as the patrimony of
certain powerful Whig families; he pays his taxes and
grumbles, but is on the whole content, so long as he is
permitted to vote for, or against the Premier. He leaves
public business to public men, it is enough for him to
attend to his own affairs. He is fond of civilians—he
places one at the head of the Admiralty, and appoints
country gentlemen to important posts in the Department

of War. He found the advantage of this arrangement in the Crimean struggle, and experience has made him wise; he is an Englishman, and both infallible and invincible. This vanity he shares, as we have seen, with the people of every other country, but he has little else in common with them. In other respects he stands almost alone; he takes sensible views of most subjects, and wherever his own personal interest is concerned, when disconnected with politics or party, he shows to great advantage. He is both able and willing to work, and attaches great value to industrious habits. For this he is mainly indebted to his climate, which, while it develops the human frame, is sufficiently temperate to admit of daily labour in the open air. It is neither too hot nor too cold, either of which extremes would confine him to his house; while the former would compel him, like the Virginian, to seek for a slave to do his work, and the latter would induce him to live like the Laplander or Esquimaux Indian, for more than half the year. It combines that happy medium that is essential to health and strength, labour and enjoyment. A grumbler, however, by nature, he is not quite satisfied with it. When at home he complains that it is too humid, and the sun seldom visible; and he longs for an Italian sky, and its transparent atmosphere. But when he reaches Italy he finds his ideas have been borrowed from poets, and remembers that he once heard, when a boy, that 'Fiction was the soul of poetry.' The seasons drive him from place to place to avoid the sirocco, the malaria, the heat or the cold, as a shepherd does his flocks in search of fresh pastures, running water, and shelter. He sees an indolent, improvident, penniless peasantry, who prefer robbing to working, and who resort to murder to prove their admiration of law, and their fitness for liberty, and who, while dreaming of the unattainable, forego what is within

their reach, and show how little benefit they have derived
from the fable of the dog who relinquished the substance
for the shadow. Yet this lazy, idle rascal, sings and
dances, talks of freedom as of a thing that dispenses with
labour as the foundation of property, but supplies and
protects riches without exacting personal exertion. He
proceeds to Greece with increased hope; for, like Byron
and Gladstone, he imbibed, in his early days, a love for
Hellenic lore, a veneration for ancient heroes, and is
spoony on the subject of its nationality; but he is soon
convinced that its climate and people have been vastly
overrated. He finds that the surface of the country,
broken by high hills and deep ravines, is more distinguished for its picturesque beauty than for its agriculture;
that the heat of the plains which ripens tropical fruits is
overpowering and enervating, and that the mountains,
covered only with the hardiest trees and shrubs, are more
fitted for the resort of wolves and bears than civilized man.
In his disappointment, while discarding all the romance of
early years, he runs to the opposite extreme, and uses
stronger language than the subject warrants. He maintains that whatever the Greeks may have been at some
remote period, they are now greedy, ungrateful, trea-
cherous, and bloodthirsty, preferring trade to agriculture,
piracy to trade, and repudiation, on account of its being
easier as well as safer, to even the greater sport of piracy
and murder.

Wherever he extends his tour he finds the climate
inferior to his own, and returns not satisfied, but grum-
bling, because he is convinced that 'bad is the best.' He
discovers, however, that there are other qualities in a
climate besides its agreeableness, which render it suitable
for the abode of man. That of England, with its many
faults, is neither too hot nor too cold to interfere with

continuous labour, and is, withal, so temperate as to promote the full development of the human frame. Green crops and corn attain their full perfection, and all the most valuable fruits are easily matured. The verdure of England is only excelled by that of the dear 'Emerald Isle,' at once so lovely and so unique. If the climate were hotter, he would be compelled to desist from work in the middle of the day, and the nights would be sufficiently warm to incline him to sleep in the open air.

If England were to drift farther south, he would require his daily siesta, and cultivate a knowledge of the guitar to serenade his mistress by moonlight. He would be poor, proud, and lazy, disinclined to exertion or thought. Less labour would procure the necessaries of life, and what he would think of equal importance, that little he would try to make others perform for him. Indolence would gradually affect his mind, even reflection would be fatiguing, he would find it irksome to think for him- self, and would probably request the Pope to save him this trouble, by providing him with a religion suited to his mind, body, and habits. He would like a spacious and cool cathedral, dreamy music, fragrant incense, beautiful paintings, gorgeous robes, imposing processions, things to delight the eye, the ear, and the imagination, but that require neither thought nor labour on his part. It is more agreeable to believe than to argue ; it is easier to get goods on tick, than to pay for them ; and it saves a world of trouble to let others decide for us, and to accept their tenets with implicit belief. If excite- ments are wanting (as they obviously would be in such a climate) bull-fights, fêtes, and above all, an *auto da fé* now and then, would diversify the monotony of life. He might have a pleasanter time of it, but he would cease to be John Bull. He would feed on figs, olives, and grapes, and drink vapid sour wine; he would eat but little meat, and cease to brew beer. Abstaining from animal food during the fasts of the Church, would be no penance to him, but rather a sanitary rule. But to renounce fruits and vegetables, would indeed be an effort of great self-denial. In like manner, if he were to apply the power of his steam-tugs to the removal of England, and tow her away to the north in search of a better climate (as it is probable he will some day when he has destroyed its constitution by adopting Yankee inventions, and pirating their patent high pressure political engines) he will have an easy time of it in winter. He will be torpid during those long, dreary months, and find the Laplander a happy, contented fellow, sustaining life, like the bear, by the absorption of his own fat, and undergoing the process of smoking, in order to his keeping through the heats of summer. As things are, however, he is the right man in the right place. To his temperate climate he owes his muscular, well-developed frame; but if it is warm enough to enable him to be abroad more days, and more hours in the day, than he could be in any other country, it fortunately does not enable him to live entirely in the open air like the inhabitants of Buenos Ayres. It compels him to have a dwelling, not as a mere shelter from the weather, but as a home to contain his family and dependents, to regulate whom, he must dwell among them, and introduce order, harmony, comfort, and economy, and cultivate the domestic virtues. To maintain them he must work, and when work ceases he seeks the seclusion of his home; he feels that it is his duty, as well as his interest, to make that home happy. He constantly boasts of it, and of its exclusive rights; he calls it *his castle*, and he defends it with as much jealousy as a sovereign does those fortified places which he dignifies with that title. England is covered with these castles, great and small, armed or unarmed, and their owners are independent each of the other, and all of the sovereign or the nobility. They severally claim for themselves that liberty which they concede to others, and in maintaining their individual rights, they unconsciously work out public liberty. From the necessity of providing means to support his family, he acquires a taste for the pursuit of gain, and becomes a merchant or a manufacturer. Nature intended that some of his children should be sailors ; his country is bounded on all sides by the ocean ; he was a good rower at school, and learned the use of a boat as well as that of a gradus or a dictionary. Whenever he obtains a view of the sea he beholds innumerable ships, he reads of their distant voyages and rich cargoes, he hears those who own them called 'Merchant Princes,' and recollects the proud and characteristic reply of his own father when this flattering appellation was first applied to him, 'I hope not,' he said ; 'princes are needy and illiberal, I trust I am neither one nor the other, I am nothing more or less than a plain English merchant.'

He has minerals on his estate, and acquires the art of mining to extract them ; and digs deep into the bowels of the earth for coals to smelt them ; and, when they are refined, sets up manufactories to convert them into articles of use or ornament. He freights his ships with these productions, and exchanges them for raw materials that his country cannot produce ; which, by the aid of mechanical skill, he exports in a manufactured state, to be again exchanged for money or cotton, for cordage or sugar, for wine or tobacco, and amasses great wealth by these several operations. He founds colonies in all parts of the globe, and peoples them with his

artisans and labourers. His language is spoken by a
great portion of the inhabitants of the earth, as America,
Australia, New Zealand, the Cape of Good Hope, and
the ports of the Mediterranean can testify. Is it any
wonder he is proud and boasts of his race, which he
firmly believes will overrun the world? Having interests
to protect everywhere, both of his own and the people
whom he governs, he is apt to interfere with his neighbours in a way to render him hated by all. Being a
strong, muscular man, and having much of the animal in
his composition, he is pugnacious—makes war without
cause; and, when his passion subsides, concludes peace
without advantage. He offers advice where it is not
asked, and sulks or fights if it is not followed. He is full
of contradictions, profuse and mean, impulsive and cold,
tolerant and bigoted, independent, yet governed by party;
learned, but not wise; good-natured, but full of fight;
fond of nobility, but democratic; full of invention, yet
slow to adopt improvements; a churchman, but refuses
to pay rates; and so on. But he is, withal, a manly
fellow—and where shall we find his equal? These very
contradictions often balance each other, and their fusion
makes the man. Such is John Bull.

On our arrival from Southampton at the Waterloo
station, Cary advised me to accompany him to the
British Hotel, Cockspur-street, which, he said, was just
the place to suit a stranger like me. 'Its first recommendation,' he observed, 'is, that it has a spacious, well-
ventilated, smoking-room; not perched up in the roof of
the house, like the cockloft used by the Long Island
Dutch for smoking hams, as if it was a thing to be
ashamed of, but comfortably situated on the ground-floor,
easy of access to those who frequent the coffee-room, or to
those who patronize the house. Nothing is so incon-

venient in England, as this affectation of associating smoking with vulgarity. In large country houses the ill-fated smokers are driven to the housekeeper's room, or to the conservatory; and in towns are either turned out to pace the street with their cigars in their mouths, or are driven to their clubs, where they have to mount to the attic, an ascent only surpassed by that of Mont Blanc. Indeed, they are lucky if they find any smoking-room at their club, for it is not every one that indulges in this luxury.

' My scientific one has none; the bishops (and they do greatly congregate there) think smoking, *infra dig.* They were once curates, and were good for a clay pipe, a screw of tobacco, and a pot of half and half; but now they are good for nothing but shovel-hats, aprons, and gaiters. Artists would enjoy a whiff, but stand in awe of these Dons. It is true they don't give "orders" themselves, but they know those who do, which is quite as good, and they have a very patronizing air; so they look at these sable dignitaries, draw a long sigh, shake their heads, and mutter, "It's a pity it's no go." A few old lords, who love black-lettered folios, because they are printed with antiquated types and are early editions, coeval with, or antecedent to, their own titles, are horrified at the sight of a "clay," which they associate with thieves and pickpockets, and the smell of tobacco, which painfully reminds them of those hot-beds of schism and rebellion, the pot-houses. The geological members of the club have a "*primitive formation*" in them; but it is either overlaid with rubbish or crops out ruggedly sometimes; still they are "*up to trap,*" and would like "a draw" if they were not overawed by these lords spiritual and temporal. Defend me from the dulness of those who point only to the future

or the past, and are not "up to the time of day." I
don't want to live with my grandfathers or my grand-
children. I have no desire to hear of Gladstone's Homer,
and the Siege of Troy, or Little Red Riding Hood, and
the Babes in the Wood. Defend me from a learned club
like mine ! The members are not genial, and they must
be incurable, when such men as Thackeray, Sam Slick,
and Dickens, who (to their credit be it spoken) are all
smokers, can't persuade them that what the white and
the black man, the Jew and the Gentile, the Christian
and the Turk, the savage and the Spanish lady do, has,
at least, the sanction of the majority, and is clearly
adapted to all tastes and all climates. The war waged
against this habit by old Dons, antiquated dames, and
pretty girls, ought to be added to the three great social
evils that afflict this country.'

'Pray what may they be,' I asked, ' for I have been
out of England the last few years, and it has been a
sealed book to me ?'

' Lawyers, doctors, and parsons,' he replied. 'I hate
a lawyer, sir; I have a natural antipathy to one as my
mother had to a cat. If I perceive one in the room I
feel faint, gasp for breath, and rush to the door. They
are so like cats in their propensities, that I suppose I
may call this dislike hereditary. I don't know if you
ever remarked it, but their habits and instincts are very
similar. They purr round you, and rub against you
coaxingly when they want you to overcome your prejudice against their feline tribe. They play before they
pounce. I was at the trial of Palmer, the poisoner. As
soon as he was arraigned, I read his doom in the look of
the judge. He had studied the examinations, and knew
what they foreshadowed. He was *gallows* polite to him ;
he ordered a chair for him, begged him to be seated, and

was very kind and condescending in his manner.   " Cock-
burn," said I (for it was he who prosecuted), " Palmer's
fate is sealed."   "Yes," he replied, " that offer of the
chair always precedes the sus. per. coll."

'How they fix their eyes and glare at their victim, just
before they finally spring upon him ! They have long
claws, and sharp, powerful nippers, and no one ever
escapes from their clutches. Like cats, too, their attachment is local and not personal; they are fond of your
mansion and estate, but not of you, and when you leave
them, they remain in possession. They begin by bowing
themselves into your house, and end by bowing you out
of it. Their bills are as long as tailors' measures ; and
when, like them, they are hung on a peg, they resemble
them uncommonly. They are very moderate in their
charges ; no man can find fault with them, the items are
so contemptibly small. As a gentleman, how can you
possibly object to two shillings and sixpence, for answering, or five shillings for writing a letter, or six and
eightpence, for allowing you to look at him, and eight and
fourpence for laying down his pen to look at you ? He
is too polite; he will attend you at your house, and
receive your signature, to relieve you of the trouble of
going to his office. Ten shillings is a small charge for
this, and two shillings and sixpence for cab hire is very
reasonable. He is so attentive and so accurate, you are
charmed with him. He takes instructions in writing,
then drafts the required instrument, then copies it in
triplicate—one for you, another for himself, and a third
for counsel ; then he engrosses it, and watches the execution of it, after which he encloses it to you, and writes to
you an interesting account of what has been done, and
you acknowledge the receipt of it, and he informs you by
return of post that your letter has reached its destination.

One charge for all this very necessary work might, in the gross, appear large, but divided into minute items, it is the essence of cheapness. "On my soul" (as Big Ben, the Jew china dealer says), "it ish a great bargain, you get it for nothing ;" and, by way of parenthesis, I may say, "Shegog, do you believe lawyers and Jews have souls? because *I* don't." 'And pray, may I ask how do you arrive at that conclusion?' said I. ' Because neither of them have any conscience; and I believe a man who has no conscience is not possessed of a soul, for man is an accountable being. Of the two, I like the Jew the better, because he runs a certain risk when he lends money, as it is only the needy or the extravagant man that borrows ; and although he charges exorbitant interest, he does give you something for your post-obit. But a lawyer's stock in trade is a quire of paper and a bunch of quills. His motto is that of the spider, "Omnia mea mecum porto." His office is none of the best dusted, (so many poor fellows come "down with the dust" there,) and none of the tidiest, so his emblem, the spider, is often seen weaving his web in the corner, an ominous sign, if his clients were well versed in natural history, and, like the clock, a quiet monitor, admonishing them that he had first to entangle a client and then devour him. The lawyer's spider is always a Cardinal.'

'What is the meaning of that?' I said, ' for I never heard the term before.'

'Hampton Court Palace,' he replied, ' which was built by Wolsey, is infested with an enormous breed of spiders, the bodies of which are nearly as large as young mice! Indeed they have spread over the adjoining country, for miles round, and are called "Cardinals" after him. For my part I never condescend to shake hands with a lawyer. Their grasp is adhesive, you can never disengage your fingers. You are trapped, as an owl is, with bird-lime. It has come to this pass now, you can neither afford to let, or to sell, or to buy land, the expenses are so enormous. This may be a free country—people say it is—but your property is not protected. The first loss is the least, and the best. If I am cheated, I follow the example of a Yankee friend of mine. He was complaining to me, in indignant terms, of having just then been swindled out of a large sum of money by an attorney, and when he had finished his story, I asked him what he intended to do. "Do, sir," he said, "I shall act as I always do under similar circumstances," and he drew himself up to his full height, and stretching out his right arm to its utmost extent, he gradually contracted his fingers on the palm of his hand, and squeezed them tightly into it, as if he had a nut to crack, "*I squash it, sir*, and never think of it afterwards." So if I am cheated, "*I squash it*." I never go to a lawyer, for that is to throw good money after bad, which doubles the loss. These fellows are not content with feeding upon living men, they devour the dead, and pick their very bones. Like vampires, they first suck the blood, and then, like ghouls, make a banquet of the body. They smother us while living, with bonds and mortgages, with charges for obtaining money for us, with bills of costs, insurances on our lives, and every sort of usury, and the breath is scarcely out of our bodies, when they open our wills, which they drew themselves, and find, that like Manchester cloth, when the shoddy is shaken out, the texture is so loose, it wont hold together. An attorney's shoddy means actions, chancery suits, issues at common law, bills, interrogatories, commissions and retainers, refreshers and appeals from the decision of one tribunal to another, until it terminates in the House of Lords. Chancellors are not much better ;

they were lawyers once themselves, or they ought to have been, and they feel for that Bar of which they were splendid ornaments in their day. But they were politicians also ; and although they were selected, as we all know, for their legal attainments, their parliamentary skill, it is more than suspected, was not forgotten. Popularity is not to be despised, even on the Bench, and all parties are satisfied that the costs should be paid *out of the estate*. Between Gladstone's succession duties, and lawyers' fees, how much of an estate goes to the heirs ? Even *Wiscount Williams* professes himself unable to answer that question. It is a crying social evil.

'Doctors are no better ; and I mean that word to embrace physicians, surgeons, *et hoc genus omne*. They have the modesty to complain in bitter terms that they are not well used. But do they do unto others as they would wish they should do unto them ? Locock says he would have been made a peer, had not an enemy traduced him, by publishing to the world that he was to be created "*Lord Deliver us*." It is as hard to lose a title by a joke, as it is for some men to perpetrate one ; and it is not a very pleasant thing to be made the subject of them, for jokes, like penny stamps, are adhesive. I don't like people whose interests are not only opposed to mine, but whose advancement proceeds from my misfortunes. If I break my leg, the surgeon rubs his hands with glee, and murmurs thankfully, "how very lucky ; it is a good chance for me." They live on epidemics. When influenza is rife, they are observed to be unusually constant in their attendance at church, not to hear the sermon, but to listen to the uproar of coughs. They can form a tolerable estimate of their future *crop*, by the number of these noisy Christians, and they return home with thankful hearts, that all things work together for the good of the righteous.

When called in for consultation, their first inquiry is not con-
cerning your symptoms, but your means, and their course
of treatment is wisely regulated by what they hear of the
state of your *chest*. It is the full purse, like the full habit of
body, that requires depletion. The poor fare better, for they
are generally left to nature, which kindly works out cures
for the ills that she bestows. Alas! we are not free agents
in this world. If we do not summon these people when
our friends are ill, and death ensues, it is at once said,
"They died for want of proper medical advice; nothing
was done for them." If the doctor is called in, and death,
like a shadow, follows his footsteps, we are often haunted
by the idea that "too much" was done for them. They
do their work in private, and not in public, like lawyers,
who, with all their faults, are jolly fellows compared to the
doctors. The former fight it out in court, in presence of
the judge, jury, and audience, and the public decide for
themselves on their respective merits. When the trial is
over, they walk off, arm in arm, in great good-humour,
dine together, laugh at the jokes of the judge, the stupidity
of the jury, and the way the witnesses were bullied and
bamboozled. The hotel bill is spread over the retainers.
It is the proper place for it. Like has an affinity for like.
Fees are attracted by fees, adhere together, and roll up,
like wet snow, into a large ball. Doctors and parsons do
not meet face to face, like these gentry, and have a regular
stand-up fight, and then shake hands, like good fellows;
but they fire long shots at their opponents when their
backs are turned; the former by inserting scalping, cutting, and venomous articles, in works devoted to science
and defamation; and the latter, by sending to religious
newspapers anonymous communications, written in a truly
charitable spirit, holding no sympathy with sinners (which
they believe all those who differ from them to be), and

H

accordingly denounce them with "bell, book, and candle," exposing them to the scorn and contempt of their so-called *Christian* friends.

'Medical men are, it must be admitted, most obliging and accommodating to those who seek them. Has an extravagant woman a penurious or selfish husband, it is an evidence of aberration of mind : the family doctor is consulted, who sends another *mad* practitioner to share the responsibility, and they certify that the poor man is unsafe to be at large. He is, therefore, received into a private asylum, the keeper of which pays the recommending physician fifteen per cent. on the amount of the annual charge for his custody and support. The unfortunate victim is outrageous at this false imprisonment, and thereby affords the proof which was before wanting of insanity. He is laced up in a strait-waistcoat, his head shaved and blistered, and he is kindly admonished to keep himself cool and quiet. Nothing can ever effect his release save poverty or death. Death does sometimes occur, not from insanity, but from a broken heart. Poverty is a specific in these cases. When the supplies fail, the patient is almost instantaneously and miraculously restored to his senses, and is not only released, but actually bowed out of the establishment ; for the governor at once discovers that it is both dangerous and wicked, to detain a man one moment after he is of sane mind. The medical attendant informs the freed man, that his disorder has assumed a new shape, and has degenerated into another complaint, for which there are other practitioners much more competent to prescribe than himself; he congratulates him on his marvellous recovery, and takes an affectionate leave of him. How can men like these complain that the world does not do them justice ? How hard these licensed quacks are on their unlicensed brethren ! They persecute and prosecute them, they hold them up to ridicule and contempt, they analyse their medicines, and sometimes deign to pronounce them harmless—can they say as much of their own? They ascribe their cures to nature, and their failures to ignorance. Perhaps they are indignant at the exposure of their own secrets; for it is *their* practice to rob nature of the credit that is due to her. Their cures are their own, and their failures almost invariably caused by the neglect of others, in not having consulted them sooner.

'The Germans managed their medical men better. They made them useful in their armies, by adding the dignity of barber and hospital nurse to that of surgeon. As English society is now constituted, they are a social evil.

'Their clerical brethren have, of late, become equally troublesome; they have thrown almost every parish in the kingdom into confusion; they have invented nicknames, and apply them most liberally to each other. One party calls the other Puseyite, and modestly assume the exclusive title of Evangelical, while they both ignore the existence of that large, sensible, pious, and orthodox body called the Broad Church, whose peace is destroyed by these two factions. The Puseyites are Romanists in disguise, and the Low Church party dissenters, while both have all the faults of extremes. If they would only let each other alone, and confine their rivalry to the amount of good they might severally do, it would be better for both of them, and for the cause of Christianity generally. If they would make "the World, the Flesh, and the Devil" their objects of attack, it would be far more appropriate and praiseworthy exercise of their clerical functions, and conduce more to the welfare of all

who eschew party dissensious, and desire to live in peace
with all men.

'Both have done, and stil do, much service in their way,
but they are equally deficient in Christian charity. If
you decline to attach yourself to one side or the other,
they both turn on you, saying you are neither "hot nor
cold," as if the fervour of religion was exclusively confined
to sectarian warfare. They appear to think that the
affairs of the Church must be conducted on the same
principles as those of the State, which require a strong
opposition. The result is, the condition of moderate men
resembles that to which a prisoner is reduced by the divided opinions of his counsel.

'The Puseyite tugs at one skirt, and says, "confess,
and throw yourself on the mercy of the priest." The
opposite party grasps the other skirt, exclaiming "do not
confess, plead not guilty, and run your chance of escape
from want of proof." One says, "confess your sins,"
and the other, "confess your virtues." There is no
escape for you, but to slip out of your coat, leaving that
and your purse in their hands. If they could understand
a joke, you might say, in affected fright, "Pray, good
men, take my life, and spare what I have got." One
would rather die, than not preach in a surplice, the other
would suffer death sooner than do so. One insists on
candlesticks on the altar, not to "lighten his darkness,"
but because it is the emblem of his party; his opponent
hereupon calls his teaching *candlestickology*, an epithet I
once heard used in a village church, where the worthy vicar
was strongly inveighing against Tractarian doctrines and
customs. The Puseyite loves the rubrick, and is as fond
of its red letters, as if he believed them stamped with the
blood of the martyrs. He has, however, a better reason,
the authority of the Episcopal Bench.

' The Militant Evangelical divine, though professing to be a Churchman, opposes the authority of his Diocesan; he wishes to be the bishop of his own parish, and to lay down the law to his own people. In short, whatever the High Churchman does, the other opposes. The former decorates his church, the latter considers it unjustifiable extravagance; it is better to give the money to the poor, and who is so ill-provided and so deserving as himself? Stones and painted windows neither eat nor drink, but clergymen, their wives and children, do both, and *their* ladies do not object to personal decoration. Women are never at a loss for reasons to justify expensive apparel. So they say, if it is expected they should go about doing good, they must be fashionably dressed; it makes their visits doubly acceptable, and their teaching far more influential, for the poor always appreciate the condescension of such very fine ladies in entering their humble dwellings. Children may possibly be of a different opinion. A Sunday-school scholar being asked by her richly-attired teacher what she understood by the pomps and vanities of this wicked world, replied, " *Them's the pomps and wanities, ma'am, in your bonnet,*" pointing to a profusion of ribbons and artificial flowers. It was considered very pert, and so it was, and something more, for it was very *pert*inent.

' These parties agree in nothing but disagreeing. They are mainly led by prejudice, reminding me of an old Yorkshire planter in Jamaica, called Ingleby. He was a member of the House of Assembly there, and as deaf as a post, but he was always observed to vote right, although he could not hear a word of the debate. My uncle asked him one day how this happened to be the case. " Why," said he, " I keeps my eye on that Scotch Radical Hume, and whichever way he goes I crosses over

to the other side and votes against him, and nine times out
of ten I find I have done right." These parties are in the
same situation, and are equally open to argument and conviction : they do not hear, they reason no more than Ingleby
did, but they make up their minds, under all circumstances,
to be always opposed to each other. For my part, I wish
they would both quit the Church—the one for Rome, and
the other for Dissent—which, severally, are more congenial
to them than the Establishment. We should then be able
to live in security if not in peace, which we cannot do while
there are concealed traitors within, and hostile hosts without
our lines. Yes, sir, I consider these three classes, lawyers,
doctors, and militant parsons constitute what is called the
" Social Evil " of England.'

'Why, Cary, my good fellow,' I said, 'you are not
only unjust but cruel to-day ; one would think you had
some personal pique against these "three black graces,"
as Horace Smith used to call them. Such severe and
prejudiced critics as you are, ought to be added to the
trio that you denominate the "Social Evil." You remind
me of the chief of the Mohawk Indians, who before re-
treating from the battle-field at Ticonderaga, stooped for
a moment to scalp a wounded French officer. Having
knelt down by his side, he drew his knife, and seizing him
by the hair of his head, he was about to cut the skin on
the forehead, to enable him to tear off the scalp, when the
whole of it came away in his hand, and left a cold, blood-
less pate exposed to view. *It was a wig*, a thing the
savage had never seen or heard of before. He was terrified at what he considered the supernatural power of the
Frenchman, who could thus cast his hair as a cockroach
does his shell, and springing to his feet, and waving the
wig by its queue, he fled in dismay, exclaiming, "Sar-
tain, Frenchman—all same—one devil." It was this in-

cident which caused the chief to be known ever after as
the "Bald Eagle." You are like him, you would use a
scalping-knife; what is the matter with you to-day?'
'Well,' he replied, 'perhaps, like the Indian, I have not
hurt a hair of their heads—the truth is, I am cross, I am
always out of temper on a hot day in England.' 'Why
in England more than anywhere else?' 'Because the
heat is more insufferable here, and so is the cold, on account of the dampness that accompanies it. When the
glass stands at 92 here in the shade, it is equal to 120 at
Demerara or Jamaica.' 'Well, keep yourself cool and
good-natured, and I will make you a beverage fit for an
emperor, not strong enough to inflame, or weak enough
to be dangerous, from causing a sudden chill.' Having
compounded this to my own satisfaction, I handed him
the tankard with that air of triumph which a man always
feels, who knows he has a receipt that pleases and puzzles
every one. 'There,' I said, 'take a pull at that, and
then make a face as if you did not like it.' 'But I *do*,
most decidedly,' he replied, as he replaced the antique
silver vessel on the table—'it's superb, it's magnificent,
perfect nectar; I could drink Milford Haven dry if it was
filled with that! what do you call it?' 'It has never been
christened yet, but as it is the first I have brewed on the
Southampton line, I shall give it, in honour of you, and
the approbation you have expressed of it, the name of

THE SEASON-TICKET.

One bottle of sound cider,
One pint and half of lemonade,
Two glasses of sherry,
One teaspoonful of orange flower water,
Two sprigs (or three) of mint,
Two lumps of sugar,
Half a pound of Wenham ice.

There, you have the name and the receipt, and let me
tell you it is the best I know of among the thousand and
one that are so much vaunted. It has the great recommendation of being very cheap and very simple, and the
ingredients are everywhere within reach. Like everything else it has a secret, and that is, the *orange flower
water*. It is that which imparts to it its delicate muscat
flavour. Champagne, claret, and moselle cup are snobbish;
the way they are generally compounded is such as to
spoil good and costly wines that are unfit for dilution.
The name sounds rich, but the beverage is poor. This
" Season-Ticket " elevates the character of the materials,
and makes a compound superior to all others. Try it
again, for ice melts quickly this weather, and your liquor
should be either hot or cold. Anything like warm is
only fit to be taken with ipecac '——' Yes,' he gasped, as
he handed me back the almost empty flagon, ' the " Season-Ticket " is beyond all praise. I am at peace now
with all the world.'

  ' If that is the case,' I said, ' recall your censures on
the professors of Law, Physic, and Divinity.'   ' I can't
do that,' he replied ; ' I neither cant nor recant. I have
the same repugnance my bailiff evinced, when sued for
defamation, to subscribe to an apology for publishing what
was not true about one of my tenants. " No, sir," he
said ; " I will never sign a lie-bill ; I'd rather die first."
I won't retract; but if you think the shadows are too
strong and dark, I have no objection to add the lights;
perhaps the portrait may then be more easily recognised
and more true to nature. Well, bring me my easel,
and give me my palette and brush, and let us retouch
these pictures. I think we began with the lawyers. It's
hard to make becoming likenesses of these fellows, their
features are so marked that, although quite perfect, their

photographs look like caricatures.   Let me see.   I will
soften down the lines of impudence, and make those of
firmness and independence somewhat stronger; keep
down the professional look of cunning, and bring out the
traits of humour, wit, and knowledge of the world for
which they are distinguished.   I could perhaps improve
the specimens by a judicious selection of sitters.   I would
choose Chelmsford and Lyndhurst in preference to
Bethell and Campbell.'   ' Why not Campbell ?'   I
asked.   ' Read his face and his Lives, and you will find
the answer in both.   He is amongst the first-fruits of the
Whigs, and men don't gather grapes from thorns.   That
party cannot boast of *feats ;* they don't aim so high; they
are content with counter*feits.'*   ' Try the cup again,' I
said ; ' it has not made you genial yet.   I hope you can
say something better for the clergy.'   ' Well,' he replied,
drawing a long breath, after having drained the flagon,
' Shegog, if all trades fail, open a " Season-Ticket Shop "
in London, and you will make your fortune.   It's capital
lush, that ; make another brew, and I will see what I can
do for the clergy.   Well, first of all, I'd paint out the
M.B. waistcoat of the Puseyites, and put in a nice white-
bosomed shirt; and then I'd cut off half a yard of his
coat, and reduce it to the peace establishment ; for now it
is a hybrid between a Romish priests's vestment and the
coat of an Irish car-driver ; and I'd fill him out as if he
was a well-fed Christian, instead of being half starved on
a miserable pittance, disgraceful to his flock, and unworthy of him.   I will say this for them—they are a self-
denying sect.   What a pity it is such good, such zealous,
and unselfish men should be a *sect,* ain't it ?   Well, then,
as for the Low Church clergy, who have " a proud look
and a high stomach," and appear as if they lived on the
fat of the land and the donations of their admiring female

devotees, I would alter their Primitive Methodistical
white chokers, and add a neat tie to them; I would give
them a shirt-collar, take away their shovel hats (to which
they have no right); substitute a morning coat for the
everlasting dress one they wear, and expunge that look
of complacency they carry about with them, as if they felt
(as the Yankees say) " good all over," and condescended
to receive the universal homage of all who beheld and admired them.   Oh, I am willing to correct my sketches. I
well know there are good, talented, and self-denying men
in all divisions of our church.'   ' Yes,' I said ; ' but your
corrections are like those of our old Harrow schoolmaster,
well meant, no doubt, but *they touch the feelings rather
painfully.*'   ' As for the doctors, they ought to be able to
take care of themselves.'   ' Never mind them at present,
the weather is too hot ; in your cooler moments I am sure
you will do them justice.   Their gratuitous services to
the poor, their unpaid, or inadequately remunerated attendance at hospitals, infirmaries, and dispensaries, are
above all praise.   I don't like to hear a whole profession
judged and condemned by the conduct of a few individuals.
Believe me, you are unjust, and it is easy for you who are
not a member of either of those learned bodies, but a man
of fortune, to find fault with them.   Recollect they might
return the compliment, by representing you as belonging
to that class which has been defined to be " Fruges con-
sumere nati."   You have charged the clergy with being
deficient in charity ; let us not expose ourselves to a similar remark.'   ' I'll tell you a story,' he said, with an arch
look, ' the application of which will furnish an answer to
your lecture.   Three or four years ago, I made a passage
from the Cape to Liverpool, and landed at the latter place
about seven o'clock on Sunday morning.   When I reached
the Waterloo Hotel, and had breakfasted, it occurred to

me that, as I was in the same town with the celebrated
Dr. M'Neile, I would avail myself of the opportunity of
attending his chapel, in the hope that I might be fortunate
enough to hear him preach. His parish was some distance from the hotel, and, when I arrived at the church,
I found not only the pews occupied but the aisles filled
with well-dressed people, who were standing there with the
same object I had in view. As I had been on deck all
night I felt too tired to remain on an uncertainty; so, addressing myself to the verger, I asked if Dr. M'Neile was
one of the two white-haired clergymen who were in the
reading-desk pulpit (for such was its shape). " Yes," he
replied, " the one on the right hand is the doctor."

' " Will he preach to-day?"

' " How do I know?"

' " It's a civil question, my friend, and deserves a civil
answer."

' " Yes, it's a civil question, but a very improper one.
People come here and ask me whether Dr. M'Neile is
going to preach. They ought to come to say their
prayers, sir, and to listen to the sermon, whoever preaches
it. The clergyman is not "——

' " Stop, my friend," I said, " I came to hear Dr.
M'Neile preach, *and not you.*"

' " Well, he is not going to preach."

' " Then good morning to you;" and I left him still
discoursing.—Now, Shegog, you may draw your answer
from that story. I came to this room to smoke, and not
to listen to a lecture.'

' How uncommon cross you are,' I said; ' that Season-
Ticket is thrown away upon you.' ' No, indeed,' he replied, ' it is not, I assure you; I am only cross because it
is all gone.' ' Try one of these cigars.' ' They are excellent. I never hear of these professional men without

remembering a scrape I got into with an old East Indian officer. He had three sons, one a clergyman, the second a surgeon, and the third a land-agent. " Ah, my friend," I said, " what a fortunate man you are in your children. They have the prayers of the church, for they represent, ' Mind, Body, and Estate.' " Instead of taking this as a *badinage,* he became furious. He said it was a joke that would stick to his family for ever. But he was still more indignant when I retracted it. " You know best," I replied, " and I withdraw it. They have neither ' mind, body, nor estate,' so I hope you are satisfied." '

Just then the smoking-room began to fill with people ; and, as I never talk freely to a mixed company, we changed our conversation to indifferent subjects, and spoke in a lower tone. ' The eleven train, for Southampton,' said Cary, ' will suit you best, so we shall meet at breakfast to-morow. I shall not return for two or three days ; but I will accompany you to the station, and see you off, and the day after to-morrow shall be there again to meet you on the arrival of the 5·50 train. Good night.'

No. VI.

BLACK JOBS AND WHITE FAVOURS.

WHEN Cary bade me good-night, as related in the last chapter, I did not leave the smoking-room immediately, but lingered a while longer, for the purpose of finishing a magnificent Havannah that I had but just lighted. My last cigar at night has always been pronounced an interminable one; I take my time to it; I fondly linger over it; it smoulders in its ashes; it never burns; it is alive, and that is all; it is genial to the last, and expires without an effort. The North American Indians measure distances by *pipes*, instead of miles as we do; but they are savages, and smoke as they travel, which, as sailors say, is 'like throwing ashes to windward.' When I indulge in a 'weed,' I do so at my leisure. I take no note of time—

    'Parting is such sweet sorrow,
    That I could say good night until to-morrow.'

Nothing concentrates one's ideas, or supplies charming reveries, like smoking. I was indulging in one of these agreeable musings, when my attention was attracted by the conversation of two Yorkshiremen who sat near me, and were sipping hot whisky toddy. One of them, lifting his glass, said, 'Mr. Dupe, I drinks to you;' 'Thank you sir, I sees you do,' was the reply, accompanied by a slight inclination of the head. 'Have you been to the Secretary of State yet?' said the first speaker, 'and secured that office you were after?' 'Yes,' replied the other, 'I have been there, but it's no go; elections are over now, and there is no getting at these gentry when they are in London. If you ask a favour of one of them beforehand, he is all smiles and bows, and patting you good-naturedly on your shoulder, he says, "Hush, my dear fellow. If I was to tell you what I am going to do, they might say I bribed you with a promise of an office; just wait till the poll closes, and then remind me of it—you understand what I mean; you know where to find me always" (and he gives me a comical look). "Doing a favour after the poll closes, is not promising it before you vote; a nod is as good as a wink to a blind horse. When you get the office, you cannot say it was a *quid pro quo*, eh? Devilish stringent act that election law; it is a mere trap for the unwary."'

'Well, after the election is over, you begin to open your eyes, as puppies do after nine days. The after-piece comes then, and a grand farce it is. Dodge first is the fortification dodge. You can't get at the great man; he is surrounded by entrenchment within entrenchment, like the circles caused by a stone thrown into the water. There are pickets, and supporting sentries, and guards supporting pickets, and an encampment in the centre, which again is a beautifully arranged labyrinth. You cannot find the clue out yourself, and when you think you know your way, some one arrests your progress, or sets you wrong. "Is Lord Tardy within?" "Don't know, sir; your name, if you please; sit down here, sir, and I will see." Well, you wait, and wait, until your patience is quite exhausted. You count the drawers in the bureaux, read their numbers, and take a mental survey of the chairs and tables, and whatever else is in the room, and when that is done, look at your watch, and begin the cata-

logue again. By way of a change, you look out of the
window, and you observe an area wall, several crooked
brick chimney heads, with iron swivel hoods to cure smoking flues, roofs of various colours, and slopes of every
possible angle, sashes of different sizes, with glass that
even the rain has failed to reach, or cleanse, since it was
first inserted there, and that appears designed rather to
let out darkness than to admit light. You then withdraw
from the contemplation of this sepulchral looking recep-
tacle of " the dead buried alive," with a chill that makes
your very flesh creep. At last your gaoler returns, looks
in at the door, starts at seeing you there (for he had wholly
forgotten you) and says, " his lordship has not come down
yet, sir ; and it is now so late, it is not probable he will be
here until to-morrow." You call the following day ; un-
dergo solitary confinement for an hour or two again, and are
informed " there is a cabinet council in the afternoon."
You try your luck a third time ; are caged as before ;
make the same enumeration of the scanty furniture, and
with an involuntary shudder look out upon the " darkness visible " of the dismal area. The only living thing
discernible is a cat, who with stealthy steps is meditating
an impromptu visit to a friend in the next street. Even
this interesting object soon disappears from view, when
you turn from the scene of solitude, and mechanically
draw out your watch to reckon the hours of your captivity.
You are about to depart, in indignant despair, when the
servitor again appears, and informs you that " his lordship has to receive two or three deputations, successively,
which will occupy him all day." Your heart fails you at
this ; at least if it don't it is made of different stuff from
mine ; you feel that if you could only get a sight of that
bird you could bring him down, whether he was on his
roost or on the wing ; but you can't even guess at his

whereabouts. By great good luck you meet him at last at the entrance, just as he alights from his carriage, when he is delighted to see you. He has heard you have taken the trouble to call upon him several times, for which he is very sorry; he invites you into his room, requests you to be seated, inquires kindly after Mrs. Dupe, and the rest of the Dupe family; "has heard Miss Dupe is about to change her name, and if so, hopes it will be an advantageous exchange." After giving utterance to this very civil speech, he smiles again blandly, and taking up a bundle of neatly folded papers from his desk, tied with red tape, he stares in well-affected fright at its great bulk, and looking grave, though very gracious, says, "My dear sir, can I do any thing for you?" You open your request, when Dodge No. 2 appears. "You are too late, my good fellow," he replies with mournful air; "why in the world didn't you apply in time? it is given away; but cheer up, better luck next time."

'Dodge No. 3, is quite as true, and equally ingenious. The office you ask for is not in your borough, the patronage belongs to the county members—"I am afraid it is disposed of, but I will inquire, and let you know." If this answer is not quite applicable, he resorts to Dodge No 4, and says, "The office is in the gift of the Board of Trade; I spoke to Wilson about it, but he assured me it was an interference on my part not usual among the heads of different departments, and got 'as mad as a hatter;'" and this is the way a poor fellow is put off. Election promises, my good friend, are like pie-crusts, short, flaky, and brittle; they won't hold together till they reach your mouth—I have done with paying court to people in office—no man shall ever have it in his power to fool me in that way again.'

'Don't be discouraged, Dupe,' said his friend, 'there-

is a mode of improving people's hearing, and their memory
too, that you are not aware of. I'll tell you to-morrow
how to put your case before him in a way he must attend
to if he wishes to retain his seat. You don't know how
to talk to a man situated as he is. Be guided by me,
and you are sure of your office,—you must not take *No*
for an answer. It is your business to ask, and it is his
interest to grant your request. You remind me of my
little boy Bob. He begged hard the other day, when
some friends were dining with us, to be allowed to come
in, and sit at the table during dessert, which I told him
he might do, provided he neither talked nor annoyed
people by asking for fruit. He very readily assented to
this condition, which he honestly fulfilled to the letter;
at last I heard the poor little fellow crying and sobbing most
pitifully—" What is the matter, Bob," I said, " what are
you crying about?" " Why, Pa," he replied, "*here I
am, asking for nothing, and getting nothing.*"

'Now, you are like that child, if you don't ask, you
won't get anything; and not only so, you must ask till
you obtain what you want. Why, my good fellow, the
whole system of representative government is founded on
a principle of mutual assurance. The elector bribes the
candidate with a vote, and expects to be paid by the gift
of some office; and the candidate bribes the government
by his support, for an appointment or a title for himself.
The only interest worth having in this country is parliamentary influence. Votes are marketable property, the
highest bidder is sure to win. Every man has his price,
but it requires tact to discover what that is, and still more
how to offer it. Money is a gross vulgar thing, and, of
course, never enters into the calculation of any but the
lowest of mankind. Office is an honourable thing; it
may be tendered freely, and accepted without hesitation.

India would have satisfied Bright; he is as well fitted for
it as any man that never saw it, and he would have got
it too, but they have an awkward trick of fighting there,
and the public would not be satisfied with a Quaker.
Others, who are less ambitious, are content with the
honour of dining with the Premier; but who can resist
the offer of an invitation for their wives and daughters to
the Queen's Ball? The higher the man, the greater the
bribe; for the thing is regulated by a graduated scale.
The office of tide-waiter will suit the son of a tradesman,.
a canonry is the measure of a popular partisan preacher,
and a bishopric may be the reward of a pamphleteer-
ing dean; an Indian judgeship pacifies a troublesome
lawyer, and a governorship a needy but influential
peer. To call these things *corrupt practices* is a perver-
sion of terms; they are simply the reward of merit.
The giver and the receiver are too high-minded and
honourable to view them in any other light. You must
read the political like the social world, by the light of
experience. As my father used to say of women,. you
must study their nature. When he lived at Sheffield,
and his establishment was small, he never rang the bell
for the maid, but when he wanted her always went out
into the street to call her, for he said women were sure
to be found looking out of the window. In like manner,
he always hired the prettiest girls he could find; they
waited for the men to run after them, but the ugly ones
always wasted their time in running after the men: one
stayed at home, and the other didn't. Now, you must
study this Cabinet Minister, and show him how important
you are to his retaining his own office; and the way to
do that, is to represent yourself as more influential, if
possible, than you now are.'

'Yes, yes,' said Dupe, despondingly, 'I may be useful

or influential, if you like, but these fellows have no gratitude in them, they never think of you after you have
served their turn. They are like the great plain we saw
when travelling in Russia, that swallows up a whole river,
and continues as thirsty as ever—drink, drink, drink, un-
ceasingly.'

'I believe you, my boy,' said his philosophic friend,
'and never drew breath the while. How I envy that
plain, this hot weather, how I should like to swallow that
river—just open my mouth and gulp down every drop of
it. How charming! oh, wouldn't I say (no, I couldn't
say it, because I should have to keep my tongue within
my teeth, but I'd think it)—

> "Flow on thou shining river,
>   But ere thou reach the sea,
> Seek Ella's lips, and give her
>   The draughts thou givest me."

Oh, dear, what fun! I never knew before the difference
between a river's mouth, and the mouth of a river. If
Ovid had seen that phenomenon of nature wouldn't he
have turned it to account in his Metamorphoses! What
a punishment for a drunkard, to transform him into a
bottomless pitcher, and what a reward to confer upon an
active, influential, obliging voter,' and then he laid back
in his chair, and laughed until his throat emitted a
gurgling sound, resembling running water. When he
recovered, he suited the action to the word, lifted his
glass of toddy to his lips, saying as before, but with unaccountable gravity, 'Dupe, my boy, I drinks to you,'
to which the other as gravely responded, 'Sir, I sees
you do.'

'No, my good fellow,' his friend continued, 'it is not
that they are so forgetful, but that you expect too much.

Talk of gratitude; why, what is your idea of that word?
why, if you "nannylize" it, as old Arkwright used to
say, you'll find it's "a lively expectation of benefits to
come." It's far-seeing, and not near-sighted, or as that
same old millionaire, when he began to study grammar
at sixty years of age, used to say to his debtors to show
off his learning to advantage, "I gives no credit, I goes
on the imperative mood, and likes the present tense—you
must pay down on the nail." Gratitude in a member of
Parliament! gratitude in a political leader! who ever
heard of it except as a figure of speech! It's a law of
nature, sir; why Jemmy Dawkins says that even the dead
are ungrateful.

'As I was coming down Cockspur-street this morning
from Pall Mall, somebody touched me on the shoulder,
and as I turned I beheld my father's old coachman,
Jemmy Dawkins.

'"How do you do, Master Jack?" said he; "you
look hearty—it's a long time since I had the pleasure of
seeing you—have you got a missus yet?" "No," I said,
"there's time enough for that; some of these days, perhaps, I may think of it, but at present I prefer to be
single."

'"Well," said Jemmy, "perhaps you are right,
Master Jack; it don't do to put hosses or men into
harness too soon, it's apt to break their spirit like. If I
might be so bold as to offer my advice (no offence, sir, I
hope)—as the old gentleman, your father, left you a
handsome fortune—if I was you, I would go in for beauty,
and not money, for as far as my experience runs (though
to be sure it's more in the *dead line* than the *white jobs*),
I should say it's better to have the wife under the whip
hand than on the lead, and to have her well under command, than for her to take the bit into her mouth and

play the devil. Shape, make, and breed is the great thing, both for hosses and wives, for

> ' An ugly woman is like a crooked pin,
> You can't get her out if she once gets in.'

But come with me, sir, if you please, I have got some beauties to show you."

' " What, women ?" I said.

' " No, sir, Lor' bless you, women couldn't hold a candle to them. I have eighty-four of 'em."

' " Eighty-four what ?"

' " Black jobs, sir—black as ink, and not a white hair on any of 'em."

' I accordingly turned and went with him to his stables, and, sure enough, there were between eighty and ninety coal-black horses, devoted entirely to the melancholy purpose of conveying the dead to their final resting-place. I assure you I felt a sort of shudder come over me when I first beheld these heralds of the grave, and listened to the jaunty conversation of their driver.

' " Beautiful animals these, ain't they, sir ? I own I feel proud when I mount the box, and take the ribbons in my hand. They are the admiration of the whole town, sir ; all eyes is on 'em, and people gather in crowds to see them walk off so stately. They have a mission, and they seem to understand its importance. It must be a great consolation to the survivors to know their friends have so handsome a turn-out as mine to take their last drive in. They are very substantial cattle for such light work. I have often thought it was a very odd custom to select such big ones; for what does one insider signify to the like of them ? Why, sir, it's mere child's play to them, and nothing more. It ain't bulk that's the cause, for in a general way people falls away in flesh at the last."

' " Perhaps," said I, " it is because of the *dead weight*."

'Jemmy paused a moment as if he were gradually comprehending the explanation of a mystery that had puzzled him so long and so often.

'"It's very odd, Master Jack," he said, "you should have found that out so quick; but I see it must be so, though I never thought of it before. But it don't much matter; we are paid by the job, and not by bulk or weight, for you see there is no luggage nor incumbrance of any kind. I never charged for overweight, sir, but once since I was in the trade, and that was this morning. I got the biggest, fattest, and most uncommon heaviest woman out of Thomas' Hotel I ever see—she weighed twenty-four stone. They grumbled a good deal about paying extra, saying what was a stone or two, more or less, to four powerful hosses like mine? 'Very true,' says I, 'and what's a trunk or two extra to a steam engine on the Great Western Railway? nothing more nor a feather,' says I; 'still they whips 'em up into the scales and weighs 'em to an ounce; and if you go for to say a word, they cram the Directors down your throat, body and breeches, and says it's their orders. Every indulgence they gives is their own, and they takes tip for it; they don't demand it, but they expect it; every snub you get comes direct from the Chairman. Now,' says I, 'I am Board and Director both in one. I lays down the law, and sees it carried into execution. So fork out; it's the rule of the institution.'

'"I have had some werry distinguished passengers amongst the nobility and gentry in my time, and it was me that had the honour of driving the great Duke to St. Paul's, though I must say that State affair they called the funeral car was so uncommon heavy, it was as much as my hosses could do to move it. But, sir, would you believe it, though I drive so safely and so carefully, and never met with an accident in all my life, not one of my passengers ever turned and said as much as I thank you, Jemmy?"

'And he gave utterance to a long, protracted chuckle of self-satisfaction as if he was delighted with his joke, which I have no doubt he had repeated a thousand times. When he recovered his wind, he said, with a knowing look :

' "Now, that's what I calls ingratitude, sir." '

'So you see, Dupe, my good fellow, gratitude is not to be expected from the living or the dead. The one utters profuse and unmeaning acknowledgments, and the other maintains a dignified silence.'

'You are right,' says Dupe, 'quite right. I will put myself in your hands, and follow your advice implicitly. I shall bother him, as a certain widow did an unjust judge, till he gives me what I ask, to get rid of me. So let us change the subject.

'What an odd fellow your friend Jemmy Dawkins must be. I wish you would show me his establishment to-morrow.' 'With great pleasure,' replied his friend, 'and I can assure you that both he and his stables are well worth seeing, for Jemmy is quite a character. When Jemmy,' he continued, 'had finished the conversation I have just repeated, I observed that the burial of the dead was too serious a subject to talk upon with such levity.'

' "Well," said he, "I used to think so too, master; but Lor' bless you, sir, when I come to see into matters, and to understand all I heerd and see'd, I come to the conclusion, sir (though it ain't for me to say so), that there is an awful sight of hypocrisy in all these outside shows and trappings of mourning. Half the time all this parade is made, not out of regard for the dead, but out of respect to public opinion, and from personal pride.

Whenever this is the case there is no money so much grudged as what is paid to me. They say it is so much thrown away, because custom lays the tax, and that it would be better to give the amount to the poor, though it's precious little the poor would ever see of it, if funeral expenses was done away with to-morrow. Housumdever, a good deal of the mourning you see comes from the heart, for a great many have to feel the loss of a home and an income, and that they do grieve for, though the dead get the credit of it ; and some cover bright eyes with crape, and conceal the beating of a joyful heart with broad cloth, for they are to get both the home and the fortune. The real mourners, sir, are the poor. They are all in all to each other ; the outer world is chilly, and drives them into a narrow circle, where they cheer, and comfort, and defend each other. They have a common lot, and a joint-stock of affection. Where there are so few to love each other, a break in that little circle is a loss that ain't repaired easy ; all they have to leave their survivors is their blessing—" their inheritance is not here," as Mr. Spurgeon says. They have nothing for affection to spread itself out on—it is concentrated in themselves, and is human love and animal instinct combined. I have witnessed such outpourings of grief among these people as would astonish you. Gentlefolks have so many friends, relations, acquaintances, indulgences, amusements, and what not of interest, that their grief is neither so strong nor so lasting. It is like dew that falls at night—it wanishes in the morning.

' " Dear me ! I shall never forget the way Parson Giles' son, Frank, frightened the people some years agone on the road from Uxbridge to London. I took his reverence down there with my best four-in-hand, and Ralph Carter drove another team of fours. After the

funeral of the old gentleman was all over, ' Jemmy,'
said Master Frank, ' I can't bear to go to the house to-
day ; my heart is broke ; it's a dreadful loss to me is the
old governor.'

' " I feels for you," said I, " but it's a consolation to
know he was beloved by all the country far and wide, both
rich and poor."

' " Yes, indeed," said Master Frank, " he was very
indulgent to me ; and nobody will miss him as much as I
shall.   I shall never handle the ribbons again any more,
I suppose ; for all he had he has left to the old lady and
my sisters, and I can't afford hosses now ; but change
places with me, that's a good fellow, and let me handle
the reins once more for the last time. '   So I gives up my
seat, and takes his, when he begins to feel the cattle, and
put them on their mettle.   It excited him so he looked
like another man.   " Clever hosses, them leaders," says
he, " look as if they had some go in 'em."   " I believe
they have," said I ; " them two mares on the lead, Sin
and Sorrow I calls em, are most too high strung for this
work ; they require a steady hand, and careful driving."
The words were scarcely out of my mouth before smack
went the whip, and off started the hosses like wink ! The
way they flew, with the plumes waving up and down, and
the manner folks stared, was something uncommon.
Whenever we came to a crowd of people he pretended to
lean back, and braced himself up, as if they were running
away with him ; and the moment we passed them he gave
the hosses their heads again, cracked his whip, and
started afresh, singing out, " Go it, my beauties ! That's
the ticket, Jemmy !   How the people stare, don't they ?
Tell them the governor has come to, and we are going for
the doctor.   What fun, ain't it ?"   Well, it took me so
by surprise, I almost forgot the ondecency of the thing

I

in the excitement of it. I couldn't believe my eyes or my ears.   At last I began to consider it might be a serious injury to me in my business, for people might think we was drunk.   So I had to interfere and put a stop to this mad frolic : says I, "Master Frank, this won't do ; it will injure my hosses, and ruin me :" and I took the reins from him, and mounted again into my own seat.   "Ah, Jemmy," said he, with tears in his eyes, for he had relapsed again into grief, and remembered his poor father's funeral, "this is the last four-in-hand drive I shall ever have."   "I wouldn't swear to that," says I, half joking and half in earnest (for I felt sorry for the poor boy), "unless you puts on the drag, and gets out of the fast line." Two years afterwards we drove down the same road together ; and it was the saddest, most sorrow-fullest, and distressingest journey I ever made, for Master Frank was an *inside passenger !*

'"As I used to say to him, sir, it's the pace that kills both hosses and men—it ain't the work. Fast animals and fast people can't keep it up long ; there must be a break-down in the natur of things at last. 'Jemmy,' he'd answer, 'when I have sowed my wild oats, I'll haul up, and be as steady as a bishop.' 'Ah Master Frank,' says I, 'it's the old story. I have heard young folks often and often talk of wild oats ; but if you sow 'em year after year on the same soil, without a fallow or a green crop, you'll soon come to what father used to call the *caput mortuum*. I have travelled the road to the grave, Master Frank, so often, I knows every inch of it. I knows what people die of as well as the crowner and his jury, or dissecting doctors and hospital surgeons do ; and mind what I say, wild oats is an exhausting, killing crop—the last sowing is the only one that ripens seed, and that seed is *Death, and the black job.*'"

' " Why, Jemmy," said I, "you are quite a moralist.
I should have thought that your very occupation would have
so familiarized you with death, that your feelings would in
time have become blunted." "Well, sir," he replied, "to
a certain extent they do ; but a thing that is ever before
your eyes, can't but occupy your thoughts a good deal
sometimes, especially when you ain't well—I feel kind of
narvous now and agin, and dream at night of the ' Black-
jobs' of the day, particularly when I don't get home till
late, and sup hearty on beef steaks, and stout.

I had a wision last week, I shan't easily forget. I
dreamed I was dead, and that I was laid out ready for my
last drive, and yet it seemed to me as if I knew all as was
passing in the room, and heard what they was a saying.
Death is a sad thing, sir, even when you are accustomed to
see it, but it is awful to *feel*. It is so cold, the heart slowly
gives up beating, and the blood don't sarkelate no more,
but thickens little by little, till all stands still, and con-
geals up solid. I'm thinking life remains there, struggling a good while after we seem dead to them that's
looking on, at least so it appeared to me. Dreams, you
know, are strange things, onpossible events happen, and
you don't know at the time, that they can't be, in the
natur of things, but you see them all, as if they was real.
Well! when Paton the undertaker, came to put me into
the coffin, says I, ' Patie, my good friend, I am "not
ready yet," don't screw me down now. Let me take my
last cast, that's a good fellow, put the coffin into the
hearse, but let me drive myself, let me see my cattle once
more, take a last look at the road I have druv so often,
and see the faces again, I have known so well. Dreadful
sudden business this, Patie, I knew it must come in course,
some day or another, but I didn't expect to be sent for so
sudden, without so much as being asked, " Jemmy, are

you ready?''   I went to bed as well as you are, and here
I am, a dead man.   But, Patie, the spirit han't set out
yet, and waits to see the " last job " done decently.   Body,
and Ghost, are both here.'   In course he was dreadfully
frightened to hear me speak so to him, but he called the
servants, and they dressed me, took me down stairs, and
lifted me on to the box, and the horses looked round, and
trembled all over, and sweated as if they had come off a
journey.   Oh, Master Jack, I see it now all as plain as if it
was real.   There was my poor Missus a standin at the
door, a sobbing and a crying of her heart out, and the
last words I heard her say, was, 'Poor Jemmy was
always a good man to me, and he was a kind friend to
the poor, that he was.'   Well, off walked the horses as
usual, only (would you believe it, Sir?) they hung their
heads as if they never would look up again in this world,
and there was the crowd at the corner as usual, only they
all took off their hats to me, and said, 'There goes poor
Jemmy, a driving of himself, how dreadful pale he looks,'
and here and there, the women folk came to the doors,
and then screamed and ran away, they was so frightened,
and I was overcome too, and couldn't speak, and felt
colder and colder, and my sight grew dimmer and dimmer,
till the horses stopped, and the last black job was over.   The
pause was awful, oh sir, I heard the coffin drag heavy as
they pulled it out, and their hands felt hot and burning,
as they took me down to put me into it, and I struggled
and fell ——————— and there I was on the floor of
the bedroom, as I rolled from the bed in a fit, and the
thought that it was a dream after all, and that I was still
alive, did me more good than all the doctors and their
bleeding put together.   It's a warning though, Master
Jack, against beefsteak suppers, and thinking too much of
the good things of this life; it makes me feel serious, sir,

I assure you ; and I often ask myself the question ' Jemmy, are you ready ?' for the day must come, when that dream will all prove true, only you will be an insider, and some one else, will put on the weeds, mount the box, in your place, and manage *the black job*."

' To change the topic, I said, "Jemmy, you talked just now of the white jobs—what did you mean by them ?" "Weddings," sir, he replied. "White is for marriages, and black for funerals. Of the two our line is the best, for we have our own customers, and in the end get theirs too. Everybody must die ; it s the law of nature ; but nobody need marry unless they please, and many of them that do like it can't get suited to their mind. It takes two to make a bargain, and it ain't every bid that's accepted. Indeed, sir, in this world, when people refuse a good offer, it's an even chance if they ever get another. That's the case in regard to hosses too—if you refuse a good price, it's a wonder to me if you don't regret it. Either something happens to the animal, or he remains on hand for a long time, and then you have to sell him at a loss. Well, sir, the white jobs don't pay well. Weddings are short affairs, and uncommon punctual. They must come off before twelve o'clock, or it's no go, and there is no time to be lost. Funerals ain't tied down by law, so though the corpse is ready, the company never is. People expect to be kept waiting, and don't arrive till they think everybody else is come. Hearses and dead people are in no hurry ; one is paid for attendance, and the other has no voice in the matter. It's a long time before processions start, and when they do, they travel slow. New-married folks are off like wink, and drive as fast as poor Master Frank did ; and since railways have come into fashion, more nor one half of them only drive to a station, and take the train into the country. Paltry white favours, and small fees is all 'white jobs' get. If charges are high, they are met by high words; but it ain't decent to dispute *our* bills, whatever people may think of them. What, fight about burying your father when you get his fortin, or disposing of your wife when she leaves it open to you to marry again? It's impossible. It ain't to be thought of for a moment. Indeed what is the loss of a few pounds, to the loss of such near and dear relations? People can't think of money, when they are overwhelmed with grief. Rich and poor *must* come to us, but they need not go to the 'whites.' The quality, besides, prefer their own carriages to hired ones, when they marry, and the poor ride in hacks, or walk quietly home from church; but the rich keep no hearses, and the poor, when they die, cannot walk, so both on 'em require us. Panics, and bad times, and broken banks, don't affect the 'black jobs.' When our bills are discharged, people may be said, Master Jack, to have paid the last debt of nature. In other respects there ain't as much difference as you would suppose. I have seen as much crying at weddings, as at funerals. Some marry for rank and some for money; some to please parents, and some to please themselves; and the last, generally displease everybody else. To my mind, weddings ain't the jolliest things in the world to the parties concerned, and they ain't always satisfactory to the job-masters. Nobody ever thinks of looking at their hosses, but all eyes are strained to look at the bride. Now, nobody ever sees our passenger; it's the hosses and the hearses that makes the show, and any man that is proud of his cattle and turn-out, can't help feeling pleased when he hears his admired. On the whole I prefers *Black Jobs to White favours.*" '

During the latter part of this conversation, several people came into the room, and talked together on various subjects—some relative to the business or news of the day, and others on general topics. One of them, an old Indian officer, recognised among the company a fellow-passenger from Calcutta. ' Ah, Colonel !' he said, ' how are you? How have you been disposing of yourself to-day ?' 'The weather, Beatson,' he replied, ' has nearly disposed of *me*. I never felt the heat so oppressive in the East as it now is in London. There the air is dry, but here it is damp, and respiration is very difficult. By way of keeping myself cool, I must needs go into a crowded place, to hear the cause of Mrs. Swinfen *versus* Lord Chelmsford. It is many years since I was in an English court, and the venerable judicial robes, the antiquated wigs, and the unvaried forms, reminded me so vividly of former days, when these paraphernalia of justice used to impress my youthful mind with awe, that the wheel of time appeared to have stood still, while all else around was changed or moulded into new shapes. If the laws are unlike those of the Medes and Persians, the forms appear to be unaltered and unalterable. For a moment I seemed to forget that I had ever been out of the country. Among the lawyers, there was the same mixture of seniors and juniors as of old ; and the same intelligence, acuteness, and humour in the countenances of all. I felt as if I had suddenly awakened from a long and fitful sleep, and as if all I had seen, and heard, and done, since I was in that place, was like the the " baseless fabric of a vision." I assure you, the sensation I then experienced, was the most extraordinary I ever felt in my life. The feeling, however, was a transient one, and I looked around me with much interest in what was going on. I must say I like lawyers, especially that class denominated barristers. In my opinion, they are the pleasantest people going. They are remarkably well-informed, full of anecdote, and up to the time of day. They possess in an eminent degree that sixth sense, tact; indeed, it may be called a professional attribute.'

'What was the trial about?' said Beatson, 'for I have suffered so much by the delays and chicanery of law, that I never read a trial, unless it is a divorce case. There never was a marriage yet, that there was not a concealment of some important fact, by one or other of the contracting parties. Things that begin in fraud, are apt to end in fight. We read of love in poetry, and in novels, but do you believe there is such a thing as pure, unalloyed love? for I don't. If there ever was such an *aqua-vitæ*, it must have been poured into a filtering machine, for when you go to look at it, you find nothing but dregs.' 'Why,' said the colonel, laughing, 'I suppose you read divorce causes on the principle some lawyers search reports; they first give the opinion the client wants, and then look up precedents to support it.' 'Was his lordship's name Swinfen?' asked Beatson. 'A divorce case, I suppose;' and rubbing his hands, said, 'come tell us all about it.'

'Not so fast, if you please, his name was Thesiger.' 'A breach of promise, then I suppose; love and fraud, the old story—liked her looks at first, then applied the magnifying glass, and converted "moles" into mountains, or the fortune disappointed him, or he saw some other victim he liked better.'

'No, nor breach of promise either, for he is a married man.'

'Oh, I have it—it was the lovely and accomplished daughter;—made love to her—offered the cup of flattery full to the brim: she was fool enough to believe him, and she drained it to its dregs; threw herself into his arms, and he ran off with her,—no, that's not the phrase, she eloped with him. It was all regular and romantic,—

post-chaise and four,—devoted lovers,—got tired of her, and left her to die of a broken heart, and the old lady brought a "per quod" for damages.

'I don't know what you mean by "quod." When we used to send a fellow in the regiment to the black hole, we used to call it "sending him to quod."'

'If you mean false imprisonment, it was nothing of the kind.'

'What do you call "quod?"'

'Why, a "per quod" is one of those numerous fictions that law is made up of: it supposes a daughter to be a servant, and gives an action to the parent for abduction, per quod, that is, by which means the aforesaid, and before-mentioned, above-named parent, mother, employer, mistress, and fifty other words that mean the same thing, lost the work, labour, assistance, and services of the young lady, so metamorphosed into a servant. All this is written out into an infernal long paper, called a "brief," as a legal joke. So now you know what a "per quod" is.'

'But what under the sun was it about? for you say a certain Mrs. Swinfen was concerned in it; now, if he has had anything to do with a woman, legally or illegally, equitably or iniquitably, at law or in chancery, as plaintiff or defendant, as principal or agent, any how or any way that it can be described or twisted by lawyers, and she has turned on him, and fought and scratched him—all I can say is, *it sarves him right.* A woman, and a lawyer, what a set-to, eh? how they would give lip, and make the fur fly between them, wouldn't they? Come, tell us all about the injured lady, and her legal adviser.'

'Well, I will tell you,' said the Colonel, 'as briefly as I can:—Mrs. Swinfen claimed an estate worth £50,000, under a will, and the question was, whether the testator was "of sound disposing mind and memory," as it is called, when he executed this will: if he was, then Madame would have it, if not, it would go to the heir-at-law. Well, Thesiger (afterwards Lord Chancellor), was Mrs. Swinfen's lawyer; the cause came on to be tried, and he saw it was going against her, so he compromised the suit for an annuity of £1,000 a-year, and the payment of the costs by the other side; and a very judicious arrangement it appeared, but she refused her consent, and repudiated his act. Well, the trial was brought on again, and by one of those chances that do sometimes occur, she gained it, and has got possession of the estate. Now she has brought an action against Thesiger, for the loss she has sustained, by what she calls "exceeding his authority" in settling the suit—do you understand?'

' Perfectly.'

' The cause came on for trial to-day, and she lost it, and it was that trial I went to hear.'

' How did she lose it?'

' Why, the gun was overcharged, burst, and damaged the man that fired it off. Her lawyer implicated the judge, Cresswell, who tried the action that was compromised, and charged him and Thesiger with combining together to do her out of the estate; talked of thimble-riggers, and used some words implying corruption, oppression, and so on. The jury at once found for Thesiger. Now it appears to me, I could have gained that cause for Mrs. Swinfen.'

' Well, what would you have done?'

' Why, in the first place I would have omitted the juage altogether, who had as little to do with it as I had; and instead of abusing Lord Chelmsford, I would have extolled him to the skies. I should have told the jury I was happy to say I had no charge to make against my learned friend, who was not only one of the ablest lawyers at the bar, and one of the best judges that ever graced the woolsack, as well as one of the most upright and agreeable men in the profession; but that I thought, with all due deference, that he had misconceived, in that particular [instance, the powers and authority of counsel in settling a cause, not only without the consent, but against the wishes of his client. That, however, was a question for the court, and they would only have to assess the damages, which would await and follow the decision of the bench, on the law. Such a course would have insured me a verdict beyond a doubt. Now, I should like Mrs. Swinfen to act on her own lawyer's opinion as to the liability of a counsel, and *sue him for losing her cause*, by mismanaging it, which in my humble opinion he most undoubtedly did. There would be some fun in that; wouldn't there, Beatson?'

'Yes, indeed, there would,' he replied. 'But, Colonel, it's a pity you hadn't been bred to the law; you would have made your fortune at it; you have a knack of putting things briefly and plainly, which very few lawyers have.' After musing awhile thoughtfully, he repeated the name 'Thesiger,' 'Thesiger,' very slowly, and remarked, 'That name is very familiar to me. I recollect when I was in the navy (for I entered that service first), there was a midshipman in our frigate of that name, and a rollicking, jolly, good-hearted, young fellow he was, too; I wonder what has become of him, for I lost sight of him after I went into the army, and have never heard of him since.' 'Lord bless you,' said the Colonel, 'the Lord Chancellor is the same man.'

'What, little Thesiger Lord Chancellor!' said the other, springing to his feet, with great animation. 'You don't say so? Climbing aloft came easy to him, it seems; and so now he is on the trucklehead, and got a Chancellor's wig on, eh? Well, I am right glad to hear it. Dear me,' he continued, resuming his seat, ' it seems to me only the other day he was skylarking in the cockpit, and up to all sorts of pranks and deviltry. I recollect we once took a Spanish prize, loaded with cigars, snuff, and all sorts of raw and manufactured tobacco. Of course, we youngsters helped ourselves most liberally. The snuff was in bladders of the size of foot-balls; but as none of us used that, we amused ourselves by shying it about at each other. The captain's clerk, who messed with us, was a sneaking sort of fellow, and used to curry favour with him, by reporting what was going on in the cockpit. So, in order to punish him, one night Thesiger and I took one of these bladders, cut it open, and spread its contents gently all over his hammock. When he came below, and turned in, as usual, with a spring (for he was as active as a cat), he sent up a cloud of snuff that set him coughing, crying, sneezing, and swearing like mad; but the worst of it was, it nearly choked the whole of us middies, upon whom it had the same effect; and when the officer came below, to inquire into the cause of the row, he tchee-hee'd and tchee-hee'd as bad as any of us; and as soon as he opened his mouth to speak, down went the snuff into his throat, and nearly suffocated him with coughing. He could do nothing but swear, stamp his feet, and shake his fist at us. There was a precious row, as you may suppose; but the best fun of all was to see the young sucking lawyer threatening to report the clerk for trying to stifle us all like rats, by attempting to conceal the snuff in his hammock. Dear me, how I should like to see him again! Oh, Colonel, those were happy days we passed afloat. I always regret having left the navy. I was fond of the sea, and for years after I quitted the service, used to sleep in a cot, that the swinging motion might remind me of the rolling of the dear old ship, and rock me to sleep, while thinking of old times and of old companions. Thesiger Lord Chancellor! Eh? Well it's better than being laid up as an old hulk of an admiral at Greenwich, ain't it? or turned out to grass, like a worn-out cavalry horse, as I am. Come, pass the whisky, and I'll drink his health in some good toddy. Many's the glass of grog we've had together, when we were midshipmen. But, bless my soul, how hot it is here. As you say, I never felt the heat in the East, as I do now, and I never suffered so much as I have to-day, even in the West Indies (which I think the hotter of the two), but once in my life, and that was at Barbadoes. In the year 1819, the 4th, 5th, 9th, and 21st Regiments went out to the West Indies. I was in the 21st, and we were stationed at Barbadoes. It was a Fusilier Regiment, the officers all wore double epaulettes, and were literally covered with gold lace. It was a crack corps, a thousand strong, and we had as much attention paid to us as if we were Guardsmen. To add to our attractions, the officers, with one exception, were single men. It was what Lord Combermere, the Commander-in-Chief, wanted for the purpose of display, so he kept us with him at head-quarters, at Barbadoes, and the other regiments were distributed among the islands. We arrived early in the morning, and as soon as possible, disembarked and marched to our barrack. The colonel, as a matter of course, immediately proceeded to Government House, and made his report, when, to his astonishment, his lordship, who was a disciplinarian of the old school, though otherwise a good sort of man, forgetting that we had but just landed from a long voyage, and had not even begun to unpack, and establish ourselves in our quarters, informed him that he would receive the officers at Government House at two o'clock that same afternoon! You may easily conceive the consternation we were in; it was with the greatest difficulty we could get at our baggage and equip ourselves full fig in our regimentals in time. But it was an order, and we were soldiers, and bound to obey the commands of our superior officers, and by dint of scolding, fretting, working, and sweating, we accomplished it at last; after which we had to walk under the broiling sun of that tropical climate, one interminable long mile to Bridgetown, cased in our heavy toggery (the gold lace of which nearly put our eyes out), our heads pilloried in the regulation stock, our feet adhering to the parched leather of our boots, and our swords actually singeing our hands. I never had such a march in my life. It was enough to have killed us all, and it did lay many of us up for a long time—in fact, it is a wonder it did not send half of us into hospital. In those days, and indeed until very lately, commanding officers seemed to be ignorant that there was any other climate in the world than that of England; and when we were sent abroad, we were clad in the same manner in the West Indies as in Canada. Is it any wonder that the mortality in our army is so great? We live by order, and die by order. What astonished us more than all was, that an old campaigner like Lord Combermere, a man who had seen so much service, and had more experience than most men, should have so pertinaciously adhered to routine. The levee, like everything else in this world, came to an end at last, but the retreat was worse than the advance, for the heat became utterly insupportable by three o'clock. You would have laughed to have seen the extraordinary figures we made on our return to quarters; coats were unbuttoned, stocks discarded, and sashes thrown loose over the shoulders. When we reached our barracks, we were more dead than alive; sangaree, lemonade, tamarind water, and the fatal punch, were called for on all sides, and vanished as quickly as a pool before a drove of camels. I had just emerged from my bath, and was lying exhausted on my bed, when I heard shouts of laughter, and the shuffling of many feet, in the next room, and a dead, heavy, irregular blow on the floor, that shook the very doors and windows of the fragile house. Far above the din sounded the well-known Scotch accents of poor Macpherson, who was raving like a madman, and, as far as I could judge, was hopping about on one leg. "Halloo," said I, to a brother officer who was passing my door, "what's all that row about?" "Only Mac," he said, "making a few *cursory* remarks" on our grand tour to Government House; his feet have so swelled, and the leather so contracted with the heat, he can't get his boots off. He has four men tugging at them, and every now and then he jumps up in a rage, and stamps and roars like a bull." "Go and cut them off," I said, "he must not commence life in this country with an inflammation, or he will soon end it with yellow jack."

‘ Poor Mac! he died soon afterwards, adding another unit to the thousands of noble fellows who have fallen victims in that fatal climate to regulation clothing. He was a great favourite in the regiment, respected for his bravery, and endeared to all by his kindness of heart, and inexhaustible fund of humour. His origin was humble, being the son of a small tenant farmer on the banks of the Tay. One night, after having indulged rather too freely (for he was a most imprudent fellow), he said to me, "Beaty, I hope I shall survive this climate, and live to return to Perthshire. *I have a mission*, and I shan't

die happy if I don't accomplish it." "And what is that?"
I said. " You recollect my poor brother, John, don't you,
who fell at Waterloo ?" " Perfectly ; I helped to carry
him to the rear myself. I suppose you want to erect a
monument to him." " No, sir," he said, " with his eyes
glaring like those of a tiger, " but to pull one down, and
to horsewhip the man that set it up, within an inch of his
life."

' " Mac, Mac," I said, " pray don't excite yourself that
way. If you imbibe as freely as you have lately done,
and suffer your passion to get the better of you, depend
upon it, you will never live to fulfil your ' mission,' as you
call it." " Well, well," he replied, "for poor dear John's
sake, I will keep myself cool. We are poor, but that is
our misfortune, and not our fault. It is nothing to be
ashamed of at any rate, especially by those who have as
good a pedigree as any family in Scotland. But if we
are poor, we are proud, Beaty ; and no man living shall
ever hold us up to the ridicule of every idle southerner
who can beg, borrow, or steal a rod, to come and fish in
the Tay."

' " Why, who has been doing that ?"

' " Colin Campbell, the parish schoolmaster, he is the
scoundrel who did it."

' " In what way ?"

' " Why, my father put up a monument to my brother,
and he got Colin Campbell to write the epitaph, which he
did, and had it cut on the stone, and there it stands to
this day, the laughing-stock of the whole country—

    ' John Macpherson was a very remarkable person ;
    He stood six feet two without his shoe,
    And he was slew at Waterloo.'

' " Well," I said, "the versification is certainly not
very elegant, though the epitaph is by no means devoid of

truth.   But if you will promise me to take better care of
yourself, I will write you one more worthy of the occasion,
and more befitting so distinguished a member of the
Macpherson clan, as your brother.   You can then ob-
literate the present doggerel, and substitute mine for it.
Now, good night, don't drink any more, and go to bed." '

The last words of Beatson coincided with the last puff
of my cigar, and both reminded me that it was also time
for me to retire, and make an entry in my journal, of
' Black jobs and White favours.'

No. VII.

A GALLIMAUFRY.

GENTLE reader, I know what you will say when you see the title of this article. You will exclaim, ' Good gracious! what *is* a Gallimaufry? I never heard the word before—what does it mean?' It is not probable you ever met with it; but I have often heard it in the rural districts of Warwickshire and other midland counties when I was younger than I am now, and it still lingers there. It means a stew of various kinds of edibles, fish, flesh, fowl, and vegetables; and when well made, and properly seasoned, let me tell you, it is by no means an unsavoury dish. The gipsies compound it to this day like all their hashes (of which they are extremely fond), in a way to tempt any man whose appetite has not been vitiated by French cooks, who pamper and provoke a delicate or diseased stomach, but do not know how to satisfy the cravings of a hungry man, or give him a hearty meal. They are not substantial fellows like Englishmen, and their fare is like themselves, all puff, froth, and soufflé. The Gallimaufry at once tempts and satisfies. Hunters of all countries have, by common consent, adopted the same process of cooking; and a similar dish is found in Spain, as olla podrida; and among the North American Indians, as Wiampanoo. I have selected it as a word that describes this portion of my journal, which includes a variety of topics and anecdotes, some substantial like solid meat, some savoury as spicy vegetable ingredients, and some fragments to swell the bulk, which, though not valuable as materials, help to compound the Gallimaufry. For instance, my journal begins from the time I leave my bed, and it terminates at Southampton, the intermediate space being filled with a narrative of all I have heard or seen, or said or done. It is, therefore, made up of odds and ends: such as it is, I now transcribe it for you. May it justify its title.

Travellers are generally early risers. In many countries it is absolutely necessary to be up long before sunrise, in order to finish a journey ere the heat of the day becomes insupportable. In towns, and on shipboard, this habit is rendered inconvenient either by the dusters and brooms of housemaids, or the holy stones and swabs of sailors; but wherever practicable, it is a most healthy as well as agreeable custom. Indeed, I have heard it asserted of those who have attained to great longevity, that nine out of ten of them have been distinguished as 'peep-o'-day boys.' Poor Richard has given us his experience in rhyme, to impress it more easily on the memory:

> 'Early to bed and early to rise,
> Makes a man healthy, wealthy, and wise.'

I cannot say that I have always strictly complied with the first part of the advice (which, to a certain extent, is rendered necessary by the latter), because the artificial state of society in which we live, interferes most inconveniently with its observance; but the early morning ought to be at our own disposal, and with the exception of the two impediments I have named, (which are by no means insurmountable,) it is our own fault, if we do not derive all the advantages resulting from it.

Long before the doors and windows of the 'British

Hotel' were unfastened, I sought the night-porter, and was released from durance vile, into the fresh open air. I strolled over to Trafalgar-square, where I was shortly afterwards joined by Cary. It was a glorious morning; there had been a thunderstorm during the night, accompanied by vivid lightning and torrents of rain; but this had passed away, and the air was cool and bracing, almost cold, while the sky was clear and unclouded, and day was fast dawning on the drowsy town. A few carts laden with garden stuff, were wending their way to their respective markets, though Cockspur-street is not their general thoroughfare; and here and there an early traveller was proceeding in his overloaded cab, to a station or a dock, about to rejoin his family, or perhaps to leave them for ever. A tired policeman paused and looked at him, more from having little else to divert his attention, than from any doubt as to the honesty of his purpose, and then he slowly resumed his weary beat, and for want of somebody to *push on*, tried to push a door or two *in* to ascertain whether it was fastened. A little farther on, he paused, and as he looked up at the sky, coughed heavily, when a coquettish cap hastily appeared at a window in the attics, and as rapidly withdrew: and in a few minutes more the same head was seen bending over the area-gate, which opened, and admitted the watchman of the night. What a safeguard a policeman is! other people are let in clandestinely to do wrong, but he is quietly introduced to detect the evildoer. No doubt he had seen a *suspicious character* in that house, and anxious to do his duty, proceeded to examine the kitchen, the pantry, and the cellar, where, strange to say, things are oftener missed, than from any other part of a house. A detective instinctively goes straight to the spot where a robbery is likely to be committed, and can tell at a glance whether there has been collusion between those within and without the building.

It is necessary to try the contents of the decanters, and to taste the viands he sees, in order to ascertain the habits of the depredator, for, unlike medical men, they make their own stomachs the tests of the contents of bottles. The policeman I noticed, must have been disappointed in his search, for he returned without a prisoner, which was evidently a relief to the maid, who, after readjusting her cap, let him out with much good humour at the contemplation of her safety from robbers; but entreated him, for the security of the family, always to have an eye on that house. A trusty servant and a vigilant policeman enable us to repose in peace; the one relies on the other, and we confide in both. Alas! there were others who had not only no house to protect, but no home to shelter them. On the steps of the National Gallery, and the neighbouring church, were several poor wretches, principally females, extended in sleep that resembled death more than repose, and who, having been first drenched by the rain, sought refuge there from its pitiless pelting. Starvation and luxury, however, if not nearly allied, are close neighbours—the only difference is the side of the wall that separates their lodgings. Within, is all that wealth, station, and connexion can confer; without, all that poverty, want, and degradation can inflict: and yet Providence holds the scale equally, and impartially, between the two. The inner wretch is tortured with gout from indolent and luxurious repose, and from faring too sumptuously every day; the outer one with rheumatism, caused from sleeping on the cold stone steps of the rich man's house, and from exposure to all weathers. The one cannot digest his food, and is dying of dyspepsia; the other has no food to 'digest, and perishes from starvation. Both are poor, the first from living too fast or too penuriously, and the other, not only from having nothing to hoard, but actually nothing to live upon; and yet the houseless poor have sometimes the best of it. The rich have proud ambition or jealous rivalry, blighted prospects of courtly honours, or an uneasy consciousness of possessing no claim beyond their money to distinction. Nature has, perhaps, denied them heirs, and they hate their successors. The poor have no prospects to encourage hope, and often experience relief when they little expect it. They have nothing to leave but poverty and rags. It is sad to think that this dreadful destitution, is too often the result of vice and dissolute habits. If temptation has been too strong and thus punished its victims, let the tempter look upon the ruin he has brought on others; and ere it be too late, make all the amends he can, to society, for the contamination with which he has infected it, and to the wretched individuals themselves, whom he has first led astray, and then left to their miserable fate.

An itinerant coffee-vender interrupted these reflections, by taking up his stand near us, and offering us a cup of his aromatic beverage, and a slice of bread and butter, 'all,' as he said, 'for only twopence.' I tasted it: it was certainly none of the best, but I have had worse at three times the price at a railway station, in one of their gorgeous refreshment rooms. It was, however, pronounced excellent by a wretched group of the houseless beings, whose slumbers the policeman had ruthlessly disturbed, as he called them from dreams of food to the sad reality of actual starvation, and bade them *go about their business.* Never before did so small a sum as the few shillings I had in my pocket produce so much immediate relief. How heavily those words, '*go about your business,*' fell upon my heart! Alas, their business of life was well-nigh over; death had set his seal upon most of them, and marked them for his own. Meanwhile the day was ad-

vancing with hasty strides. The tide of foot-passengers
was rapidly increasing and flowing eastward; the sound
of many wheels was swelling into a continuous rumble,
like distant thunder; and the city, like a huge monster,
was shaking off its slumber, and preparing for its daily
toils. The sun shone out brightly, and the homeless
poor, I have mentioned, vanished from view like spectres
of night, and were seen no more. All was hurry-scurry,
but without confusion; each one was intent on his own
affairs, and only regarded others to avoid contact. As
we were about returning to the hotel, Cary said, 'How
coolly you and your new acquaintances took the storm in
the early part of last night. It was very violent while it
lasted: it was one continued illumination of lightning,
and the thunder was awful. Like everything else in this
country, there was a truly British earnestness about it.
England is so thickly peopled, I shouldn't be much surprised if we heard of some sad accidents having occurred.
After I left the smoking-room last night, I encountered a
lady and her maid at the first landing, both of whom were
in a dreadful state of alarm, the former entreating that
her *crinoline* might be taken off, and the latter afraid to
touch it, having known, as she said, a man to be killed in
consequence of carrying a scythe on his shoulders, which
attracted the lightning. Each flash was followed by a
scream, and one peal of thunder was so heavy that it appeared to shake the house to its very foundation. Their terror
rendered them speechless for a minute or two, when I heard
the lady mutter in great agitation and agony, the words,
" 'So especially for both Houses of Parliament, under our
most religious and most gracious Queen at this time assembled——' Oh, dear! that was very vivid! I am sure it
has affected my eyes——' ordered and settled by their
endeavours on the best and surest foundations.' Oh, that

bolt must have struck the house—how awful this is."
The maid, with equal incoherency, imitating her mistress,
repeated the first words her memory supplied her
with—

    ' " How doth the little busy bee improve each shining hour,
      And gather honey all the day from every opening flower." '

Poor things, it was evident what their object was, but
equally so that they were unconscious of the application of
the words they were uttering. " Oh, sir," said the lady,
when she perceived me, " how dreadful this is ! I am
always so alarmed at thunder, that I lose all self-posses-
sion. Do you think there is any danger ?" " Not the
least in the world," I answered ; " nobody was ever killed
by lightning yet." " I have known many, many," she
said, with the greatest earnestness. " They died of
fright," I replied, " it is fear, and not lightning that kills,
—so it is in drowning—you have heard of people being
restored to animation, after being submerged for three-
quarters of an hour, and others who have expired in a few
minutes ; the latter have invariably died from fright, which
has caused apoplexy ; their faces always exhibit marks of
extravasated blood." " Oh, dear," she said, " I wish I
could be assured of that ; but trees, you know, are not
afraid, and yet they are often struck, split, torn to pieces,
and set on fire——Oh, that clap is nearer still—the lightning and thunder came together simultaneously that
time ;" and then clasping her hands, she resumed,
" ' peace and happiness, truth and justice, religion
and——' " " Calm yourself, madam, I beseech you," I
said, " there is no danger but in fear — this is my
sitting-room, pray be seated, and allow me to offer
you a smelling-bottle. Don't be alarmed ; as for
trees, you know, they have vegetable, and not animal
life, which makes all the difference in the world."

"Well, I never thought of that before," she replied, "I see it all now. It is, I know, very foolish to be so nervous, and for the future I will think of what you are so good as to say, and endeavour to be calm and collected." In a few minutes more the storm passed away, and we separated, with mutual good wishes, to our respective rooms.' ' You didn't mean what you suggested, did you?' I inquired. 'Of course not: it was all I could think of at the time to allay her fears. In my opinion it was a very justifiable piece of deception, it could not possibly do any harm, and, as you see, it did good by calming her anxiety and fright. It is what we conventionally call "*a white lie*," as we desire our servants to say " not at home," when we do not find it convenient to see our friends.' 'Well,' I replied, 'I do not know that deception is ever justifiable—truth, in my opinion, is always to be preferred. If we order our domestics to state what they know is not the fact, do we not induce them, by our example, to take the same liberty with us, and for their own convenience, tell us also what is not true ? We know that the custom is sanctioned by the usage of society, and means nothing more than we are not at home to visitors; but servants are unsophisticated, and understand things literally. Would it not be better to copy the French in this matter? They say, " Madame ne reçoit pas," or " Madame n'est pas visible ;" this is at once truthful, and conveys the information that is required.' ' Do you mean to lay it down as imperative,' said Cary, ' that you must upon all occasions say exactly what you think ? If that is the case you had better *think aloud*, as old Lord Dudley used to do. Upon one occasion when he saw a young dandy approaching him, he exclaimed, " Oh, here comes that insufferable young puppy : I suppose I must ask him to dinner." To which the

K

other rejoined, "If this old bore asks me to dine, I suppose
I shall have to accept the invitation."   It is a well-known
story, and I only allude to it as an apt illustration. What
sort of a world would this be, if we all acted upon such a
rule as you propose?—why we should all be at loggerheads,
one with the other, in no time.' 'No,' I replied, 'I mean
no such thing; we may think what we please, but we can't
say whatever we choose; my rule is this—"it is not
always expedient to say what you think, but it is not admissible ever to say what you don't think."' 'Well,' he
observed, laughingly, in order to turn the conversation,
'if I must say what I think, I am bound to state that I am of
opinion it is time breakfast was ready, so let us cross over
to the hotel.' As we entered the coffee-room, he spied an
old acquaintance reading near the window the *Times*
newspaper. 'That,' he whispered, 'is General Case. His
family consists of himself, his mother, and two daughters;
they are a queer lot.   He is one of the best shots in Lincolnshire, and can talk of nothing but field sports; he is
called "Gun Case."   His eldest daughter, who is goggle-
eyed, is known as "Stare Case," and the other, who is as
ugly as sin, and sets up for a blue, bears the sobriquet
of "Book Case."   His mother, who is an enormous
woman, and uncommonly cross, has been nicknamed
"Case us Belli."   They are neighbours of mine, so I must
go and speak to him, though it is not very pleasant to do
so before strangers, he is so very deaf; but "what can't
be cured must be endured," so here goes.'   Cary accordingly went up to him, shook him by the hand, and inquired
how Mrs. Case, his mother, was.   As usual the general
didn't hear him, but supposed he was talking of a poor
woman who had been killed by lightning the previous
evening.   He said, with a very solemn face, 'she was
in the streets very late last night, I hear, not very sober,

and was drenched with rain. Just as she was making for
the colonnade of the Opera-house for shelter, she was
struck with lightning, and though her clothes were all
wet, they were set on fire, and she was killed and dreadfully burnt. The police ought to take better care of such
people.' 'Ah,' said Cary, turning to me, 'ain't this too
bad; nobody in this house seems to understand what they
are talking about. That lady I encountered last night
didn't know what she said herself, and this man can't
comprehend what anybody else says. Nothing is more
disagreeable than to talk to a man who can't hear your
conversation, and compels you to repeat it in a louder
tone. It draws attention to you, and you can't help
feeling, that you are rendering yourself ridiculous to the
rest of the company, when shouting out at the top of your
voice some commonplace observation, of which one-half of
general conversation is composed. I recollect once a
ludicrous instance of this at the table of the late Lord
Northwick. He had this infirmity of deafness, so painful
to oneself and so distressing to others. He recommended
to the notice of a lady some sweet dish that was near
him, when she replied, "Thank you, my lord, I have
some pudding." Not apprehending her answer, he again
and again, at short intervals, urged her to taste the dish,
and received the same inaudible reply, when the lady's
servant, a country lout, considered he ought to explain
matters. He therefore approached Lord Northwick's
chair, and putting his mouth close to his lordship's ear, vo-
ciferated with all his lungs, " My lord, *missus says as
she'll stick to the pudding.*" The effect was electrical, but
no one enjoyed the joke better than the deaf lord himself.'

After breakfast we proceeded to the Waterloo terminus, to await the train for Southampton. 'There are few
stations in England,' said Cary, 'so inconvenient, so crowded,

K 2

and so badly arranged as this of the South-Western. At
times, and especially on an excursion day like this, it is almost impossible to make your way through the complicated
crowd of arriving and departing passengers. Here you
stumble over luggage that obstructs the platform, there
you run against some distracted female who has been separated from her party. Having recovered from the fall,
and the collision, your shoulder is nearly dislocated by a
trunk, carelessly carried on the back of a porter, or your
foot is crushed by the iron wheel of a handbarrow.
There are no means of getting across the interminable
station, you must go round it. Having effected, with great
fatigue, this long pedestrian journey, you are nearly
squeezed to death by an impatient and selfish crowd, that
assemble round a pigeon-hole, from whence tickets are
issued. All tidal currents exhaust themselves at last,
and having waited for your turn, just as you demand your
" passport," the stagnant stream is flushed by a fresh flood
of late comers, sweeping you from the port, into the
estuary beyond, from whence you seek the eddy again,
cross to the " custom house," and, if you are lucky, get
your " clearance." No doubt the directors have very
good reasons for not opening the narrow pane through
which these documents are issued, till ten minutes before
the departure of each train, among which, perhaps, the
best is, that it is their sovereign will and pleasure.
Railways were made for the emolument of chairmen,
directors, and engineers, and not for the advantage of
stockholders, or the convenience of travellers. One line
yields little or no dividend, while it pays its chairman
some two or three thousand a year ; but he is a nobleman,
and nothing can be done in this country without a peer.
Snobs in the city are so narrow and contracted in their
ideas, that if left to themselves, I have no doubt they

would select a man of business to manage an extensive and complicated affair like an enormous trunk line, having countless branches, ramifications, and suckers (miscalled feeders). But what can you expect from people in trade, who have no ideas beyond " the main chance ?" Government acts on the same principle : the Duke of Somerset directs the Admiralty Board, whose business it is to build line-of-battle ships, and then razee them into heavy frigates, and afterwards cut them in two, lengthen them, and put in steam-engines. If the navy is very expensive, see how much is done : you build a ship—that counts one ; you razee it—that makes two ; you convert it, and that counts for three ships. The John Gilpinites " of credit and renown," in the city, say you have not three ships after all, but only one, which costs as much as three ; but what do they know about ships ? It's a pity shopkeepers won't stick to their own business, which they do understand, and not meddle with affairs of state, which are above their comprehension. Well, the Colonial Office has nothing to do, and a Duke is placed at the head of it, with heaps of under secretaries, head clerks, under scribes, and an immense staff to help him. Lord John Russell has radicalized London to that degree that its citizens slap their breeches pockets, which are full of sovereigns, and say " money is no object, as far as that goes, but don't pay people enormously for doing nothing, who to avoid the name of idleness, strive to bring something to pass, and always do it wrong. Let them play if you like, but don't let them play the devil." Lord Elgin, who *put up* the Canadian rebels, and *put down* the loyalists, is rewarded with the command of the Post-Office, a self-acting "traction carriage," with four wheels, representing the four quarters of the globe, of which he is the very necessary and useful "fifth wheel." These cavillers say he

is a mere ornamental appendage, for the working officials
are so devoted to their duties, that a child of one of the
responsible officers was recently born with the impression
of a penny stamp upon its back.   In short, the whole
Whig Government professes liberal principles, and evinces
its sincerity by filling every high office with dukes, earls,
and aristocratic scions.   We are a consistent people, and
no mistake.   Well, if the government of the country is
all wrong, is it any wonder the management of our iron
roads is not right?   If secretaries of state don't know
their business, how can you expect secretaries of railways
to be wiser or better than their superiors?   Dockyards
cost twice as much as they are worth, why shouldn't our
"great line."   The public are taxed to support government, why should not holders of railway stock be taxed
to support chairmen, directors, and engineers?   The
famed confusion of Balaclava is equalled, or at any rate
rivalled at a great terminus like that of Waterloo.   See
what is going on now: the bell has rung, the time for
departure has arrived, and passengers seek the train.
But, alas! the first carriage is full, and so are the others;
one by one they visit them all in rapid succession.   The
more sturdy and pertinacious travellers are quietly
seated, and regard the anxiety of the outsiders with calm
indifference; while one perhaps, unworthy of a seat in the
first class, *chaffs* them as they inquiringly look into the
carriage, and says, "There is plenty of room here, if you
could only find it!"   The porters are so accustomed to
this admirable arrangement, they cease to be surprised at
anything that occurs.   Finally, one solitary seat is found
for the last "place-hunter," vacant, but not empty, appro-
priated, but not engaged.   It is filled with parcels, shawls,
parasols, and cloaks.   Two or three ladies, with looks of
great dissatisfaction, and evident feelings of ill-usage,

remove their general assortments, and the luckless
traveller occupies his place with many humble apologies
for the inconvenience he has occasioned them, but with an
internal conviction, that if there had been more vacant
seats, the ladies would have filled them all in a similar
manner.'

Fortunately for me, I had my 'Season Ticket,' and had
the convenience of leisurely securing a seat, that gave me
the command of the window, whence I had an opportunity
of observing the accuracy of many of Cary's strictures on
the inconvenience of the station, and the inadequacy of its
arrangements to meet the requirements of such an extensive line. These were palpable enough. The analogy,
however, between the management of the affairs of a
railway company and those of the government, though
amusing, was not quite so obvious to me, who am no
politician. I prefer listening to others to venturing
opinions of my own—'semper auditor tantum.'

The carriage was rapidly filled by seven other persons,
four ladies and three gentlemen. The four first appeared
to constitute a separate party, while the other three and
myself were unknown to them or to each other. 'Good-
bye, Shegog,' said Cary, shaking me by the hand, 'I shall
expect to meet you to-morrow night again at the British
Hotel.' 'Shegog!' whispered one of the ladies in my
carriage to her nearest companion, 'what a funny name!
I wonder if he is any relation of Gog and Magog?'
'Why,' said the other, 'he is a male, you see, otherwise
I should think he was Gog's wife,' a sally which was
repressed by a subdued *hush* from the elder lady, and
followed by a general titter. It is not the first time my
name has attracted inconvenient attention, so I am accustomed to this sort of thing, and rather enjoy the jokes
it gives rise to. Still, like ladies of a certain age, I

am ready to change it for a fortune, and am open to an offer. Bright said the other night, in the House of Commons, that a gentleman he had never seen or heard of had left him a large sum of money on account of his advocacy of peace principles. I wish he would introduce me to such a friend, for I too am for 'peace at any price,' and I would condescend to accept his fortune, and adopt his name.

No name, however, can escape from being turned into ridicule by adding to it a droll prefix. *Lyon*, whom I knew at college, a great coxcomb, was everywhere greeted, to his serious distress, as '*Dandy Lyon.*' No man was ever more annoyed than he was by this ridiculous joke, and great was his relief when he inherited an estate, with the privilege of assuming the name of '*Winder.*' Had he laid aside his absurd style of dress, it is possible he might thus have escaped the ridicule to which he had exposed himself; but his relentless companions merely altered his nickname, and he was ever afterwards known as '*Beau Winder.*' I have always thought my parents did me great injustice, as they could not give me a fortune, they might at least have bequeathed to me 'a good name.'

The first thing after adjusting and settling yourself in a carriage is to take a rapid reconnoitring glance at your fellow-travellers; and I have observed that the survey is generally one of disappointment, judging from the manner in which people close their eyes and affect to sleep, or search for a paper or a book with which to occupy themselves. The family party had all the talk to themselves; one, whom the others addressed as 'Aunty,' had, as appeared from her conversation, been a great traveller in her day, and, like most travellers, every incident she related had happened to herself, every anecdote referred to parties whom she knew personally, and every witty speech was either addressed to her, or uttered in her presence. 'Didn't you find a great inconvenience, aunt,' inquired one of the younger ladies, 'in travelling in Russia and the north of Europe?' 'I never let little matters disturb me, my dear,' she replied; 'if everything went smooth with you, life would be like a calm day on the water at Venice, a level glassy surface, sails flapping against the mast, your bark maintaining its monotonous roll, a burning sun, and a listless existence. We need excitement, my dear; we require change, even if it be a gale, a thunder-storm, or a white squall. The delays, privations, discomforts, and even dangers of travelling, by the alternation with their opposites, render the reminiscences of these things most charming. If we could go round the world on a railway like this, it would be the most insipid tour imaginable, too tame, too easy, and too unvaried. "*I took my satisfaction with me,*" my dear, as poor old Sally Philips used to say, which, I believe, is the only true way to enjoy travelling, and most other things in this world. You remember old Sally, don't you? She lived in our village, near Chickweed Hall, and used to assist the gardener in weeding, sweeping the lawn, and such matters. Well, I once gave her an outing to London, and when she returned, I asked her how she liked it. "Well, ma'am," she replied, "*I took my satisfaction* with me. I always does, and in course I always returns home pleased. Oh! it did me a power of good, too; for I had been ailing for some time, and at last I was so bad, I was three days in bed with the doctor. Oh! ma'am," she continued, "it was a grand sight every way was London; I knowed it from all accounts before I went, and yet all I heard did not come up to the truth." Poor old Sally, she was an honest,

K 3

faithful creature; but when angry or excited, she made a strange jumble of her stories. I recollect her once coming to me in great haste, curtsying down to the ground, in spite of her agitation, and exclaiming, "Oh! dear, ma'am, a most dreadful thing has happened to me, and, saving your presence, I will tell you all about it. When I came home from market this evening, I brought my head with me, as I generally do, when I find it is reasonable. Well, ma'am, my husband, you see, split my head for me." "Good gracious! how dreadful," I said. "Yes, indeed, ma'am, it was dreadful, as you say, for he had washed it nicely afterwards, and taken my brains out, and put them altogether into a bucket, and I had just left him for a minute, to go into the next room to straighten myself, when I heard an awful smash. 'Ruth,' says I, to my daughter, 'as sure as the world, there's my head gone, brains and all.' So I rushes back to the kitchen just in time to see Mrs. Davies's unlucky dog run off with my beautiful head in his mouth, and all my brains on the floor. The moment I saw him I screamed out, 'Drop my head, you nasty brute;' but no, off he runs with it in his mouth, and never stops till he gets under Mrs. Davies's haystack, and begins to gnaw at it. So on I goes to Widow Davies, and says I, ' Mrs. Davies, your dog has made away with my beautiful head and spilt all my brains.' ' If he saw any beauty in *your* head,' said she, tossing her ugly face up with scorn, 'it's more than ever I could; and as for brains, you never had any.' Says I, ' It's my sheep's head.' ' Oh! the sheep's head, is it? Well, you ought to have taken better care of it, that's all I have to say. But I never interfere with nobody's business, not I indeed; as we say in the north —

'Who mells with what another does,
   Had best go home and shoe his gooze.'

Says I, 'Mrs. Davies, that's not the question; will you
make proper amends, and give me another head as
handsome as mine, with brains too?' With that she flew
into a tearing passion, and, saving your presence, ma'am,
she said, ' Go to the devil,' so of course I came right off
to you." Poor old woman, she died in Chickweed Hall
hospital, as my father used to call the house he built for
his pensioners.' ' Aunty,' said one of the young ladies,
to whom Aunt Sally did not appear half as amusing as
her namesake did to the Duke of Beaufort, ' look at this
photograph of Charles, is it not a capital likeness?' 'It's
justice without *mercy*, my dear,' replied the old lady, ' as
all photographs are; they diminish the eyes, and magnify
the nose and the mouth, and besides, they make people
look older.' ' Then they are neither just nor merciful,'
was the retort of the sharp young lady. ' No, dear, they
are not,' continued the aunt, looking sentimental, ' neither
are they flattering. But what does it signify after all, for
in a few short years they will fade away, and be forgotten,
like ourselves. I was very much shocked by a conversation I overheard the other day, at Brighton. I was in
Smith's, the old china dealer's shop, near the Pavilion,
when I saw Sir John Mullett approaching, and as I did
not feel inclined to talk to him, I slipped into the back
room, but had not time to close the door after me, so I
was very reluctantly compelled to listen to his conversation—" Smith," said he, " have you got rid of my father
yet?" " No, Sir John," he replied, " I have done my
best for you, but nobody wants him, they say he is too
large; but I'll tell you what I have been thinking, Sir
John! how would it do to cut his legs off below the knees,
there would be enough of him left then, for it appears to

me, they are by no means the best part of him." "By
Gad!" said the other, " that's a capital idea : have his
legs taken off immediately, tho' let the job be done neatly,
don't let him be disfigured, you know.   But stop! don't
talk about it," he continued, "for ill-natured people
might make a good story out of my cutting off my father's
legs, and all that sort of thing, eh ?"   And away he went,
laughing to himself, as if he had said a good thing.
When the coast was clear, I returned into the shop. " For
goodness gracious sake, Mr. Smith," I said, " what was
that wicked, heartless man, Sir John Mullett, directing
you to do with his respectable old father ?" " Why,
ma'am," said Smith, " he has a full-length portrait of his
late father, presented to the old baronet for eminent services; it is too large for his rooms, at least he fancies so,
and he wants to sell it, and I advised him to reduce the
size, which would make it more saleable, for it really is a
good picture, by Sir Thomas Lawrence." " Yes," I replied, " that is very true, but if reduced in size, it would
suit his rooms, as well as those of others."   He shrugged
his shoulders, and observed, " *that* was a matter of taste."
" It may be," said I, " but it certainly is not a matter of
feeling."   I shall never have my likeness taken, dear, I
have no idea of my legs being cut off, that I may not occupy too much space on the wall, or be made a target of,
as my great-grandmother's portrait was by my younger
sisters in the archery ground.'

' Yes, but you know ladies are not painted in a picture
like gentlemen; but how funny it would be if'—

' Hush, dear, don't be silly now.'

' Well, you might have a miniature taken, you know,
and that occupies no room.'

' Yes, but even that, if done by a first-rate artist,
would sell for money, and sold I should be to a certainty;

and what is worse, ridiculed for the extraordinary way
old women arranged their hair in '59, for the bad taste
with which I was dressed, and the total absence of dia-
monds. Last week I was at Storr and Mortimer's, and I
saw on the counter some very beautiful miniatures, most
exquisitely painted. "These," I said, "are sent here to
be reset, I suppose?" "No, madam," was the answer,
"they are for sale. They are likenesses of Lord South-
cote's ancestors, taken by the first artists in Europe, of
the different periods in which they lived. This (exhi-
biting one in particular), is an enamel of the Louis
Quatorze period, a portrait of that far-famed beauty,
the wife of the second lord. She was reckoned the hand-
somest woman in England of her day." I turned from
contemplating them, with feelings I cannot express. Ah,
my dear, succeeding generations are like the succeeding
waves of yonder vast Atlantic. They gather strength
and size with the storms that lift them from their calm
existence, and urge each other onward in their ceaseless
course, till they successively break on the rugged shores
that imprison them, recoil into the immensity of ocean
from which they sprung, mingle with its waters, and are
lost to view for ever. They leave no trace behind them.
One generation has as little sympathy for that which pre-
ceded it as one wave has connexion with another. We
look forward with hope, but regard the past with awe or
regret. We may control the future, through the agency
of the present, but the past is irrevocable. Our sympathies are with our own contemporaries, and our living descendants. The dead are dreams of other days, dark
dreams too, and full of mystery. No! paint me no portrait; when the reality departs, let there be no shadowy
unsubstantial picture! Few would recognise the likeness; it would be but a face and nothing more, and one,

too, that borrows or assumes an expression for the occasion. Memory wants no aid from an artist, it engraves the image of those we love on the heart, and it retains the inward qualities as well as the outward lineaments. We live while those who love us live, and we perish with them; posterity knows us no more than if we had never been. We must die, dear, and be forgotten, it is the law of our nature ; but I neither wish to be painted when alive, *razeed* when dead, nor sold as " the Lord knows who," by a London jeweller.'

'By-the-by, Aunty,' said one of the young ladies, by way of changing the conversation, 'did you buy one of those wonderfully cheap gold watches, in the city, yesterday, for me, at that great bankrupt sale, near St. Paul's?' ' No, my dear,' said the old lady, with great animation, ' I bought nothing, I was only too glad to get safely out of the shop. Never go to these large advertising establishments that promise such extraordinary bargains, they are all cheats. I never was in such a place before in my life. I saw placards in large black and red letters, stuck up everywhere, that the effects of a bankrupt had been purchased at a discount of sixty per cent. below prime cost, and that as the sale was positive, they were to be disposed of at an enormous sacrifice. So, as I had to go through the city, on my way from the Shoreditch station, I confess I was silly enough to be tempted to look in, intending to make a purchase for you. As soon as I entered, two ill-dressed men, out of a crowd of attendants or conspirators, beset me, one on one side, and one on the other, talking and boasting as loud as they could. I was shown, or nearly forced up stairs, and, on my way there, passed a lady who appeared quite alarmed, though she had a gentleman with her, and if I had had my wits about me, I should have joined them, and made my escape ; but, as

I am not easily frightened, (having travelled so much,) on
I went, and found myself in a large upper room, filled
with every kind of showy, trashy stuff. I had hardly
reached this place, when a shopman shouted out from below, "Have you any more of those diamond rings?"
"No," was the answer, delivered in an equally loud
tone, to attract attention. "No, they are all sold; Lady
Grosvenor took the last four this morning." And again,
"Have you sent those six court dresses to the Austrian
Ambassador's?" "Yes, and his excellency will be obliged
if one of the young ladies will wait upon him with some
more this evening." "Send down one of those splendid
Turkish hearth-rugs for a lady to look at, also one of the
fifty guinea dressing-cases." "All sold, except one, and
that the Duke of Wellington has just sent for." All this,
and much more stuff of the same kind, passed between
them. "Have you any gold watches?" I asked, "I observe you advertise them?" "Sorry to say, madam, you
are too late; we had many hundreds yesterday, but
Savory and Co. came this morning and bought them all
up; they said they were so dirt cheap they would ruin
the trade; cost twenty pounds a-piece, and sold them at
four. But here are some clocks," showing me some Sam
Slicks, put into tinsel and varnished cases. "Capital articles! Can afford to sell them for next to nothing.
Tremendous sacrifice for cash!" "Thank you, I do not
want one." "Keeps wonderful time. Mr. Gladstone
bought one; we call the new movement the Gladstono-
meter, after him." "I tell you I don't want a clock, I
asked for watches." "Beautiful India shawl, ma'am, just
look at it," spreading before me a wretched affair, only
fit for a kitchen maid. "That," said I, resolutely (for I am
a judge of India shawls), "is neither Indian nor French,
but a miserable Norwich imitation, and is made of

cotton, and not silk." "Pray may I ask you," said the fellow, most impatiently, " are you *in a position* to purchase an Indian shawl?" "I am in a position, sir," I said, "not to put up with insolence." The door was obstructed by several of these people, so I said in a firm voice, " Allow me to pass, sir, or I shall call a policeman." "Which, if you do not," replied my persecutor, "I most certainly shall. Make room for this lady. What was the cause of your intrusion here, ma'am, I know not, you certainly never came *to purchase*, whatever your real object may have been. Smith, see this lady out. Below there, *two upon ten*," which I believe is a slang term that implies "keep two eyes on that person's ten fingers." I never was so rejoiced as when I found myself in the street again, and was enabled to draw a long breath, and feel assured that I was safe. I must say it served me right; I had no business to go there. I have always heard those places were kept by scoundrels and cheats; but I could not bring myself to believe that they dared to do such things in such a public place, and in so unblushing a manner. Many a timid lady is plundered in this way, by being compelled to purchase what she does not want, and to accept some worthless article in exchange for the money she is bullied out of. The form of sale is adopted to avoid the technicalities of law, and to divest the affair of the character of a larceny ; but in fact it is neither more nor less than a robbery. If you want a good article, my dear, you must pay a good price ; and if you desire to avoid deception, go to a respectable well-known shop. But here we are at Winchester ; I think I see Charles on the platform. Now see that you don't leave your things behind you, Jane, in the carriage, as you so often do. I have only thirteen packages, and they are easily found.' In a few minutes the family party left us, the

bell rang, and we were again on our way to Southampton.

The gentleman who sat opposite to me returned me
the *Times* which I had lent him on leaving Waterloo,
and I said, 'What do you think of the news to-day, of the
Emperor reducing his military and naval forces to a
peace establishment?' 'I think it is a very significant
hint to us,' he replied, 'to be prepared for an invasion.
Napoleon never makes an assertion that is not calculated
to induce a belief of its being the very opposite of what
he really thinks or intends. He is one of those who fully
believes in the saying of an old epigrammatist, that "language was given to men to conceal their thoughts." I
regard his acts and not his protestations; one are facts,
the other delusions. If I must interpret his language, I
do so by comparing what he says to Frenchmen with what
he addresses to foreigners. He proclaims to his people
that the defeats at Moscow and Waterloo are to be
avenged, and that all those who occupied Paris, and
overthrew the empire, must in turn be punished. His
mission, he says, is to effect this grand object. The first
part he has fulfilled by humbling the pride of Russia, by
the destruction of Sebastopol, and the capture of the
Redan; the second by driving the Austrians out of Italy.
Prussia and England are still to be humiliated. The
Rhine provinces will appease his anger against the former,
who will have to fight single-handed, and will probably
purchase her peace by the cession of her frontier possessions. England has a long series of victories, by land and
by sea, to atone for. Every Frenchman will rally round
the Emperor in this struggle for life and death, and ex-
pend his blood and his treasure to gratify the long
cherished revenge, " *Delenda est Carthago.*" To Europe
he says, " the empire is peace," and in proof of his pacific

intentions, he has reduced his military and naval forces. What does he call a peace establishment? Before the Italian war he solemnly denied that he was arming, and yet every arsenal in France was occupied day and night with preparations for war, both by sea and land, while rifled guns and their carriages, packed in heavy cases, were shipped to Italy as merchandise, to elude observation, and every arrangement made for a sudden and successful invasion. For the maintenance of his enormous army there may be plausible reasons assigned. It may be said, that as a continental power he must be ready for every contingency, where his neighbours pursue the same suicidal course of expending their resources on their military establishments; but what is the meaning of the enormous increase of his navy? One quarter of his fleet is more than sufficient to annihilate that of America, and one third of it is able to cope with that of Russia, which can never be a formidable maritime nation. Austria, Prussia, and the other great powers have no navies worth mentioning. What, then, is its object? Can any reasonable man doubt that it is a standing menace to England, and that as soon as it can be raised to a numerical majority, it will be let loose upon us? If this is his peace establishment, nominally reducing his forces means being ready for every emergency, and making no alteration whatever that will interfere with immediate action. Sending soldiers to their homes *looks* pacific, but is an artful dodge to save for a time the expense of paying them; for though they are absent on leave, a telegraphic message would bring every one of them back to their respective regiments in ten days. In like manner, his foreign commerce is limited, and his sailors can be reassembled at a moment's notice. It is a well-conceived, but ill-disguised trap laid for us, in hopes that we shall be induced by our credulity on the one hand, and our Manchester politicians on the other, to accept his promises as honest, and disarm also. But even if his reduction were real, and not nominal, disarmament by the English would be followed by very different results. If you disband your soldiers you can never lay your hands upon them again. If you pay off your sailors, as you did at the termination of the Crimean war, the consequence would be equally disastrous, for when wanted they will be found scattered, like our commerce, over every part of the world. Napoleon, on the contrary, has nothing to do but to stamp his foot on the ground, and up will spring five or six hundred thousand soldiers, together with all the sailors of France, trained, disciplined, and effective men. In the mean time, every ship in ordinary will be kept in readiness to put to sea. She will be strengthened, refitted, and her guns ticketed and numbered, as they are deposited in store, or other rifled and improved ones substituted in their place. Portions of other ships will be prepared, fitted, and marked, so as to be put together at a moment's notice, when required, while stores and materials will be accumulated in the arsenals, and the yards, furnaces, and smithies enlarged, arranged, and fitted for immediate action. There will be nothing to be done but to issue the orders and "let slip the dogs of war." Are we prepared for such a sudden emergency—I may say, for such an explosion—for when it does come, it will be his interest to lose no time? If we are to be beaten at all, he knows his only chance is to take us by surprise, to assault us, as a burglar, in the night, and to plunder the house before the shutters are closed, or the watchman is at his post. Steam has bridged the Channel, we no longer use nautical terms in reference to it, we do not talk of the distance across in knots, or miles, we estimate it by hours.

Cherbourg is five hours from Southampton. I left it at six, and landed at the dock of the latter at eleven o'clock in the forenoon, and by two o'clock was in London. The most foolhardy of the present administration, even Palmerston himself, says this is inconveniently near, should Napoleon become an assailant. Now I am no alarmist, which is a very favourite name given to those who desire the use of ordinary precaution. I exclude from my consideration any junction of the Russian with the French fleet, which, it is admitted on all hands, we are not at present able to resist. But I do maintain that we ought to be in a position to retain the command of the Channel, besides detaching large squadrons to the Mediterranean, and to other naval stations; and that if we are unable to do this, we lie at the mercy, and invite an invasion of the French. It is impossible to fortify all our extended coasts, or effectually to defend the country against a large invading force; they must be protected by the navy. "Britannia rules the waves." When she ceases to rule them, she ceases to exist as a nation. If the French can achieve maritime supremacy, an invasion would be as easy as that of the Normans, and a conquest as complete; and I can see no reason, as a military man, why it should not be annexed to France, and become an integral part of that empire, as much as Algeria.'

No. VIII.

OUR NEIGHBOURS AND DISTANT RELATIONS.

MY fellow-passenger, ascertaining that I was going to
Radley's Hotel, at Southampton, proposed to share my
cab, and also, if I had no objection, to join me at dinner.
This arrangement was most agreeable, for nothing is so
uncomfortable or uninviting as a solitary meal. Indeed,
I think, conversation is absolutely necessary to digestion.
It compels you to eat slowly, and enables you to enjoy
your wine, which you are never inclined to do when alone.
Talk is an excellent condiment. A dog prefers to retire
to a corner with his food, and if a comrade approaches
him he snarls, and shows his teeth, and if he persists in
intruding his company, most probably fights him. But dogs
cannot communicate their ideas to each other; if they
could they would, no doubt, regard the quality of their
food as well as its quantity. Man is a reasoning animal,
and delights in a 'feast of reason and a flow of soul,' as
much as in his material food; he equally dislikes a
crowded or an empty table. The old rule that your
company should not be less than three, or exceed nine, is
a fanciful one, founded on the limited number of graces
and muses. Now, in my opinion, the arrangement should
be made by couples, from two to ten. Three is a very
inconvenient limitation, constituting, according to an old
adage, 'no company.' If more assemble the table should

be round, which admits of your seeing all your friends at once, avoids the necessity of talking across any one, and enables you to hear more distinctly. Straight lines are always formal, but never more so than at a convivial board; indeed, I should prefer to have the dining-room circular : you can then say, with truth, that you are ' *surrounded* by your friends,' or that you have ' gathered your friends *round* you,' expressions which are either unmeaning or inapplicable to our ordinary arrangements. But this is a digression.

My new acquaintance, Colonel Mortimer, had seen much foreign service, and was a well-informed and pleasant companion. He was acquainted with many people I had known in the East, and with several of my friends in North America. Nothing is more agreeable than such a casual meeting with one who has travelled over the same ground as yourself. It enables you to compare notes, and has the advantage of presenting the same objects in different points of view. After dinner I reverted to our conversation of the morning, as to the state of our national defences. 'This place,' I said, 'is imperfectly fortified, and open to attack both by land and sea, and the number and value of the steamers in the docks invite a visit from our neighbours, if we should, unfortunately, be at war with them. Do you really think there is any fear of a French invasion ?'

'Fear,' he said, 'is a word, you know, we Englishmen don't understand. Nelson, when a boy, asked what it meant; but I do think there is reason to apprehend that the invasion of England is seriously contemplated by Napoleon. Time and opportunity are alone wanting for him to make the attempt. As I observed this morning, what is the object of the great and incessant naval preparations in France ? I asked the question, the other day, of a

Frenchman; he shrugged his shoulders and said, "We are at war with the Chinese, and we think it necessary to be prepared for an attack from them!" The real design, however, is too obvious to be denied. The Emperor is a sort of diplomatic Jesuit, who says one thing and means its opposite, who conceals his objects until the proper time arrives to unmask them, and who by his skill acquires your confidence without giving you his own in exchange for it. He is not an "ally," but "a lie" to England, and an enigma to Europe. His naval preparations point to us; they may be meant as a blind to withdraw public attention from his designs upon Belgium or Prussia, and, judging by his past acts, it is not improbable that such may be the case; but as neither of these countries possesses a navy, it is not reasonable to suppose that such an enormous expenditure has been incurred for such a purpose. We must look at things as they are, and draw our own conclusions. At this moment he has twenty line-of-battle ships on the stocks, plated with steel, and fitted with every modern improvement. He has completed the construction of a coast line of telegraphs, all centering at Cherbourg, so that no ship can leave any harbour on this side of the Channel without being signalled to the fleet stationed at that port. These preparations for war are not confined to France: he has a greater military force at Martinique and Guadaloupe than we have in all our West India Islands put together. He has fortified St. Pierre and Michelon, which lie between Newfoundland and Canada, contrary to the express terms of the treaty; and under pretence of meeting at Cape Breton the French mails, conveyed by the Cunard steamers, he sends men-of-war thither, who return to those places heavily laden with coal from the Sydney mines. This is pretended to be for the use of the ships themselves, but every now and then a *sailing* vessel takes a cargo on account, it is said, of the merchants there, but in reality for the Government. He has an immense store of coal there ; and every vessel laden with fish, that sails thence to the French West Indian Islands I have named, quietly conveys a certain portion of this fuel, to form a depôt there also, for his Atlantic fleet.

'The Island of Cape Breton, as you are aware, is one vast coal field, and was conquered from the French. Its capital, Louisburg, was taken by General Wolfe. Most of the inhabitants of that colony remained there after its formal cession to England, and their descendants are, to this day, a separate race, speaking the language of their forefathers ; they are mainly occupied in the fisheries, and are excellent pilots. Their descent, their religion, their traditions, and their sympathies, naturally incline them to think favourably and kindly of their mother country ; and though not actually disloyal to England, they are not unfavourably disposed towards the French. It has been observed of late that their friendship has been systematically courted by the latter, who engage their young men in their fisheries, encourage them to trade with them, and, under one pretence or other, continually visit their harbours. During the past year, while that valuable colonial possession has been entirely neglected by the admiral on the Halifax station, in consequence of the limited number of ships under his command, three French men-of-war have been at anchor a great part of the time, at Sydney, as if it were a French port, and their flags, and that of their consuls, were the only ones that were seen by the inhabitants. Cape Breton, on its eastern side, presents many harbours, and numerous hiding-places for French men-of-war, not merely on its coast, but by means of the great Bras d'Or Lake (which is an arm of the sea that nearly divides the island into two parts) affords nooks of concealment in the very heart of the country. The coal-mines are wholly unprotected, and could be either held or rendered useless at the pleasure of an aggressor. What renders this more alarming is, that *Halifax, and the whole of our squadron* at that station, are entirely dependent upon these very mines for their supply of coal; so that in six-and-thirty hours' sail from St. Pierre, one ship of war could reach Sydney, and render the English fleet utterly powerless to move from their moorings. On every foreign station, whether on the Atlantic, or Pacific side of America, or in the East, the French naval force has been quietly and unostentatiously increased, so that if war were to break out, they would be in the ascendant in every quarter. In these days of telegraphic communication, when news of hostility can be transmitted with the rapidity of lightning, it is not too much to say, that the Emperor, by his foresight, judicious preparations, and well-concealed plans, could sweep the commerce of England from the seas in six weeks.

'As I said before, I am no alarmist; I conjure up no phantoms of a junction of Russian or American fleets with those of France, because that probability is too painful to contemplate; but, despite the frivolous pooh-poohing, and imbecile policy of those who ridicule patriotism, and throw cold water on the formation of defensive independent corps, which they style the result of a "rifle fever," I think there is every reason to apprehend that our country is in imminent danger. An invasion of England is a traditional idea in France. Napoleon the First, as is well known, very nearly attempted it; Louis Philippe had it much at heart. The Prince de Joinville, you are aware, published a pamphlet on the subject, and kept alive the national feeling by describing to his countrymen the facility with

L

which London could be taken by a *coup de main*, and
excited their cupidity by pointing out to them the
enormous booty it contained, to reward their successful
attack.   To prepare the public mind for such an attempt,
and to awaken and revive the naval ardour of the nation,
our flag was everywhere insulted, and in one instance he
fired into one of our gun brigs, in South America, forcibly
took away her pilot, a Brazilian subject, and compelled
him to transfer his services to the French ship.   From
the time of the first Empire to the present, every exertion
has been made by every successive government to increase
the French naval force, not merely by building ships,
accumulating naval stores, and enlarging their dockyards,
but by giving bounties to their vessels engaged in the
foreign fisheries, especially those of Newfoundland, which
are great and growing nurseries for their seamen.   There
are more than thirty thousand well-trained sailors engaged
in this business alone.   Now you must recollect that
France, possessing but few colonies, and much less commerce than we have, has, of course, very much less to
defend, while our distant possessions and immense foreign
trade require a force for their protection nearly equal to
what is necessary to insure our own safety.   The French
navy is aggressive, and not defensive; its business is to
burn, sink, or destroy, not to guard, protect, or defend.
Its employment will be piracy—its reward plunder.
The past and present neglect of our navy is, therefore,
altogether inexcusable; we must maintain our maritime
supremacy, whatever the cost may be; and if our fleets
have the command of the channel, we may safely
intrust our defences to them, with a certain conviction that our native land will never be polluted by
the presence, or ravaged by the hordes, of a foreign in-
vader.'

'I am entirely of your opinion,' I said: 'I have been so much abroad lately, that I am not very—'

'Well posted up, eh, Squire Shegog? Well, if you ain't, I want to know who is, that's all? And how are you, stranger? I hope I see you well.'

'Quite well, Mr. Peabody' (for it was he). 'And how is my friend, the Senator?'

'Hearty as brandy,' he said, 'but not quite so spirited; looks as sleepy as a horse afore an empty manger, but is wide awake for all that. He'll be here directly; great bodies move slow; he worms his way through a crowd, as perlite as a black waiter. "Permit me to pass, if you please, Sir." "By your leave; will you be good enough to allow me to go on," and so forth. I make short metre of it. I took up a porter by the nape of his neck, and stood him on one side, as easy as if he'd been a chessman. It made people stare, I tell you; and I shoved one this way, and another that way, and then put my two hands together before me like a wedge, and split a way right through the crowd. One fellow, seeing what I was at, just scroodged up again me, so as to hold his place: "Take your hand off my watch-chain," said I; "what do you mean by a-hustlin of me that way?" The fellow squared round, and so did others, and I pushed on, saying I should not wonder if my purse was gone too. They had to make room to feel their pockets, and that made space enough for me. There is no use a-talkin of it, stranger, people must keep off the track, unless they want to be run over. Here comes Senator, at last, I do declare, a-puffin and a-blowin like a wounded porpoise, when h e whole shoal of 'em are arter him.'

'Well, Senator,' said Peabody, 'you seem to have had a tempestical time of it at the station, among the excursionists a-goin to see the Great Eastern. Take a chair, and sit down, and rest yourself, for you look like a fellow that's sent for, and can't come, and sittin is as cheap as standin, when you don't pay for it. So let us all heave to, and cast anchor, it saves the legs, and depend upon it, they wern't made always to hang down, like a Chinaman's tail, or dangle like old Sharmon Fluke's queue. If you want them to last out the body, you must rest them, that's a fact; you must put them upon a chair, or out of a winder, or cross them in front of you, like a tailor. Is it any wonder the English go about limpin, hobblin, and dotangoone in, when their feet hang down for everlastin, like those of a poke, when it's frightened from a swamp, by a shot from a Frenchman, who hates him like pyson, for poachin among his frogs. Blood won't run up hill for ever, you may depend. I don't wonder you are tired, threadin your way through these excursionists. Don't the British beat all natur in their way? they will go anywhere, stranger, to see anything big. What's curious ain't no matter, it's size they like—a hugeacious ship, a big glass palace, a mammoth hog, an enormous whale, a big ox, or a big turnip, or Big Ben (that's cracked like themselves). Any monster, fish, flesh, or fowl, is enough to make the fools stare, and open their mouths as if they were a-going to swallow it whole, tank, shank and flank. Fact, I assure you—now jist look a-here. Senator is a far greater man than I be anywhere, he has more larnin, more sense, and the gift of speech of ten women's tongues, reduced and simmered down to an essence; talks like a book: we call him a " big bug" to home. Well, he is undersized, you see, and they think nothen of him here, but stare like owls at a seven-footer like me. As one of them said to me to-day, " If you are a fair specimen of your countrymen, Mr. Peabody, I must say the Americans are a splendid race of men." " Stranger," said I, " I

am just nothen, I am only seventeen hands high, or so;
I am the leastest of father's nine sons; you should have
seen my brother Oby : when he was courtin Miss Jemime
Coffin, of Nantucket, he used to lean on the winder sill
in the second story, and talk to her as easy as if he was
a-lollin on the back of her chair.   One night he went, as
usual, to have a chat with the old folks—of course he did
not go to see the young ones; such a thing is onpossible,
who ever heard of that in all their born days !   Visits is
always to parents, and if a lady comes in by accedent,
and the old ones go out, or go to bed, why, accordin to
reason and common sense, young people remain behind,
and finish the evening; natoral politeness requires that,
you know.   Well, this time he was a little bit too late ;
they had all gone to roost.   To home in our country,
folks don't sit up for everlastin as they do here, but as
soon as it is daylight down, and supper over, tortle off to
bed.   Well, this night, the fire was raked up safe, the
hearth swept clean and snug, the broom put into a tub of
water, for fear of live coals a-stickin to it, and they had
all turned in, some to sleep, some to dream, and some to
snore.   I believe in my soul, a Yankee gall of the right
build, make, and shape, might stump all creation for
snoring.'

'And pray,' said I, 'what do you call the *right build*
for that elegant accomplishment ?'

'Why,' said Peabody, 'a gall that is getting old, thin,
and vinegary, that has a sharp-edged bill-hook to her
face, with its sides collapsed; they act like stops to a
key-bugle, and give great power to that uncommon
superfine wind instrument, the nose.   Lor' ! an old spinster
practitioner is a caution to a steam-whistle, I tell you.
As I was a-sayin, they had all gone to the land of Nod,
when Oby arrived, so as he didn't like to be baulked of his

chat with the young lady, he jist goes round, and taps
agin the glass, and she ups out of bed, opens the sash,
and begins to talk like all possessed, when he jist puts his
arm round her waist, hands her right out as she was,
throws his cloak over her, whips her up afore him on his
hoss, and off to Rhode Island, and marries her quick stick.
It gave her such an awful fright, it brought on a fever,
and when she got well, her face was as red as a maple
leaf in the fall. Gracious! what a fiery daugertype it
gave her; she always vowed and maintained it warn't the
fever that throwed out the scarlet colour, but that she
blushed so, at being hauled out of the winder all of a
sudden, afore she had time to dress, that the blushes
never left her arterwards. Give a woman modesty for a
title-page, and see if she won't illuminate and illustrate,
and picturate it to the nines. Yes, if you want to look
on a model man, you must see Oby. He was near
eighteen hands high, fine lean head, broad forehead, big
eye, deep shoulder, perdigious loins, immense stifle, splendiferous fists, knock an ox down a'most, and a foot that
would kick a green pine stump right out of the ground;
noble-tempered fellow as ever trod shoe leather, never
put out in his life, except when he warn't pleased; in
short, he was all a gall could ask, and more than she
could hope for. Poor fellow! only to think he was tied
for life to one that looked as scarlet as the settin sun
arter a broilin day in summer, hot enough to make water
bile, and red enough to put your eyes out. It all came
from bein in an all-fired red-hot haste. Still, I won't say
but what there are shorter men than me in the States,
and specially among the French in Canada. I was
drivin, between Montreal and Quebec, winter afore last,
in a little low sleigh I had, and I overtook a chap that
was a-jogging on along afore me, as if he was paid by

time, and not distance; sais I, "Friend, give us room to
pass, will you, that's a good fellow;" for in deep snow,
that's not so easy a job as you'd think.   Well, he said he
couldn't, and when I asked him again, he said he wouldn't.
We jawed a little grain faster than our horses trotted,
you may suppose, when all of a sudden he stop't straight
in the middle of the track, atween two enormous snow
drifts, and said, "Since you are in such an everlastin
hurry, pass on."   Well, there was nothen left for me to
do but to get out, throw the little chatterin monkey into
the snow bank, and his horse and sleigh arter him; but
when I began to straighten up, the fellow thought there
was no eend to me; it fairly made his hair stand, starein
like a porcupine's quills; it lift up his fur cap—fact, I
assure you.   "So," sais he, "stranger, you needn't
uncoil more of yourself, I cave in;" and he scrabbles out
quick stick, takes his horse by the head, and makes room
for me as civil as you please.   But, stranger, sposin we
pre-rogue this session, and *re*-rogue again, as they say in
Congress, to the smoking room.'

We accordingly all proceeded thither, with the exception
of the Colonel, who said he never smoked, and had
an appointment with the officer commanding at the
battery.

'Now,' said Peabody, producing a case of cigars; 'I
feel to hum—talking and smoking is dry work; when I
want to build up a theory, I require liquid cement to mix
the mortar, moisten the materials, and make them look
nicely.'

'When you joined us,' I said, addressing the Senator,
'my friend the Colonel and myself were discussing the
probability of a rupture with France; do you think there
is any prospect of an interruption in our friendly relations
with America?'

'That,' said he, 'is a question easier asked than answered. Under ordinary circumstances, I should say, no ; but inconsiderate and unprincipled people may compromise the United States in a way to make the President think that concession may be mistaken for fear, and that recourse must be had to hostilities for the sake of national honour.'

'Well, supposing such an occurrence to take place, for instance, as has lately happened by your taking forcible possession of the island of St. Juan, and a conflict were to ensue, what would be the conduct of the colonists? Do you suppose that they would defend themselves, and remain loyal to England, or would they sympathize with the invaders?'

'There is not the slightest doubt in the world,' he replied, 'that they would retain their allegiance. Few persons in this country are aware of the value and extent of British America, its vast resources and magnificent water privileges, or the character and nature of its population. The British possessions in North America cover the largest, the fairest, and most valuable portion of that continent. They comprise an area of upwards of four millions square geographical miles, being nearly a ninth part of the whole terrestrial surface of the globe, and exceed in extent the United States and their territories, by more than 879,000 miles. The Old Atlantic colonies consist of Canada (east and west), New Brunswick, Nova Scotia, Newfoundland, and Prince Edward's Island, and to these countries alone has public attention been hitherto occasionally directed. The history of the rule of Downing-street over these valuable dependencies, since the peace of 1783, is a tissue of neglect or ignorance, of obstinate conflicts or ill-judged concessions. Nothing has preserved them to you but the truly loyal and British feeling of the

people, and a continued and marvellous prosperity, that
has triumphed over every difficulty, and overpowered the
voice of politics by the noise of the axe, the saw, and the
hammer. They have been too busy in commercial to
think much of political speculations, and too familiar with
free institutions to be intoxicated with power, like those
who have but recently acquired their rights. However
large the accretion by emigration may be from Europe,
the bulk of the people are natives, who are accustomed to
the condition of colonial life, and the possession of responsible government, and desire neither absolute independence of England nor annexation to the United States,
but who feel that they have outgrown their minority, and
are entitled to the treatment and consideration due to
adult and affectionate relatives. The day for governing
such colonies as those in North America by a few irresponsible head clerks in Downing-street has passed away,
and something more efficient than the present system
must be substituted in its place. As these countries
increase in population and wealth, so do the educated
and upper classes, who, although they deprecate agitation,
will never consent to occupy a position of practical inferiority to their brethren in England, or their neighbours in
the United States. They are contented with the power
of self-government that they possess within the limits of
their respective provinces; but they feel that there is no
bond of union between the Atlantic colonies themselves;
that they have five separate governments, with five several
tariffs, five different currencies, and five distinct codes of
municipal laws; that the supreme power is lodged in
Downing-street; that the head of the department with
which they are connected is more occupied with imperial
interests than theirs, and goes in and out of office with
his party, while the business is delegated to clerks; that

L 3

they not only have no voice in matters of general intercolonial and foreign interest to all the colonies, but that
as individuals, or delegates, they have no personal status
here, and no duly constituted medium of transacting their
business with the imperial government. This inconvenience is generally felt and lamented, and there are not
wanting unquiet persons, both here and in our country,
who point out to them that their neighbours have a
minister in London, and a consul at every large seaport,
and many of the manufacturing towns in Great Britain,
while even Hayti has its black ambassador, and every
petty German state its accredited political agent. This
is as obvious to you as it is to them, and common prudence,
if no higher motive, should induce you to apply a remedy
before it grows into an established grievance of dangerous
magnitude.'

'He talks like a book, Squire, don't he?' said Mr.
Peabody; 'if you only had the like of him for a colonial
minister, I reckon he would make English secretaries rub
their eyes and stare, as if they felt they had been just
woke up out of a long dreamy sleep. Why, would you
believe it, not one of these critters ever saw a colony, in
all his born days, and yet the head man, or Boss, as we
call him, sends out governors that know as little as he
does. When he gets the appointment himself, he is like
a hungry lean turkey being prepared for market—he has
to be crammed by the clerks. "Tell me," says he,
" about Canada, and show me the ropes. Is Canada
spelt with two n's?" "No, my Lord Tom, Dick or
Harry," (as the case may be), says the underling; " it
ought to be, but people are so poor they can only afford
one. "Capital," says secretary, "come, I like that, it's
uncommon good. I must tell Palmerston that. But
what is it remarkable for? for I know no more about it

than a child." "Big lakes, big rivers, big forests," says clerk. "Ah," says he, "*when will the government be vacant?* I have promised it already. Now, New Brunswick, what of that?" "Large pine timber, ship-building, big rivers again, and fisheries." "Grey wants that for one of his family; but the Eliots threaten to go against us, if we don't give it to one of their clan. To settle the dispute, I shall appoint my brother. Now, tell me about Nova Scotia." "Good harbours, Halifax is the capital, large coal-fields, lots of iron ore, and fish without end, quiet people." "Ah, that will just suit Mulgrave." "Now," says the clerk; "if any colony feller comes a-botherin here, the answer is, 'you have a responsible government, we should be sorry to interfere.' That s our stereotyped reply, or 'leave your papers to be considered.' I will then post you up in it agin he calls next day. All colonists are rascals; no principle—they pretend to be loyal—don't believe them; unless they are snubbed, they are apt to be troublesome "—— By golly, I do wonder to hear Senator talk as he does, when he knows in his heart we couldn't stand them when we were colonists, and just gave the whole bilin of them the mitten, and reformed them out in no time.'

'Now, my good friend,' said the Senator, 'how do you know all this? You were never in Downing-street in your life, and it's not fair to draw upon your imagination, and then give fancy sketches as facts.'

'Lyman Boodle,' said the other, striking his fist on the table with much warmth; 'I am not the fool you take me to be. Didn't our Ambassador to the Court of St. James's, Victoria, tell both you and me so, in the presence of John Van Buren and Joshua Bates, word for word what I have said; and didn't you break through your solemncholy manner, and laugh like a slave nigger (for

they are the only folks that laugh in our country)? So
come now, what's the use of pretendin'; I like a man
that's right up and down, as straight as a shingle.'

'Mr. Peabody,' said the Senator, with well-affected
dignity, 'I have no recollection of the conversation you
allude to ; but if it did take place, as you say, nothing
can excuse a man for repeating a piece of badinage, and
abusing the confidence of a private party.'

'Ly,' said his friend, looking puzzled, 'you do beat the
devil, that's a fact.'

The Senator, without pressing his objections any farther,
turned to me, and with great composure, resumed his observations. 'There are now,' he said, 'about three
millions of inhabitants in British America, and in justice to
them I may add, that a more loyal, intelligent, industrious
and respectable population is not to be found in any part of
the world. Their numerical strength is about the same
as that of our thirteen revolted colonies in 1783, when
they successfully resisted England, and extorted their independence. But there is this remarkable difference
between the two people. The predilection of us Americans,
with some few exceptions, was ever republican. The
New England States were settled by Cromwellians, who
never fully acknowledged English sovereignty. From the
earliest period they aimed at independence, and their
history is one continued series of contests with the preroga-
gative of the king, the power of parliament, and the jurisdiction of the ecclesiastical courts. From the first they
claimed the country as their own, and boldly asserted
their exclusive right to govern it. They altered the
national flag, assumed the right to coin money, entered
into treaties with the native tribes and their Dutch and
French neighbours, and exercised sovereign powers in defiance of the mother country. Aware of the advantage

and strength derived from union, the New England
Colonies confederated at a very early period, and elected
a representative body of delegates, who settled all dis-
putes of a religious, territorial, or defensive nature,
arising either between their respective provinces, or between them and their neighbours of foreign origin.   In
this tribunal we find the embryo Congress of the United
States, and the outline of the government which now prevails in that country ; it required but time and opportunity
to develop it.   The control of the parent state was ever
merely nominal, and when it ceased to exist, the change
was little more than converting practical into positive independence, by substituting forcible for passive and obstructive resistance.   The unjust as well as impolitic attempt to impose taxation without representation, afforded
them what they ardently desired—a justifiable ground for
organizing an armed opposition, and a deep-rooted disaffection, and sectarian hatred, infused a vigour and a bit-
terness into the contest, that the assertion of a constitutional right would alone have failed to inspire.   When
an object is predetermined, it is not often that folly furnishes so good an occasion for effecting it as the Stamp
Act.   Had the people been originally loyal, resistance
would have ceased when it had been successful ; but the
repeal of the Act, while it removed the obnoxious tax,
failed to appease disaffection, and the contest was continued,
not for principle, but for independence.   The present
British provinces are peopled by a totally different
race.   They were never the refuge of the discontented,
but the asylum of the loyalists, who were either driven
from their homes by us, or voluntarily followed the
flag of their sovereign into the British territory.   The
great bulk of the original settlers of Upper Canada,
New Brunswick, and Nova Scotia, had carried arms on

the British side in the American Revolution, and those who subsequently removed there, selected the country because they preferred retaining their allegiance to their sovereign to becoming subjects of the Republic. Most of the loyalists were men of property and education, for such are seldom revolutionists, and their descendants have inherited the feelings of their forefathers. It is from this cause that they are morally, and from the salubrity of their climate physically, fully equal, if not superior, to their English brethren—a fact that is patent to all who have travelled on that continent, or mixed with the population on both sides of the Atlantic. It is necessary to keep these facts in view, whilst speculating on the destiny of these noble colonies. It is a settled conviction with a certain class of politicians in this country (who hold that colonies are an incumbrance), that as soon as they are able, they will separate from the parent state ; and they point to the United States as a proof of the truth of their theory. This has been loudly and offensively proclaimed by such men as Duncombe, Wakefield, and Buller, who have wounded the susceptibilities of the colonists by their offensive personal remarks, and weakened the interest which the people in this country have hitherto felt in their transatlantic possessions. It is, however, manifest, that separation does not necessarily follow from the power to sever the connexion, but that to the ability must be superadded the desire ; and that where there is a good and cordial feeling subsisting, that desire is not likely to arise, unless it is the decided interest of the colonies to become independent. In what that interest can consist, it is difficult to conceive, so long as this country pursues a wise, liberal, and just policy towards so important a portion of the empire.'

'I will tell you,' said Peabody, 'what their interest is,

and you know it as well as I do. Their interest is to jine us, and become part and parcel of the greatest nation in all creation; to have a navy and army of their own, and by annexation to the United States, to feel they are able to lick all the world. Now they are nothing; no, not half nothing, but just a nonentity. Invaded and insulted by us, they can't help themselves for fear of England, and England daren't go to war, for fear of the cotton spinners of Manchester. Big fish were never found in small ponds. Let them jine us, and I'd like to see the power that would dare to hurt a hair of their heads. They haven't got one member to Parliament, no more than footmen have; if they belonged to us, they would send a hundred Senators to Congress. Who ever heard of a colonist being appointed a governor anywhere? Catch the English a-doing of that! No; they give them the great and glorious privilege of paying British governors, and actually make them fork out to Sir Head, in Canada, a salary much larger than we pay to the President of the United States; and while they support all the consuls east of Philadelphia, by fees levied off their ships, only one colonial consul is to be found, and Lord Clarendon was bullied into that. I tell you I know it as a fact, they are shut out of every appointment in the empire.'

'You forget,' said the Senator, 'that Mr. Hincks was appointed a governor.'

'No, I don't,' said Peabody, 'but he warn't a colonist; he was an Irishman that went to Canada to seek his fortune, and he was promoted for two reasons: first, because he was an Irishman; and secondly, because he waded into the troubled waters Lord Elgin got into, and carried him out on his back, or he would have gone for it. But show me a native that ever got that commission! You say the critters have some intelligence; well, if they had, wouldn't they show their sense by jining us, and being made eligible to be elected President, or Foreign Ambassador, or Secretary of State, and so on?   What sort of birthright is a farm in the woods, half swamps, half stumps, with a touch of the ague, and no prospect before them but to rise to be a constable or a hogreave, catching vagrant thieves or stray pigs?   Bah! the English are fools to expect this to last, and Canadians are still bigger fools to stand it. But go on: some of these days you will say, "Peabody warn't such a fool as you took him to be."'

'All you have advanced,' said the Senator, 'amounts to this : the provinces require a new organization, and so does the Colonial Office.   I understand both these bene- ficial objects will soon be obtained by the mutual consent of Great Britain and her dependencies ; and to the very great advantage of both.   I do not deny that the evils of the present system require removal, but I have no doubt the remedy will soon be applied.   I was talking of the country and the loyalty of its people, and not of its con- stitution.   Much has been said,' he continued, 'of the rapid growth of the United States.   No sooner was their independence acknowledged than they became the resort of all who sought a refuge from political strife in Europe ; a safe and wide field for the investment of capital ; a market for their labour, and a new home in their vast and unoccupied territory.   They absorbed, to the exclusion of other countries, nearly the whole emigration, not only of Great Britain but of Europe.   The continued wars that grew out of the French Revolution gave them, as neutrals, a very great proportion of the carrying trade of the world.   It was a popular country ; a realization of the theories of French philosophers and English reformers. It was neither burthened with the expenses of royalty, the tithes of an Established Church, nor the entails of an

hereditary nobility.   Freedom and equality were inscribed on their banners, and their favourite maxim,
" Vox populi, vox Dei," was realized in the assumption of
the whole power by the people.   Direct taxation, except
in municipalities, was unknown.   Customs duties and the
sales of public lands maintained their then frugal government, and supplied a large surplus for works of public
defence or improvement

' The first-fruit of this system was a vast increase of
population and wealth.   The growth of the country,
however, stimulated by the causes just mentioned, has
been prodigious; and it is for this reason I select it as a
standard wherewith to measure the growth of Canada,
and I think the comparison will astonish you, if you have
not taken the trouble to institute an inquiry for yourself.'

Turning to his pocket-book, the Senator read as
follows :—' " The last Census of the United States was
taken in 1850, when the population (after deducting that
of recent territorial acquisitions) was upwards of twenty-
three millions.   In 1840 it was only seventeen millions,
or thereabouts.   In ten years, therefore, the increase was
upwards of six millions, or thirty-five per cent.

' " The Census of Upper Canada in 1841 gave 465,000.
In 1851 it was 952,000.   Increase in ten years 487,000,
or about 104 per cent.   It may be said it is not fair to
take the whole of the United States for a comparison
with Upper Canada, much of the former country being
comparatively old and long settled.   It will be seen,
however, from the United States Census, that the three
States of Ohio, Michigan, and Illinois, which have had
the most rapid increase, contained in 1830, 6,126,851 ;
in 1850, 8,505,000, or a little over 320 per cent. in
twenty years.   Now the increase in Canada West, from
1840 to 1849, was over 375 per cent. for the same

period, so that the increase in these three choice States was 55 per cent. less than in Canada West during that time, while in the Far West of Canada, the counties of Huron, Perth, and Bruce, have increased upwards of 571 per cent. in ten years—an increase almost beyond comprehension.

'"This immense advance is not confined to the rural districts, for the cities and towns will equally vie with those of the United States. Between 1840 and 1850 the increase in Boston was 45 per cent., but in Toronto, 95 per cent. The increase of New York, the emporium of the United States, and a city which, for its age, may vie with any in the world, thus stands as compared with Toronto, 66 per cent. between 1840 and 1850, against 95 per cent. of the latter. St. Louis, which had in 1850 70,000 inhabitants, had increased it fifteen times since 1820. Toronto had in 1850 increased hers eighteen times that of 1817. The population in Cincinnati was in 1850, 115,590, or twelve times its amount in 1820 (thirty years before); and Toronto had in 1850 eighteen times its population in 1817 (or thirty-three years before).

'"Nor is the comparative statement of cereal production less favourable. The growth of wheat is very nearly one-sixth of that of the whole Union; of barley more than one-fourth; of oats one-seventh; and in all grain, exclusive of Indian corn, about one-sixth."'

'Oh, of course,' said Peabody, 'they deserve great credit for all this, don't they? They had great tracts of good land; emigrants came and settled there; the country grew, and the population increased. They couldn't help it, nohow they could fix it; but naterally they are a slow conceiving, slow believing, slow increasing people when left to themselves. There ain't a smart city in Canada.'

'What do you call a *smart* city?' I asked, 'for I never heard the term before.'

'Well, I'll tell you,' he said; 'I was goin' down the Mississippi oncet in a steamer, and the captain, who was a most gentlemanlike man, was a Mr. Oliver (I used to call Oliver Cramwell, he was such an everlastin' eater), and we passed a considerable of a sizeable town. Sais the captain to me, "Peabody," sais he, "that's a smart town, and always was. Ten years ago, when I was steward of a river boat, we wooded at this place, and there didn't seem to be any folk there, it looked so still: so as I walked down the street, I seed a yaller cotton oil coat a-hangin' out of a shop door; I tried it on, and it fitted me exactly, and as there was nobody there to receive the pay, I walked off, intending, *of course*, to pay for it next time I came that way. I hadn't gone a few yards afore I was seized, had up afore the justice, tried, convicted, received thirty-nine lashes on my bare back, and, upon my soul, it was all done, and I was on board the steamer agin', in twenty minutes." Now that's what I call a *smart place*. They han't got the go-ahead in them to Canada we have. Their lead hosses in the State team, their British governors, are heavy English cattle, with a cross of Greek and Latin, and a touch of the brewer's dray. They are a drag on the wheels, made of leaden links, that the colonists have to gild. The only airthly use they can be put to is to sink them at the mouth of a river in time of war, for they are the grandest obstruction to a new country that ever was invented.'

'Pooh, Pooh,' said the Senator, 'don't talk nonsense. Such, Mr. Shegog, is this magnificent country, through which the proposed route to the Pacific is to pass from the Gulf of St. Lawrence, having a vast continuous chain of navigable waters from the Atlantic to the head of

Lake Superior. Four hundred and ten miles of steaming from the ocean, and you reach Quebec, the great seaport of Canada, with a large and increasing foreign commerce ; 590 miles more bring you to Montreal. From thence seven canals of different lengths and great capacity, fitted for sea-going vessels, enable you to ascend 116 miles of river, and at 168 miles above Montreal, you are in Lake Ontario. Swiftly traversing this vast body of water, which is 180 miles long, you pass by the Welland Canal into Lake Erie, and thence through Lake St. Clair, and its river, into Lake Huron, 1,355 miles from your starting point, the entrance of the Gulf. By means of St. Mary's River, and a gigantic canal, you now enter Lake Superior (a fresh-water sea as large as Ireland, and the recipient of 200 rivers) which enables you to attain a distance of 2,000 miles from the mouth of the St. Lawrence. I do not speak of what *may be,* but what *has* been done. Vessels of large burden, built and loaded in Lake Superior, have traversed this entire route, and safely reached both London and Liverpool.

'Such is the navigable route to Lake Superior. There is nothing in England, or indeed in Europe, that can furnish by comparison an adequate idea of this great river, the St. Lawrence. Of its enormous tributaries I have not time even to enumerate the principal ones. I must refer you to maps and statistical works for fuller information. I shall only mention one, and that is the Ottowa—it falls into the St. Lawrence near Montreal. It drains with its tributaries a valley of 80,000 square miles, commanding the inexhaustible treasures of the magnificent forests of the north-west of Canada, that cover an area of six times the superficial extent of all Holland. One of the tributaries of this noble river, itself a tributary, the Gatenaux, is 750 miles long, and nearly as large as the Rhine, being 1,000 feet wide, 217 miles from its junction with the Ottowa. Imagine innumerable other rivers of all sizes downwards, to the limited extent of those in England, and you have an idea of the rivers of Canada.'

'Lyman Boodle,' said Peabody, rising suddenly, and drawing himself up to his full height, 'Lyman Boodle, I like to see a feller stand up to his lick-log like a man, and speak truth and shame the devil. You are an American citizen, and we all have the honour of our great nation to maintain abroad. My rule is to treat a question I don't like as I treat a hill, if I can't get over it I go round it; but catch me admitting anything on the surface of this great globe in rips, raps, or rainbows, or in the beowels of it, or the folks that live on it, to have anything better than what we have, or to take the shine off of us. Don't half that river St. Lawrence belong to us as well as them, and hain't we got the right to navigate from that half down to the sea? Don't we own half of every lake as well as them, and all Huron besides? Hain't we got the Mississippi, that runs up over two thousand miles right straight on eend, and only stops then because it is tired of running any farther? and don't the Ohio fall into that, and, big as it is, seem only a drop in the bucket? If you like it so much you had better go and settle there, give up being a senator, and sink down into a skunk of a colonist. I'd like to hear you talk arter that fashion to Michigan, and unless you wanted to excite people to board and take Canada, why they would just go and lynch you right off.'

To give a turn to the conversation, which, on Mr. Peabody's part, was becoming warm, I said, 'Has Canada the power to maintain itself against the United States?'

'I think,' he said, 'in the event of a war, in which our population was united, we should overrun it.'

'Well done, Ly,' said his friend, slapping him cordially on the back, 'you are clear grit after all—you are a chip of the old American hickory block. Overrun it! to be sure we should, and I should like to know who would stop us? Why, we should carry it by boarding; some we should drive into the sea, and some into the lakes, and the rest we should tree. If the telegraph ain't built afore then, the first news they'd get here would be that Canada is taken, the British flag hauled down, the goose and gridiron run up, damages repaired, prisoners down the hold, and all made ready for action agin. It would all be over directly—arrived—saw it—drew a bead on it, brought it down and bagged it. England would feel astonished as the squirrel was Colonel Crockett fired at when he didn't want to kill the poor thing. He drew on it, let go, and took its ear off so sharp and slick the critter never missed it till he went to scratch his head and found it was gone—fact, and no mistake.'

'Yes,' said the Senator, not heeding the interruption, 'we should overrun it, but whether we should be able to hold it is another matter; perhaps not.'

'Ah, there you ago again,' said Peabody, 'rubbin out with your left hand what you wrote on the slate with your right—you are on the other tack now; I hope it is the short leg, at any rate.'

'Mr. Shegog,' said the Senator, 'it is almost incredible how Canada has been neglected by this country. There is much truth mixed up with the extravagant talk of my eccentric friend here. I have reason to believe that the greatest possible ignorance prevails in Downing-street as respects this noble colony. It is inaccessible to ships in winter, and for mails all the year round. Would you believe it possible that all European and intercolonial mails pass through the United States to Canada, with the exception of a few that are sent to Quebec during the summer months by provincial steamers? There is no road from Nova Scotia or New Brunswick to Canada. We grant permission for the British mails to be sent there from Boston or New York, through our territory, but at a month's notice (or some very short period) this permission can be withdrawn, and Canada in such a case would be as unapproachable for a certain season as the interior of Africa. In a military point of view this state of things causes great uneasiness in the British provinces, and, I may add, to all discreet and right-thinking men also in the United States. If war were to be declared by us in the early part of November, not a soldier could be sent to the relief of Canada till May, nor any munitions of war conveyed thither for the use of the people, while their correspondence with the mother country would be *wholly suspended*. This state of affairs is well known to our citizens, and the defenceless condition of the country invites attack from a certain restless portion of our population, consisting of European and British emigrants, to whom plunder has more allurements than honest labour. It is surprising that the lesson taught by the Crimean war has been so soon forgotten. You may recollect that during that anxious period the British Government wanted to withdraw a regiment of the line from Canada, and send it to Sebastopol, and also to draw upon the large munition of war accumulated at Quebec. The winter meanwhile set in, the navigation was closed, and there were no means of transporting them to Halifax; so they lost their services altogether. The artillery and other military stores were of still more consequence, and it was determined to send them by means of the railway (leased to an English company) to Portland, and thence ship them to their place of destination : but the question arose, whether they could legally be transported through our country, that was at peace with Russia at the time. The English Crown Officers were of opinion that they would be liable to seizure.'

'And we are just the boys to seize them too,' said Peabody, 'for we are great respecters of law.'

'Yes,' I replied, 'when it happens to be in your favour.'

'Stranger,' he said, 'you weren't born yesterday, that's a fact; you cut your eye-teeth airly; I cave in, and will stand treat. I am sorry they han't got the materials nor the tools for compounding here; and Boodle is a temperance man, and never drinks nothing stronger than brandy and whisky; you shall have your choice, try both, and see which you like best.'

'Peabody,' said the Senator, 'I wish you would not keep perpetually interrupting me in this manner—I almost forget what I was talking about.'

'Smuggling ammunition and cannon through our great country,' said Peabody.

'Ah,' continued the Senator, 'the consequence was they could move neither troops nor military stores. This state of things, if suffered to continue, may cost Great Britain the most valuable colony she possesses.'

'How,' I asked, 'do you propose to remedy it?'

'You are aware, sir,' he replied, 'that the great through line of railway in Canada is completed to a point about ninety miles below Quebec, called Trois Pistoles; an extension of this line for four hundred and fifty miles will connect it with the Nova Scotian line, and then there will be an uninterrupted railway from Halifax through New Brunswick and Canada to Lake

Superior. This is the only link now wanting to complete the intercolonial communication.

'If once constructed, Great Britain and her colonies will be independent of us for the transit of their mails, and the former will be relieved of the burden of maintaining a military force in Canada as a precautionary measure in time of peace. In twelve days a regiment may be conveyed from England to Halifax, and thence by railway to Quebec, accompanied by its baggage and stores; and the very circumstance that the country can obtain such ready and efficient aid, will, of itself, put an invasion of Canada by us as much out of the question as a descent upon England itself. The three colonies of Nova Scotia, New Brunswick, and Canada, have severally undertaken to carry out this great national object, if aided in raising the funds under an imperial guarantee; but the apathy with which it is viewed in Downing-street has almost exhausted the patience of the provincials, who feel that as colonists they are unable to obtain that loan, which, if they were independent, they could raise without difficulty. A feeling of dependence is not very congenial to the Anglo-Saxon mind; but it is the worst policy in the world to make that dependence more galling than it naturally is. Commercially it is of the utmost importance to the traders to have a safe and cheap mode of conveyance for themselves and their productions, and a new and extended field opened to them in the Lower Provinces for the exchange of their mutual commodities. At present we derive an enormous advantage from intercepting this trade, and directing it through canals and railways to various parts of our Union. While the British Government are either indolently or wilfully negligent in promoting their own interests, our people are fully alive to the importance of monopolizing the trade of the

M

upper country. The navigable lakes above Canada are bounded by a coast of many thousand miles, connected by canals and railways from the Mississippi, Missouri, Illinois, Wabash, and Ohio rivers. Twenty American Railways are already in operation, leading from those rivers to Chicago, one of the largest exporting ports for food of every description in the world. In addition to these, there are the great Erie Canal, extending to the Hudson River, the New York Central Railway, and that to Boston *viâ* Ogdensburg, as well as several others. Now, you must recollect, that while all these works have been constructed for the express purpose of diverting the trade to us, the same routes furnish us with so many channels for transporting troops for the invasion of the country, to the different points at which they terminate. Now three things result from this state of affairs—First, we are in possession of your only mail route. Secondly, we divert the colonial trade to us, and thereby increase the interest the provincials and ourselves feel in each other, and render annexation not a thing to be dreaded, but to be desired, as one of mutual advantage. Thirdly, our railways and canals afford every means of overrunning the country at a season of the year when it is inaccessible to you. The completion of the unfinished portion of the line between Nova Scotia and Canada is, therefore, a matter of vital importance, both in a military and commercial point of view, and when I consider that the British Government is not asked to do this at her own expense, but merely to assist by a guarantee the several provinces in raising the necessary funds, I am utterly at a loss to understand why she does not perceive that her duty and her interest alike demand it at her hands. The truth is, the Colonial Office is a dead weight on the Empire. Instead of facilitating and aiding the progress and development of the colonies,

it deadens the energies and obstructs the welfare of the
people.   It is almost incredible that the Home Government actually subsidize two several lines of ocean steamers
to run to Boston and New York, and convey hither their
first-class emigrants, their mails, and their valuable
merchandise, the first to swell our population, and the
two latter to be first taxed and then conveyed by us to
the boundary line ; while Canada is treated more like a
foreign and rival country, and left to maintain steamers
at her own cost as best she may.   It is an undeniable fact
that these ocean steamers have driven out of the field the
passenger and freight ships that used to run to Quebec,
and thereby diverted the stream of emigration from you
to New York.   Up to 1847, emigration had increased at
Quebec to 95,000 against some 80,000 to New York,
while in 1850 it had diminished to some 30,000 at the
former, against an increase of 200,000 at the latter.
The diminution of direct exportation from Quebec has
also arisen from the circumstance of its having no outlet
in winter.   The Halifax Railway will supply this difficulty,
and by its harmonious action at an early period make
that capital the greatest city of the West.   In summer
it will possess the advantage of being 250 miles nearer
Liverpool than New York, and in winter it can avail
itself of Halifax harbour, which is also 300 miles nearer
England than our empire city.   How is it that a minister
of state knows so little, and a colonist effects nothing ?'

'I'll tell you,' said Peabody, ' it's as plain as a boot-
jack ; it's six of one, and half a dozen of the other ; one
darsn't, and the other is afraid.   One don't know what to
do, and t'other don't understand how to do it nohow he
can fix it.   There was a feller came over here from Montreal, to complain that the Newfoundlanders, who are a
set of donkeys (the Roman bishop there used to call them

kings of the rabbits) had granted a monopoly of setting up telegraphs in the island to a Yankee company, whereby New York would get European news before the British provinces. So he goes to the Colonial Office, and asks for the Boss, to protest against this act getting the assent of the Queen. Well, the gentleman that tends the door made a gulp of a bit of bread and cheese that he was a-takin' of standing, told him his Lordship was in, and piloted him up, threw open the door, and said,] "Mr. Smith, my Lord, from Madawisky." "Mad with whisky," said Lord, stepping back, and looking scared, "what does all this mean?" "Mr. Smith, from Madawisky," repeated the usher. "Sit down, sir," said Lord (for he didn't half like a man who had "mad" and "whisky" to his name), "glad to see you, sir, how did you leave Doctor Livingstone? had he reached the great inland lake beyond the desert, when you left him?" "What lake?" said Colonist, looking puzzled, for he began to think minister was mad. "Why the Madawisky," said Peer, "I think you called it by some such name: I mean that lake in Africa, that Livingstone has discovered." "I am not from Africa," said poor Smith, looking sky-wonoky at him; "I never was there in my life, and I never heard of Doctor Livingstone. I am from North America," and he was so conflustrigated he first turned red, and then white, and then as streaked as you please. "Oh! North America is it?" said the skipper, "well here is a map, show me where it is." Well, while he was looking for it, Lord stoops over him, and he had a great long ugly stiff beard, as coarse as a scrubbing brush, and it stuck straight out, like the short dock of a horse, he tickled him so with it, he nearly drove him into a conniption fit. "Oh! now I see," said Lord, "pray what may your business be?" So he ups and tells him about the Newfoundlanders, and their telegraph, and Cape *Race*, and the Basin of Bulls, and so on. " Strange names," said Secretary, " I had no idea they had *races* there, and as for the other place, I *have* heard of the fat Bulls of Basan, but I never heard of the Basin of Bulls. That place must be inhabited by Irishmen, I should think," and then he laid back in his chair, and haw-hawed right out. Smith was awfully scared, he never sot eyes on a lord afore in all his born days, and expected to see some strange animal like a unicorn, and not a common-looking man like him. He was wrothy too, for he thought he was a-quizzin' of him, and felt inclined to knock him down if he dared, and then he was so excited, he moved to the edge of his chair, and nearly tilted it and himself over chewallop. He got nervous, and was ready to cry for spite, when Lord said, " Show me where the Basin of Bulls is." "Bay of Bulls," said Smith, kinder snappishly, and he rose, and pointed it out to him on the map, and as Lord stooped down again to look at it, he gives a twirl to his beard, that brushed across Smith's mouth and nostrils, and set him off a sneezin' like anything. Then, from shame, passion, and excitement, off he went into the highstrikes, and laughed, sneezed, and cried all at once. They had to lead him out of the room ; and Lord said, " Don't admit that man again, he's either mad or drunk." Creation! what a touss it made among the officials and underlings. Would you believe it now, Senator, that monopoly Act *was* passed by the Newfoundlanders, *was* approved by the Colonial Office, and *did* receive the Royal assent, just because the asses in Newfoundland found kindred donkeys in Downing-street ; so the interests of Great Britain and the North American colonies were sacrificed to the ignorance and negligence of this useless—nay, more than useless—obstructive department.'

'Good gracious!' said Mr. Boodle, 'what nonsense you do talk.'

'I tell you it ain't nonsense,' said the other: 'President Buchanan told me so himself, the last hitch I was to England. He was our minister to St. Jim's at that time, and says he, " Peabody, how long do you think we would stand such a secretary in our great country?" "Jist about as long," I replied, " as it would take to carry him to the first sizable tree, near hand, and then lynch him." And now, Senator, don't you think all this insolence, and slack, and snubbing colonists get, comes from their not being so enlightened and independent as we are, nor so well educated?'

'As regards education,' replied the Senator, ' you will be surprised when I tell you that they have made better provision for instructing the rising generation than we ourselves. Of the social benefits to be derived by a nation from the general spread of intelligence, Canada has been fully aware, and there is not a child in the province without the means of receiving instruction, combined with moral training. In fact, the system of education now established there far exceeds in its comprehensive details anything of the kind in Great Britain.

'In 1842, the number of common schools in Upper Canada was 1,721, attended by 66,000 pupils; and in 1853, the number had increased to 3,127 schools, and 195,000 pupils. There are now in the upper province, in addition to the above, eight colleges, seventy-nine county grammar schools, one hundred and seventy-four private, and three normal and model schools, forming a total of educational establishments in operation of 3,391, and of students and pupils 204,000. But to return to what I was saying when Mr. Peabody interrupted me, you may take what I *now* say as incontrovertible—

' 1st. Transatlantic steamers, subsidized by Great Britain, should be in connexion with her own colonies, and especially Canada.

' 2ndly. The completion of the Quebec and Halifax line of railway is of vital importance, both in a defensive and commercial point of view; and any delay in finishing it may be productive of infinite mischief, if not of the loss of Canada.

' 3rdly. As soon as possible, after this railway is finished (which will complete the line from Halifax to Lake Superior), immediate steps should be taken to provide a safe, easy, and expeditious route to Frazer's River, on the Pacific.   Had such been now in existence, you never would have heard of the invasion of St. Juan, for an English force could leave Southampton on the 1st of November, and on the 16th of the same month arrive at Vancouver Island. *An ounce of precaution is worth a pound of cure.* But this is your affair, and not mine. I hope you will excuse the plain unreserved manner in which I have spoken. I have said what I really think, and given you as candid an opinion as I am able to form.

' But it is now getting late, and as I feel somewhat fatigued I must *retire*.'

As the Senator left the room, Peabody put his finger to his nose, and whispered to me, ' Didn't I put him on his mettle for you beautiful?   He is a peowerful man that, but he wants the spur to get his Ebenezer up, and then the way he talks is a caution to orators, I tell you. Good night.'

No. IX.

THE LIVING AND THE DEAD.

EARLY the following morning, Colonel Mortimer called upon me, and proposed that we should visit the various objects of interest in and about the port of Southampton, and defer our departure for London to a later train in the afternoon. To those who think with me, that no view can be perfect that does not include a considerable quantity of navigable water within it, Southampton presents great attraction. What, indeed, can be more beautiful than the prospect exhibited to the admiring eye of a stranger, as he approaches it from Basingstoke, embracing at once the town, a large portion of the New Forest, and the extensive bay, protected by the Isle of Wight?

My old friend, Commodore Rivers, was our guide on this occasion. He was an enthusiastic admirer of the place (with every part of which he was well acquainted), and had many interesting anecdotes connected with it, which he told in his own peculiar style. As a seaman, the docks stood first in his estimation, not only for their utility, but for their beauty. Now this is a quality, I confess, I could never see in them, any more than in foot-tubs; we may admire their magnitude, their usefulness, their wonderful construction and importance, but their beauty, if they have any, is discernible only to a nautical eye. On our way thither we passed the 'Great Carriage-building Factory' of the late Mr. Andrews.

'A clever man that, sir,' said the Commodore ; 'did a vast deal of good to the place, employed a great many hands, and was a hospitable and a popular man, too. He was three times Mayor of Southampton, and boasted that he was the greatest coach-builder in the kingdom. Says I to him one day—"Andy, how is it you build so cheap ?" "Come in, and take a glass of brandy and water with me," said he, " and I will tell you." And that,' remarked the Commodore, 'puts me in mind that I don't feel very well to-day. The last time I was at *Alexander*, in the Simla, I had a touch of cholera, and I have never been quite free from pain since ; I will just go on to the Royal, "above bar" here, and take a thimbleful neat, or, as More O'Ferrall used to call his whisky, "the naked truth."'

When he rejoined us, he continued : 'Andrews said, " I will tell you, Commodore, the secret of my success. I first took the hint from you." " From me," says I ; " why I know nothing about any wheel in the world but a paddle-wheel, and that is built with floats, not spokes, and has an axle, but no hob ; or a helm to steer by, that makes a vessel turn round, but not go ahead. How could I know anything about coach-building ?" " Why," says he, " I caught the idea from a story you once told me of the black preacher." " Oh, I remember it !" said I ; " he was one of the 'mancipated niggers in Jamaica, that was too lazy to work, so he took to itinerant preaching. When he returned from one of his circuits, as he used to call them (for his old master was a lawyer), he was asked what he got for his day's work. 'Two-and-sixpence,' said he. 'Poor pay,' replied his friend, 'it ain't as much as I get for hoeing cane.' 'Yes, Pompey,' he said, 'it is poor pay, but reck'lect, it's berry poor preachin' I gibs 'em,

M 3

berry poor, indeed ; for I can't gib 'em Latin or Greek
as church minister does, and I can't talk dic (dictionary)
—niggers is always berry fond ob what dey can't understand. When I can't 'swade 'em, I frittens 'em—dat is
de great art, and white preacher don't always understand
de natur ob coloured folks. Now, Pompey, dere is one
natur ob nigger, and one natur of Massa Buckra. You
can't scare our people by telling 'em dey'll go to berry
hot place if dey is sinners, for no place is too hot for
dem dat sleep on pillow of hot roasted sand in de
broilin heat ob day, wid dere faces turned up to it, like a
sun-flower. I scare dem by cold : I talk ob frozen ribbers
dat dey must walk on barefoot, and ob snow drifts, and
ob carryin' great junks ob ice on dere bare heads for eber
and eber, like dischargin' cargoes of Yankee ice from
Boston vessels, which kills more ob dem dan yaller fever.
I can't talk book larnin', 'cause I can't read ; nor eber-
lastin' long words, 'cause I can't pronounce 'em. But I
fritten dem to death amost, so dey call me " Old Scare
Crow." Yes, half a dollar a day is poor pay, but I
must 'fess it's berry poor preachin'.' Is that the story
you mean ?" " Yes," says Andrews, " that's the story ;
' poor pay, poor preaching,' started the idea in my mind
of ' cheap work, cheap price.' Now I won't say I charge
low because my work is indifferent, for it is very good
for the price ; but I don't build my vehicles to last for
ever—that is the grand mistake of the trade. In a general way, carriages outlive what is called ' all the go,'
though they are as good as ever for wear after they become
unpresentable. Old coaches don't suit new bonnets, fine
birds must have new cages, a coat is of no use after it is
too long or too short waisted, or too high or too low in the
collar, however good it is ; it is then only fit for the Jew's
bag, or for Rag fair. I build my traps to last as long as the

fashion does, it saves labour and material, and suits both buyer and seller. Then I take my pay generally by three annual instalments, which is an investment of two thirds of the capital at five per cent."

'It's a pity that the trade hadn't his honesty, and talked truth and sense as he did. Poor man! he died of a broken heart, he never held up his head after Palmerston jockeyed him out of his election. The grand mistake Andrews made, was, *he forgot who greased his wheels,* turned against the aristocracy who made him what he was, and joined the Radicals, who, my washerwoman declares, are not "carriage people." He didn't know what you and I do, that the Whigs use the Radicals to get into power, and then, in their turn, forget who *greased their wheels* for them.'

'I was not in the country at the time,' I said, 'and do not know to what you allude—what is the story ?'

'Why,' said the Commodore, 'Andrews heard that the Government was using its influence in the Southampton election for the Whig candidate who started in opposition to him. So he wrote to Palmerston, for whom he had fought through thick and thin, to ask him if it was true. What does his lordship do, but instead of answering his question, writes back in his usual supercilious way, "Since you ask my opinion, I think *you* had better stay at home and mind your own business." You never heard such a row as that kicked up at Southampton, in all your life. The Tories crowed, and said, "sarved him right ;" the Whigs laughed, and said he might know something of the spring of a carriage, but not of the springs of government ; and the Radicals threw up their hands in disgust, and said they could do nothing without *court cards.*

'It's astonishing what gamblers these fellows are, they

always expect the knave to be turned up trumps. Poor
Andrews! he was never the same man arterwards. I
used to try to rally him, for he was a good-hearted fellow
as ever lived, though he was a Radical. "Andy," I used
to say to him, "you see you have been chucked over, my
boy, to lighten the ship: you are what we call at sea a
'jutsum,' but bouse up the mainstay, and have pluck
enough to be a' floatsum ;' hold on by your eyelids, you'll
come ashore safe yet, and then show fight, and we will all
vote for you, because you have been ill-used." But it
was no good. Then I tried him on another tack. Says
I, "Did you ever hear, my old friend, of a tarantula?"
"No," says he, "I never did—what is it?" "Why,"
says I, "it is a great big speckle-bellied spider, that is
common in the Mediterranean countries. Captain
Inglesby, the great Conservative here, calls it a Whig,
for it turns on its own small fry if they cross its path,
snaps them right up, and lives on 'em. Its bite, if not
attended to, is said to be certain death. When an Italian
is stung by one of these creatures, he sends for musicians,
and dances and sings till he falls down exhausted on the
floor, it's the only cure in nature there is for it. Now,
cheer up! *you* have been bit by a tarantula; and so
was Inglesby himself once at the Admiralty, and he
capered and hopped about like a shaking Quaker, till the
pison was thrown off by perspiration."

'But it was no go, Andrews shook his head—"My
wheels is locked," said he, "I can never see the pole of
a carriage again without thinking of the poll at the hust-
ings, or how can I make seats for others, who have lost
my own? It's *bootless* to complain, and it's all *dickey*
with me now." And so on, and he tried to laugh and
joke it off; but Pam had put the leak into him, and he
felt the water gaining on him; so he just drifted away

towards home and foundered, and it was the last time I ever saw him.

'Poor fellow! I lost a great friend in him, and so did Southampton too, I can tell you. But as Inglesby said to me one day (and there ain't a more sensible man in this place than he is), "Rivers," said he, "his life and death ought to be a warning to Radicals who volunteer for the forlorn hope, die in the breach, and open the way for the Whigs to enter, gain the victory, and bag all *the prize money*. What," said he, "did the party ever do for Joe Hume, who fought their battles for them with the Tories? Why, they sent his picture to his wife, and then raised a paltry subscription for a lying monument to himself—one made him handsomer, and the other a greater man than he was. *They paid him in flattery*, a cheap coin, like Gladstone's adulterated halfpenny that passes for more than it's worth. Yes, and when they had done these two paltry acts, one of their wittiest members said, 'We have now paid our debt of gratitude to this eminent man, and the "tottle of the hull" (and he mimicked his Scotch accent to please the Irish) is, we ought, from respect to so great an economist, not to ask for a *stamped* receipt." '

'Curious world, this, Mr. Shegog,' continued the Commodore, 'this country is fooled in a way no other nation of the world is. Yesterday I dined on board of yonder man-of-war, the captain of which I knew at Balaclava, and we were talking over old times and the present state of things. Says he, "Rivers, what a muddle the Whigs made of the Russian war—didn't they? and what a mess they will make of it again, if we should ever have a set-to with France. I can't think this country would trust them in such a case; but if they do, depend upon it we are lost for ever. We don't want tricksters, but men of honour and men of pluck. We require the right man in the right place—a thorough-going Englishman is the only one that is fit to stand at the helm in such a crisis as the present. The Whigs rely on Conservative votes to defend them against the great Liberals, and on the support of the Radicals, because they outbid the Tories. They play off one against the other: and though hated and distrusted by both, they win the game, for their trumps are all marked, and they ain't above looking into the hands of their adversaries. There are three parties in this country—Conservatives, Whigs, and Radicals. The Whigs are the weakest and smallest, but they cheat at cards, and come off winners. Talk of Lord Derby being in a minority—so he was, by half a dozen; but that was a *minority of the whole house.* The Whigs are nowhere, they are numerically so few, but by good tactics, they so manage matters as to govern the country by a minority that is actually less than either of the other parties."

'I agree with him entirely,' said the Commodore, 'though I couldn't express it as well as he did. But here we are at the docks. Beautiful docks, these, sir, as you will see anywhere, and lovely craft in them, too—ain't they?'

'Do you mean those beautiful young ladies on the quay?' I said. 'For if you do, I am of the same opinion —they are the best specimens of English girls I have seen since my return.'

'Ah,' he continued, 'go where you will, sir, where will you see the like of Englishwomen? I am an old man now, but I have a good eye for "the lines," as we call them in a ship. Beautiful models, ain't they? real clippers; it's impossible to look on 'em without loving 'em. Poor dear things! how many of them I have had under my charge afore now, taking them to Lisbon, Gibraltar, or

Malta, or to *Alexander*, to go to the East. I could tell you many very queer and some very sad stories about some of my lady passengers that I took out with me in the Peninsular and Oriental steamers. Some don't go out, but are *sent* out to India to try their fortune; others are engaged by letter to old friends they had once known at home, who had offered to them through the post-office, and were accepted. They often changed their minds on the way out (for a quarter-deck is a famous place for love-making), and got married in the Mediterranean. I will give you the histories of some of them one of these days.

'Now, ain't these splendid docks? They were incorporated in 1836, and have a space allotted to them of 208 acres. The quay line extends 4,200 feet. There are two portions, one enclosing sixteen acres, having eighteen feet of water at the lowest tides, with gates 150 feet wide; and the other, a close basin for ships to deliver their cargoes afloat. It is one of the noblest establishments of the kind in Europe; and all this has sprung up from our Peninsular and Oriental Line using the port, which has been the making of Southampton. It was here that Canute sat in his arm-chair, to show his courtiers (after he gave up drinking and murder) that though he was a mighty prince, he could not control the advance of the sea.'

'Well,' I said, 'what Canute could not do, your Dock Company has accomplished. It has actually said to the sea, "Thus far shalt thou go, and no farther;" and the waves have obeyed the mandate.'

'They tell me,' said Rivers, 'that this has always been a noted place for expeditions to sail from, and for our enemies to attack. It was sacked in Edward the Third's time; and the son of the King of Sicily lost his life while plundering it. Henry the Fifth rendezvoused here, for the invasion of France; and it's my belief that these Johnny Crapauds, some foggy day or dark night, will pay us a visit from Cherbourg. If they do, I hope they won't fire a gun from the forts till every ship has got inside; and then we'll let them know, that those who licked them at the Nile have left behind them children that can thrash them as well as their fathers did. The breed hasn't run out, I can tell you. But it is time to move on. Let us go now to Netley Abbey; it is only three miles from the town!'

'What a beautiful ruin!' I exclaimed, when we reached the lovely spot; 'I could linger here for hours. What a place to meditate in; to give licence to the imagination; and to endeavour to realize it as it was in the olden time!'

'It is like an old man,' said the Commodore, 'venerable for its age, and noble even in its dilapidations; but it don't do to inquire too closely into its past life. If you had seen such places as I have on the Continent, peopled as they now are, and in the way that this once was, it would knock all the romance out of you, I can tell you. If these abbeys had been in the same hands, and continued in full occupation of the Church to this day, England would have remained stationary too. If Netley Abbey had continued as it was, so would Southampton (or Hanton, as it was then called). Poets and artists may have the abbey all to themselves, if they like; but give me the docks! I dare say it does make a good drawing; but to my mind a bill of exchange, or a cheque on Coutts', or Childs', is the prettiest drawing in the world. The docks feed more men than all the abbeys and monasteries in this part of England put together ever did; but if you intend to go up by the afternoon train, it is time for you to think of returning. We must finish our tour of inspection some other day.'

On reaching the Southampton station, there was such a crowd of passengers that our party could not all be accommodated in one carriage, and we severally seized upon any vacant seats we could find. I thus became separated from my friends of the previous evening, and found myself among a party returning to Winchester, who had been to see the Great Eastern, whose merits and defects they discussed in that decided and satisfactory manner which those who have never seen a vessel before are alone competent to do. They were quite unanimous in their opinion that, when resting on the top of two waves, she would break asunder in the centre, collapse, and founder; or, that if by any chance, while leaping like a kangaroo from one mountain wave to another, she should fail to reach 'the preceding one, she would inevitably plunge head foremost into the intervening gulf, and vanish from sight altogether; that she would either pitch into the waves, or the waves would pitch into her, and that as her model was that of an egg, if she had ever the misfortune to be in a rolling sea, she would certainly roll over; although it was very doubtful whether her flat deck would permit her to come up again on the other side. A young lawyer, of a poetical turn of mind, amused the party by declaring she would in that case make an excellent submarine palace for Neptune; and expressed his determination, if she ever foundered, and her exact position could be ascertained, to visit her in a diving-bell. He hoped, he said, to be present at the first ball given by his marine majesty to the sea-nymphs of his court, and the young mermaid ladies, of whose luxuriant hair and extraordinary beauty so much had been said and sung. He grew quite animated on the subject—'Only think,' he said, 'of John Dory swimming through a quadrille with Miss Ann Chovy, giving his neighbour a flip on the shoulder, and saying, " *Stir, John,* your fins, and give us a Highland fling." ' He was of opinion that of flat fish there would, as a matter of course, be as many as in other courts, and cross old crabs too. Common plaices, he was sure, would be in abundance, as well as 'good old soles.' Bloaters, the aldermen of the sea, enjoy good eating, and are sure to be found at civic feasts. 'What a glorious thing,' he exclaimed, 'it would be to hear a real syren sing; wouldn't it ?'

'I suppose,' said the young lady with a wicked smile, 'that sharks, like lawyers, would also be plentifully there, seeking whom they could devour. But pray tell me,' she continued, 'do you believe in mermaids ?'

'Do you believe in mermen ?' replied the barrister, 'because, you know, there can't be one without the other.'

'If that is the case,' she said, 'I do. A merman must be a lawyer-like creature; an amphibious animal, neither fish nor flesh—at once, a diver and a dodger. But really now, and without joking, do you believe there are such things or beings as mermaids ?'

'Why not ?' replied the young lawyer, who bore the allusions to his profession with great good-humour— 'Why not ?' A beaver, you know, is an animal, and a most clever and ingenious one too; an engineer, and builds a dam to make an artificial lake; an architect, and designs a house; a carpenter competent to build, and a mason, to plaster it; and yet the tail of the beaver is a fish's tail; has scales on it like a fish; and requires to be kept continually submerged in water. Why shouldn't a mermaid be a link between us and fishes in the same way that a beaver is between animals and them ?'

'I didn't ask,' the young lady retorted, with some

warmth, 'why such creatures should not be, but whether you believe they really do exist.'

'Well,' he said, affecting to look wise, 'not having seen, I don't know; and not knowing, I can't say; but their existence appears to me to be as well authenticated as that of the sea-serpent. Hundreds of people declare they have seen the latter, among whom is a captain in the Royal Navy; and Mr. Grattan, in his recent work on America, states, that all his family beheld the marine monster from their window at the inn at Nahant, in Massachusetts Bay, as plainly as they saw the water, or the ships in the harbour. Now, Miss Mackay, the daughter of a Scotch clergyman, the minister of Reah, in the North of Scotland, whose letter is preserved in the Annual Register, declared on oath that she and four other persons had the pleasure of contemplating a mermaid for a whole hour, while disporting itself within a few yards of them, for their particular instruction and amusement. It was so near that they saw the colour of its eyes and hair; and she describes it most minutely: says she was particularly struck with its long taper fingers, lily-white arms, and magnificent neck and bust. This mermaid was, most probably, crossed in love, for it often placed its hand under its alabaster cheek, and floated pensively and thoughtfully on the water. So you see its existence is as well authenticated as that of the sea-serpent.'

'Then you believe in them both?' asked the young lady.

'No, indeed,' he replied, 'I do not. Professor Owen has proved that they not only do not, but that they cannot exist.'

'Well, I don't thank him,' rejoined the young lady, 'for his demonstration. I like to believe in sea-serpents, and mermaids, and ghosts, and dreams, and all that sort

of thing; it excites and thrills me. I wouldn't give up
the Arabian Nights' Entertainments for all the wise books
Professor Owen ever wrote, or ever will write in his life.
Now, there is that legend about Netley Abbey—perhaps
it may be an invention, if you come to criticise it and ask
for proof; but still it is a pretty little antiquarian story,
and I like to believe it; *I* don't want to be undeceived.
There is a moral attached to it, showing that consecrated
ground cannot be desecrated with impunity.'

' I am not aware,' said the lawyer, ' to what you allude ;
but recollect I never believe any thing that is not proved.'

' No,' she said, ' nor do you believe it when it is.
Smethurst, you know, was found guilty of murder, so
thought the judge, so thought the jury, and so did the
public; but Sir Cornewall Lewis said, "If you call that
man guilty of poisoning the body, what will you say of
agitators who have poisoned the *minds* of the public?
One is as innocent as the other, for no noxious drug can
be found in the stomach of the one, or the brain of the
other;" *that*, I suppose, you will call Home-Office logic ;
won't you ?'

' Uncommon good,' said the lawyer; ' but what is the
tradition of Netley Abbey, that you wish to believe, if you
can ?'

' Well,' she said, ' Netley Abbey, about the beginning
of the last century, was sold by Sir Bartlett Lacy to a
Quaker builder, who had bought it for the purpose of
using its materials in the way of his trade. Shortly afterwards, the purchaser had a dream that he was taking
down the arch over the east window, when the keystone
fell upon him and killed him. He related this dream to
the celebrated Dr. Isaac Watts, who was a native of
Southampton, and, though a dissenter, was educated by
a Churchman, and attached to the Establishment. When

he heard of his dream, he advised him not to have any thing to do with the demolition of this house of the Lord. The Quaker, however, ridiculed the idea of consecrated ground, as his successors, Bright and others, have since done, and while proceeding to take down the building, a stone from the east window fell upon him, and killed him. Netley Abbey still stands, but what would it have been without this tradition? Now, I like this little legend; it is charming, and I strive to believe it. The removal of the body of St. Swithin (who is our patron saint at Winchester) amid continued rains, gave rise to the popular story or prejudice, that should St. Swithin's day, the 15th of July, be wet, it will rain for forty days consecutively. I dare say you laugh at all this; but I wish to think it true; and, what is more, half the world believes in it. If I gave that up, pray what have you to give me in its place for a creed? It is safer and pleasanter to believe too much than too little. For instance, what a delightful thing it is to think we are under the protection of invisible agents! depend upon it, it has a beneficial influence on the mind. Who would wish to be without a guardian angel— would you?'

'No, indeed,' he said, with an admiring and affectionate look, 'but I like a visible one, not spiritual, but substantial;' and then he continued in an under tone, 'such a one I know, and almost worship, but the worst of it is, I believe I am more afraid of her than I should be of one from the other world. When I attempt to address her, and entreat her to take me under her guardianship, the words die ere they pass my lips,' [the young lady hung her head and blushed,] 'I stare, stammer, and look and feel like a fool.'

'What a coward you are!' she replied, giving him a look of encouragement that invited confidence; 'I should

have thought that a lawyer like you, who advocates the
causes of others, would be eloquent when pleading his own.
If you cannot speak, surely you can write. But, dear
me! here we are at Winchester.'

What an opportunity was thus lost! He had evidently
screwed himself up to the point, when his speech and his
journey were thus unexpectedly brought to an end.
They both appeared loath to depart and to separate, but
time and trains wait for no one.

This party had hardly left the carriage before their
seats were filled by the ladies with whom I had travelled
the preceding day, and I heard the word 'Shegog,'
accompanied by a titter, repeated again among the young
ladies as they recognized me as 'the man with the funny
name,' who had travelled with them the day before.

'Ah,' said the elder lady, apparently resuming a conversation that had been interrupted by the stoppage of
the train, 'it was an extraordinary scene, and one I can
never forget.'

'To what scene do you allude, Aunt,' asked one of her
young companions.

'The annual election for the admission of idiots into
the asylum. It was held in the London Tavern, in
October last, and I attended it with a friend. As we
ascended the stairs, of which there were three or four
flights, printed placards were fastened to the walls, and
even tied all round the hand-rail of the stairs. They
consisted of earnest recommendations of the various distressing cases—"Vote for A. B., aged thirteen years,
parents dead, supported by an aged grandfather, who is
now out of work."—"Your vote is earnestly entreated
for C. D., Father dead, Mother keeps a mangle." And
so on, up to one hundred and thirty-two equally afflicting
cases, of which only twenty could be admitted into the

asylum on this occasion. When we reached the election room, it was covered with at least a hundred small tables, some of which exhibited two placards, others only one, similar to those on the staircase. At these tables were seated the friends of the different unhappy candidates, for the purpose of receiving and collecting votes and proxies, which from time to time were transmitted to the polling officers at the upper end of the room. But the touters played a prominent part in this strange scene, and their language sounded very extraordinary to my uninitiated ears. "I want twenty idiots," said one, "have you any to spare? I'll give you twenty infant orphans for them." "No, I want a hundred idiots myself." "Well, I'll tell you what I will do, I'll lend you ten idiots if you can give me fifteen indigent blind." "Done! write out an I O U, and I'll sign it, and give me the idiots at once."

'One of the most touching incidents was a poor, dear little deaf and dumb child, perambulating the room with a relative, soliciting votes for her own admission into a Deaf and Dumb Asylum, by talking with her fingers. I think she was one of the most beautiful and interesting little creatures I ever beheld. The election continued from twelve till two o'clock; I did not wait to see its close, but as the time drew near for its termination, tears of disappointment and distress were visible in the eyes of the friendless and unsuccessful poor.

'It is an excellent institution, but, like many others in this charitable country, is susceptible of improvement in its management. For instance, I think the poor idiots, when once admitted, should be maintained through life, instead of being liable to dismissal, unless re-elected at the end of every five or seven years. But none of these suffering people gave vent to their grief as Lady Sarah did this morning. "Oh, Martha," she said, as she burst

into my room, " this is a dreadful business. Lord Polebury is quite dead, Lady Middleton as black and soft as
if she had been boiled, and Prince Frederick William
will never recover! What terrible destruction!" ' This
observation seemed to wake up an elderly gentlemen from
a reverie in which he was indulging. He was evidently
a clergyman, and of that class, too, which commends itself
to our affection by its total exemption from party badges
of any kind. He was attired neither in the distinctive
dress of the High, nor Low Church party, but habited like
a parson of the old school. His manner and general
appearance indicated the gentleman, while his placid
countenance and expansive forehead exhibited at once
benevolence and intelligence. He looked like an ingenuous and simple-minded man, clever, but not acute; a
man of God, but not a man of the world : in short, it was
impossible to look upon him without seeing who and what
he was.

'Is it the cholera, Madam?' said he, in great alarm;
' what is the cause of this sad and sudden mortality?'

' Frost,' replied the lady, who seemed to think her companion was not quite sane. ' Frost, sir; it has ruined
the gardens for the year. Even the chrysanthemums are
all injured.'

' Oh,' he said, with great apparent relief, ' is that all?'

'You would not say that, sir, if you were fond of a
flower garden. I cannot conceive a greater infliction in
its way. After you have spent all the winter and spring
in planning out your garden, arranging the edgings,
inventing ribbons, producing effects, and harmony of
colours, having worried through the labours of planting
out, and settled which are to occupy the same bed'—here
a slight smile passed over his reverence's face, as if
he was amused at her excitement, or her phraseology;

but he instantly repressed it, and she proceeded without
noticing it)—'having fought and conquered your gardener, vanquished slugs, overcome drought, checked
thrips and caterpillars, removed the dead and dying, and
supplied their places, producing thereby a blaze of
beauty; after having satisfied your own critical taste,
and astonished and delighted your friends, to find on
waking some fine sunshiny morning, that a frost, like that
of last night, had destroyed it. Oh, sir, you wouldn't say,
"is that all?" It precipitates the winter: it is sudden
death.   Dying, falling leaves are enough to try the
patience of any floriculturist in the world. Sweep, sweep,
sweep, and still the lawn is untidy; every puff of wind
scatters them like flakes of snow; but that,'—she remarked, with a supercilious toss of her head, which
showed that she had not forgotten his exclamation, 'is
that all '—'but that, 1 suppose, you will say, is the order
of nature, and if they add to our labours, their variegated
hues, ere they fall, contribute also to the beauty of the
scene.   But, sir, an early and unexpected frost, like that
we have just experienced, brings death and destruction to
plants, and is indeed a calamity that requires a large
stock of philosophy to bear.'

    ' I can easily understand your feelings, madam,' said
her clerical friend, 'for I am very fond of gardening
myself; it is an innocent, an interesting, and instructive
pursuit.   When you spoke of Lord Polebury being dead,
and Lady Middleton *in extremis*, I took it literally, and
not in reference to geraniums and verbenas.   I beg your
pardon for the mistake; but at the time I was thinking of
something else, and the suddenness of the remark, though
not addressed to me, startled me; for his Lordship,
though deficient in judgment, means well, and is, I believe,
a very good man.   His zeal is without knowledge, and

N

not always tempered with discretion; but his energies are directed to laudable objects, and he would be a serious loss to the country.' He then discussed the respective merits of all the varieties of roses, calceolarias, dahlias, &c., &c., in a manner that showed he was quite a master of the subject. 'Yes,' he said, 'I can well sympathize with you, madam, in the destruction occasioned by the frost of last night; but it is emblematical of that death which terminates all our fondest hopes and dearest affections. Everything reminds us of this invariable law of nature, whether it be gradual decay or sudden destruction.'

'Oh, yes,' she said, 'we know that; but still it is no less vexatious. I lost all my wall-fruit this spring by a late frost, and now our flowers are all destroyed by an early one. It is very easy to say, "is that all?" but you little know the truth of your statement. "It is all," fruit and flowers together; what is there left worth having, when you are deprived of both? and you must excuse me for saying it is not the law of nature; if it was, we should provide against it, or submit to it with patience. It is an unexpected irregularity that makes it so vexatious.'

He bowed civilly to her, but went on, without replying to her testy observations—'The laws of the seasons are not immutable; and yet there is no reason, because all is transitory here below, why we should not interest ourselves in everything around us. The garden survives many more active pursuits, and furnishes occupation and amusement at a period of life when excitement ceases to minister to our pleasures. Flowers are the gift of God; and His infinite wisdom, goodness, and power, are as discernible in them as in the stars that glitter in the firmament—they both delight and instruct us. In their fragrance and beauty, they are emblems of purity, and in their decay and vernal reappearance, they are typical of a resurrection. It is a conviction of this nature that has induced mankind from the earliest period to plant them on the graves of their departed friends.'

' Then,' said the lady, pointing to the cemetery at Woking, with a mingled feeling of pique and civility, ' that place, I should suppose, is one that would excite the most agreeable and tender thoughts in your mind.'

' No,' he said, ' I approve of it, but I do not admire it. It is a necessary provision for the relief of a metropolis like London, or any other large city, for intramural burials are found to be destructive of health ; but they fail to attract us like the old rural churchyards to which we and our forefathers have been accustomed. The more you decorate them, the more repulsive they become. Rare exotic trees, and shrubs, gay flowers, and the tricks of landscape gardening are not in keeping with the place. We forget that we are wandering through the city of the dead, the last resting-place of mortality ; and yet there is something in the tombs, urns, and tablets around us, that destroys the illusion of ornamental pleasure-grounds. It is neither a burial-place, nor a garden : it is too gay and smiling for the one, and too lonely and melancholy for the other. Our reflections are diverted by the gaudy parterres, and our enjoyments destroyed by the mementoes of death. Bridal flowers decorate the tomb ; and headstones, with learned or rustic inscriptions, label the rhododendrons and azaleas. These cemeteries are in most cases too distant to be visited by the relations and friends of the poor ; and in all countries the affections of the heart are more intense and more durable where the soil is not sufficiently rich to force up luxuriant weeds to choke their growth. In the great estuary of an over-

grown city like London, men are drawn into the vortex of
a whirlpool, in which they disappear, and are forgotten
for ever. People are too busy to think, and where there
is no reflection there is no feeling. The grave receives
the body, and the cemetery engulfs the grave. Death is
an incident—food and shelter, a necessity. Grief is,
therefore, a luxury that is denied to poverty. All are in
the current at the same time, and self-preservation leaves
but little opportunity to watch the struggles or disap-
pearance of others. No; the cemetery has no attraction
for me. Its gaudy decorations are not in keeping, and do
not harmonize with a widow's weeds, or the mourning of
orphans or parents. But there is something in the dear
old rural churchyard that has an indescribable effect on
me. My earliest recollections are connected with it; my
thoughtless childhood was first awakened to a sense of
mortality by the mournful processions that repaired
thither, and the sad and lonely visits of those, who,
bereaved of their relatives, poured forth their sorrows and
affections over the graves of those they had loved so well.
The churchyard has a moral effect on the mind; it
suggests to us the frail and uncertain tenure of our own
lives; it bids us prepare to follow our departed friends,
to emulate their virtues, and to fix our hopes on a reunion in a better and happier world. It is, besides, the
greeting-place of the villagers and parishioners, where
their mutual afflictions receive mutual sympathy, where
the voice of discord is unknown, and "the short and
simple annals of the poor" are registered in the memory
of those who will deliver them as traditions to succeeding
generations. The place has a holy and a salutary
influence that prepares the congregation for entering the
sacred edifice, in which as children they were brought to
the baptismal font, and made members of the Church of

God. All these incidents and accessories of a rustic churchyard do not exist in a cemetery. The "Dead Train" at once distracts your attention and appals you, as an evidence of great mortality. The number of corpses, like those on a battle-field, attest the awful contest between life and death that continually rages in the city; but the heart becomes hardened by the daily spectacle, and the gaudy appearance of the place withdraws your attention from the moral it should suggest. Grief seeks seclusion; and though it may be alleviated by the presence and affectionate sympathy of sorrowing friends, it instinctively shrinks from the public gaze.

'The speed of a railway is so unlike the slow and measured tread of the rustic procession, one cannot but feel that it bears too strong a resemblance to the ordinary business of life; while the short and hurried sepulture, and the rapid departure of the mourners, gives the affair more the appearance of the *embarkation*, than the burial of a relative. The graves are seldom visited again—time and expense, in most instances, deprive the poor of even this sad consolation—and they are compelled to regard the loss of a deceased friend in the light of one who lies buried in a foreign land. As I have before said, the affections of the poor are more intense and more durable than those of the rich, because they are more dependent upon each other. They have but few to love them, and of those few not one can be spared, without the rupture of many ties. These distant cemeteries are grievous affairs to them, I assure you, and it is only those who, like myself, have ministered among them, that can fully comprehend and enter into their feelings.'

All this was said with a simple earnestness and mildness of manner that showed how habitual such thoughts were to his mind, how little accustomed he was to travelling, and to the desultory conversation or constrained silence of railway passengers. The ladies who had been so impatient and excited by the account of the destruction of the garden the previous evening, now listened with deep interest to those observations of the old clergyman, who, by the softness and sweetness of his voice, and his unaffected and winning demeanour, had interested us all in his favour.

'I never considered the subject in that light,' said the old lady. 'We know that the increased and increasing population of large towns demand the formation of cemeteries; but still it does appear to me that the decoration of them is well suited to the object for which they are formed; they cannot be viewed without a certain degree of approval—they evince, at least, a respect for the dead; but as you say, much of the salutary effect of the churchyard is lost. The graves are so numerous that individuality is as much destroyed as it is in the crowds of the metropolis; the moral, as you justly observe, is gone.'

'Talking of the "moral," madam,' he inquired, 'were you ever in the churchyard of Montgomery, in North Wales? or were you acquainted with the rector of the adjoining parish, the Reverend Mr. Pryce's?'

'No,' she said, 'I never was in Montgomery; but I had the pleasure of knowing the gentleman to whom you allude. He was a remarkably clever, well-informed person, and one of the most striking and effective preachers I ever met with. Poor man! he is now dead, and I am not acquainted with even the name of his successor.'*

'Yes,' continued the clergyman, 'he was a man of rare endowments; he was an old college chum of mine.

---

* The Rev. Mr. Pryce furnished the author with these particulars, and some further details, which are too minute for insertion.

If you were intimate with him, madam, he, perhaps, may have told you the remarkable story of the "Robber's Grave."'

'No,' said the lady, 'I never heard it; would you be obliging enough to relate it to me?'

Bowing assent, the clergyman proceeded:—'In the year 1819 there was, in the neighbourhood of Montgomery, an ancient manor-house, called Oakfield, which, like many of those old structures, losing its original importance from the increased size and convenience of modern buildings, had been converted into a farm-house. The late occupant, one James Morris, had been an indolent and somewhat dissipated man; the farm consequently fell into neglect, and became unprofitable, and he died in debt, leaving his wife and an only daughter in possession of the place. Shortly after his death, the widow took into her employment a young man from Staffordshire, of the name of John Newton, the hero of this little story, who had been strongly recommended to her by her brother; and well and faithfully did he discharge his duties as bailiff, fully justifying the praise and recommendations she received with him. He was an utter stranger in that part of the country, seemed studiously to shun all acquaintance with his neighbours, and to devote himself exclusively to the interests of his employer. He never left home but to visit the neighbouring fairs and markets, and to attend the parish church, where his presence was regular, and his conduct devout. In short, though highly circumspect in his behaviour on all occasions, he was a melancholy, reserved man; and even the clergyman of the parish, to whom he was always most respectful in his demeanour, entirely failed in his endeavours to cultivate an acquaintance with him. The farm, under his management, had improved, and become

profitable ; and the circumstances of Mrs. Morris were, by his assiduity and skill, both prosperous and flourishing. In this manner more than two years had passed, and the widow began to regard him more as a friend and benefactor than a servant, and was not sorry to observe her daughter's growing affection for him, which appeared to be reciprocal. One evening in November, 1821, being detained longer than usual by business at Welshpool, Newton set out about six o'clock on his return to Oakfield. It was an exceedingly dark night, and he never reached home again. The family became very anxious, and upon inquiring early the following morning at Welshpool, they ascertained that he had been brought back to that town, not long after his departure from it, by two men, named Parker and Pearce, who charged him with highway robbery, accompanied by violence, an offence then punishable with death. At the trial at the next assizes he was pronounced guilty, on the testimony of these two persons, which was clear, positive, and consistent throughout, was sentenced to be hanged, and left for execution. He employed no counsel, and called no witnesses in his defence ; but upon being asked by the judge, in the usual form, "if he had anything to say why sentence of death should not be passed upon him ?" he made in substance the following extraordinary speech :—
" My lord, it is evident all I could say in opposition to such testimony would be vain and hopeless. The witnesses are men of respectability, and their evidence has appeared plain and conclusive, and my most solemn protestations of innocence could avail me nothing. I have called no witnesses to character, and upon such evidence the jury could pronounce no other verdict. I blame them not. From my soul, too, I forgive those men, upon whose false testimony I have been convicted.

But, my lord, I protest most solemnly before this court, before your lordship, and above all before that God in whose presence I must shortly appear, that I am entirely guiltless of the crime for which I am about to suffer. I have produced no one to speak in my behalf. Two years have scarcely passed since I came into this country an utter stranger. I have made no acquaintance here beyond the household in which I have been employed, and where I have endeavoured to discharge my duties faithfully and honestly. Although I dare not hope, and do not wish that my life should be spared, yet it is my devout and earnest desire that the stain of this crime may not rest upon my name. I devoutly hope that my good mistress, and her kind and excellent daughter, may yet be convinced that they have not nourished and befriended a highway robber. I have, therefore, in humble devotion, offered a prayer to heaven, and I believe it has been heard and accepted. I venture to assert that, if I am innocent of the crime for which I suffer, the grass, for one generation at least, will not cover my grave. My lord, I await your sentence without a murmur, without a sorrow, and I devoutly pray that all who hear me now may repent of their sins, and meet me again in heaven."

' The unfortunate man was condemned and executed, and was buried in Montgomery churchyard. *Thirty years* had passed away when I saw it, in company with poor Eliot Warburton, and *the grass had not then covered his grave.* It is situated in a remote corner of the churchyard, far removed from all other graves. It is not a raised mound of earth, but is even with the surrounding ground, which is, for some distance, especially luxuriant, the herbage being rich and abundant. Numerous attempts have, from time to time, been made by some who are still alive, and others who have passed away, to bring

N 3

grass upon that bare spot. Fresh soil has been frequently spread upon it, and seeds of various kinds have been sown, but not a blade had there ever been known to spring from them, and the soil soon became a smooth, cold, and stubborn clay. With respect to the unhappy witnesses, it appears that Parker's ancestors had once owned Oakfield, and that he had hoped, by getting rid of Newton, to remove the main obstacle there was to his repossessing it, and that Pearce had, at the time of Mr. Morris's death, aspired to the hand of his daughter, in whose affections he felt he had been supplanted by poor Newton. The former soon left the neighbourhood, became a drunken and dissolute man, and was ultimately killed in some limeworks while in the act of blasting a rock. Pearce grew sullen and dispirited; his very existence seemed a burden to him, and as the old Sexton of Montgomery expressed it, " he wasted away from the face of the earth." '

'What a strange and interesting story, sir,' said the lady; 'do you know in what condition the grave now is?'

'I have not seen it,' he replied, ' since the period I mentioned, which, I think, was in 1850; but I have heard that some person has since covered it with thick turf, which has united itself with the surrounding grass, except at the head, which is still withered and bare, as if scorched with lightning. The prayer, however, of poor Newton, that his grave might remain uncovered for at least one generation, has been heard, and his memory vindicated in a most remarkable manner. The name given to the grave was singularly inappropriate, it should have been called " the grave of the innocent." The widow, with her daughter, left Oakfield, and went to reside with her brother. For some weeks after poor Newton's burial, it is said his grave was from time to time found strewed with wild flowers, by an unknown hand. But it was observed that after Jane Morris had left the neighbourhood, not a flower was found upon it!

'As I said before, poor Eliot Warburton went with us to see it. He gazed upon that bare spot with a hallowed, reverential emotion. What sacred thoughts passed through his mind during those few brief moments I cannot tell. But he promised me he would, when he next came into the neighbourhood, visit it again, and write and publish the story. Poor fellow, he came not; the relentless waves have closed over him! What a beautiful and affecting story would the simple facts, told by him, have given to the world!'

He had hardly concluded his narrative, ere we reached Kingston, where he took leave of us.

'Aunty,' said one of the young ladies, 'what a dear old man that is! did you ever hear a more interesting story? I wonder what his name is! How could you be so rude to him, when he misunderstood you about the flowers? Couldn't we find out from the rector who he is, and all about him? Do try, aunt.'

But her entreaties were cut short, by the re-appearance of Mr. Peabody, from another part of the train, who was so convulsed with laughter, he could scarcely speak. Taking the seat recently occupied by the clergyman, he bent forward, and striking his open hand on his knee with great animation, he said.

'By gum, Squire Shegog, we have had the greatest bobbery of a shindy in our carriage you ever knowed in all your born days. Did you hear the hurrush?'

'No,' I said, 'we heard nothing extraordinary here.'

'Well,' said he, 'the train was so crowded this morning, that though I had a first-class ticket, I had to put up with a seat in the second, or be left behind. We got rid of all those that were in our box at Winchester, but two—one was a thin, pale, student-looking-chap, who, if he hadn't seen his best days, wasn't like to find them here below at all. He was an inoffensive kind of a feller that wouldn't say boo to a goose—the other was a cap sheaf critter, that thought himself a beauty without paint, and was better and finer than his neighbours. He had a beard that wouldn't acknowledge the corn to no man's, and the way it was beargreased, or iled, or Cologned, or musked, or what not, was a caution to a tar-brush. Every now and then he passed the thumb and forefinger of his right hand over his lips as if to give room for showing his teeth to advantage ; and, I must say, his mug resembled a Skye terrier's as near as could be, while a pair of little ferret eyes watched over all as if they were guarding his precious anointed face. Well, what does I do, but take out my cigar case, and make preparation for smoking, in that cool way, you know, that nobody but us, Yankees, can do. Sais I to the invalid, " Have you any objection to smoking ?" " No," sais he, " I rather like the flavour of a good Havannah." Well, if he had said no, I'd have given up, for I scorn to take advantage of helpless people like women, niggers, and hospital folks. Then I turned to Skye, " have you any objection ?" sais I. " Most decidedly," he said. " Well, I know some does dislike it," sais I, and I struck a light and began to smoke. " Didn't I tell you I objected to it ?" sais he. " You did." "Then why do you persist in such an indecent manner ?" " Because," sais I, " I never could bear parfumes, they make me faint; and your beard is so scented, I am obliged to use tobacco in self-defence. If you will stick your beard out of the window on that side, and let the breeze sweep away its horrid smell, I'll put my head out of the one on this side, and let the odoriferous smoke go clear." " If

you don't take that cigar out of your mouth," sais he,
"I'll take it out for you." " My friend," sais I, " (oh!
how that horrid perfume chokes me), before you go to try
that game, recollect two can play at it. Look at me and
take my measure, and see if I am a man that you can
handle (phew! what is that tarnal scent you have about
your pendable? it beats all natur.)" " We shall settle
this," he said, " when the train stops, I have no idea of
being insulted in this way." " Nor I either," sais I ; " I
have paid for a seat in the first-class, where gentlemen go,
and here I am thrust into this second-rate carriage along
with a man that looks for all the world as if he had just
escaped from his keeper." Seeing bullying was no go, he
put on his cap, folded his arms, shut his eyes for fear the
smoke would make them look more bloodshot than they
were by nature, pressed his lips together as tight as if he
had put an hydraulic screw on 'em, and composed himself
for a nap. When we got to Basingstoke (wasn't that the
name of the last place?) he and the pale-faced man were
both fast asleep, so I slips out quietly and gets into the
next division of the carriage. Arter a while, I peeps over
the back, and seeing they were still in the Land of Nod,
I lights a Vesuvius match, pitched it through the division,
let it fall on his beard, and then dodged down again and
told the people in my carriage what I had done, and why
I did it, and they all entered into the joke as good-natured as you please. In less than half no time, I heard
an awful row between the two I had left in the next
division; both were singing out murder at the top end of
their voices. Skye terrier woke up, feeling the frizzle in
his beard, and thought 'tother fellow had been tryin to
cut his throat, so he yelled out murder, made a spring at
sick man, caught him by the neckcloth, and nearly choked
him, while invalid thinking he was mad, and expecting to

be killed right off, squeaked out murder too. There they were, like two dogs, standin on their hind legs, showin' their teeth, snarlin', snappin', and biting like all possessed.

' "Your beard is afire," said Paleface. " It was you that did it, then," said Skye. " No, it warn't," said I, looking over the division that separated us, " it's spontaneous combustion. The spirit of the Cologne has set the bear's grease in a flame, shut your mouth, or it will burn your innerds. Here's my Arkansas toothpick, stranger, give Skye a dig in the ribs with it, or he'll be the death of you. No, stand on one side, I'll give him a shot with my revolver, he is as mad as a polar bear dancin on hot iron. I knew he was crazy when I first see'd him, he's dodged his keeper, and slipt out of an asylum. Creation! Man, says I to Skye, why don't you put out the fire that's frizzlin your beard? You look for all the world like a pig that's gettin his bristles singed off." Then we all set up a great shout at him, and even Paleface laughed.

' When we stopped at the station, he charged me with smoking, and invalid with setting fire to him; but we both agreed and affirmed he was an escaped lunatic, and everybody larfed like any thing, and there we left him, lookin like a caution to a singed cat. If he warn't a madman, when he came into the carriage, I'll be hanged if he didn't rave like one, when he left it. Why on airth can't people go through life like sensible folks? The voyage we have to make is soon over; why not lay in a large stock of good-humour, patience, and above all, consideration for the other passengers? Storms, tempests, accidents, and what not, will occur in spite of us; but why not enjoy fine weather, fair winds, and the fellowship of others, when we can?

' That's my philosophy at any rate. It's no use for

folks to stick themselves up above their fellow-travellers. High peaks are covered with ice and snow, and are everlasting cold. But the glades that lie at the foot of the mountains, bear grapes, and produce oranges, figs, and all manner of pleasant fruits. Them that like to go up, and soar aloft with the eagles and vultures, are welcome to their cold perch and their grand views; but give me the brook and the valley, and the happy and genial folks, that inhabit the lowlands.'

' A very pretty idea,' said one of the nieces.

' And a very charming young lady that says so,' replied Peabody.

' Tickets, if you please.'

We all know what that means. The journey is over.

No. X.

THE OLD AND THE NEW YEAR; OR, QUAKERS AFLOAT AND ASHORE.

AFTER dining at the British Hotel, I sauntered as usual into the smoking-room, where I found the Senator, Mr. Peabody, and many others, whom it was difficult to distinguish in the fragrant cloud that filled the apartment. 'Well, Mr. Shegog,' said the Senator to me, ' the old and the new year are now about to shake hands together, as the Lord Mayor and his successor did on the 9th of November last. The former abdicated the throne, after a brief tenure of office, and surrendered his mace and insignia to the new incumbent. Both he and his pageantry have passed away, and are already forgotten. His court, and his parasites alone remain, and they are transferred to the new magnate, who in his turn will play his part as civic sovereign, and in twelve short months retire and be lost among the crowd who have " passed the chair." What a picture of life is this! At his official dinners, like those of royalty, are to be found ministers of state, foreign ambassadors, chancellors, judges, commanders-in-chief of the army, lords of the admiralty, *et hoc genus omne.* The guests praise and ridicule the possessor of power, as is their wont, and as soon as he is *functus officio* pay the same courteous, but insincere homage to his successor. An ex-Lord Mayor and a dethroned king

know how to estimate mankind at their true value, better
than any other people in the world.   Those who condescend to accept the invitations, and receive the hospitalities
of the former, affect, as soon as he retires into private
life, to forget both him and his name ; and those whom
the latter delighted to honour, while they retain the rank
and titles he conferred upon them, ascribe their success to
their own merits, and feel that but little gratitude is due
for a mere act of justice.   As the old year was, so will be
the new.   There is a general similarity in them all.   One
is marked by war, and another by peace : this by the
death of a king, and that by the accession of an heir or
an usurper, and both are varied by an irregular course of
monetary or political panics—strikes—rebellions in the
east or west — reform bills, agitators like O'Connell,
Bright, Wat Tyler, and Smith O'Brien; shocking Irish
assassinations, lamentable suicides, or awful shipwrecks.
What has been will occur again annually.'

'Zactly,' said Peabody, 'but that only happens in
Europe.   We are more sensible in our great country.
What turns up this year in England, don't happen in the
United States but once in four years ; an' the things you
have totted up as the incidents of the past twelve months,
are mere by-play there, and give just excitement enough
to show that Jonathan is alive.   One administration it is
true, follows another here, like a flock of geese, Indian
file ; and folks think the nation is getting ruined all the
time.   Now Derby is in, and some say England is going
to the bad, for he won't give a vote to those he don't
deem fit for it.   Then Palmerston succeeds him, and
t'other side vows that he will upset everything, for he
will lower the franchise below what is safe, and increase
the number of representatives, so that no room in London
will hold half of them.   Then some say that Lord John

Russell, who bids at a political auction (where long credit is given on renewable paper), like a feller that has no real capital to trade on, is going to destroy the constitution by letting in just as many outsiders as will swamp all the real estate in the kingdom, and to my mind they ain't far out in their reckoning either. No man need tell me, after seeing him, that bleeding ain't good for the human frame. That man's feelings are so tender, and his innards are so thin-skinned, his heart has been bleeding without stopping for thirty years, for the unrepresented class. It would have burst its boiler long ago, if that large safety-valve hadn't been fixed in him originally hard and fast. What a wonderfully constructed system he must have, for his heart to have sustained such a continued drain of blood from it; and, great as the demand has been, the supply has always been equal to it! He looks as well (indeed, some folks say better) than ever he did. The tears also that he has shed over small boroughs, especially those of the Tories, would actilly float a river steamer; still there are fellers who say he is a dangerous and venturesome critter, and that he is too small a man to wade into such troubled waters as those of reform. Then there is John Bright, the Quaker, everybody says that fellow is a republican, double-dyed in the wool, and I believe he would revolutionize this country if it warn't for his temper—Quakers have no means to let off the steam like other folks—it's agin their creed to fight. If you give one on 'em a sock-dolager under the ear he is in duty bound to turn round and say, "Try thy hand on the other side, my friend, will you?" They are made of the same stuff as other folks, and have the same feelings and passions, and commonly are a little grain stronger, too, from being temperate and keeping good hours (for that saves both fire and candles); but they have, in a

general way, to bite in their breath, and gulp down their
rage; and it nearly sets them hoppin', ravin', distracted
mad. I have often expected to see them explode, for they
have to look as calm and mild as if butter wouldn't melt
in their mouths, and cheese wouldn't choke them. They
can't relieve the pressure by swearing either, which I
must say is a great privilege, for it's like a spoonful of cold
water thrown into a maple sugar kettle, it stops the bilin'
over in a minute. Nothin does an angry man so much
good as that.'

'Now, Mr. Peabody,' said the Senator, 'don't talk
nonsense that way; you know I don't like to hear such
assertions; and more than that, you don't approve of that
abominable practice yourself. It is a shocking and disgusting habit; but unlike most other objectionable things,
it has not one redeeming quality about it.'

'I am not approving of it,' he replied, 'as you well
know. I am only talking of it as a man of the world;
but when you say it has no one redeeming quality about
it you go to the other extreme,' and he gave me a sly
wink, to intimate that he was only drawing his friend out
for his amusement. 'It does let the steam off, that's a
fact. Now, hot iron is not a redeeming thing, as you call
it, and yet it is necessary to burn out the pyson of a snake.
But for the matter of that, I have heard as good a Quaker
as ever you see, one of the real Foxites (and there could
not have been a better founder for that sect than a Fox,
for they are as sly as e'er a Reynard that ever cleared a
hen-roost), swear like a Mississippi rowdy, make your
hair stand on end, and stiffen it so, you could no more
smooth it than a grove of pines. I have, upon my soul.'

'Mr. Peabody, all I can say,' rejoined the Senator (and he appeared by the emphatic way he used
the word *Mister* to intimate that he disapproved of

his style of conversation), 'all I can say is, he must have been an impostor and not a real member of the Friends, for a more moral, discreet, and respectable sect is not to be found in our great nation. Although I differ from them in their religious notions, I entertain the highest opinion of them, both individually and collectively. So universal, indeed, is this feeling among us, that un-principled people adopt their dress and use their phrase-ology for the purpose of deception, knowing that, as a body, they are men of great probity, and that the word of a Quaker is as good as his bond.'

'Yes,' said Peabody ; 'but if his bond is no good, and his word is equal to that, how much is his word worth ? Try it by the Rule of Three, and the answer is nil. Now, were you acquainted with old Jacob Coffin, of Nantucket, the great whaler ?'

'I was,' said the Senator, 'and a more honourable, upright, and pious man was not to be found in the United States. I do not know any one that stood higher in the estimation of the public, or of the Society, of which he was a member and an honour.'

'Well,' said Peabody, 'the way he swore was a caution to a New Orleans witness, and they can swear through a nine-inch plank. I have heard a western stage-driver go it : and it isn't every one that can ditto him, I can tell you; well, he could afford to give them four moves a-head, and beat them both at their own game. I'll explain to you how I found him out. A sailor, you know, always fancies farming, for it is the natural occupation of man—ploughing the deep turns his mind to ploughing the land. He gets tired of the ocean arter a while, and longs for terry firmy, and he has visions of a cottage with a nice verandah to walk in in wet weather, or to enjoy his cigar, and a

splendiferous gall for a wife, with cheeks of white
and red roses crushed on them—perfection of complexion—in rig, a rael fore and after, and in lines a doll
of a clipper, all love and affection for old Whalebone to
splice with. Then he imagines a brook, with pastures leading down to it, and cows coming and asking to be milked,
and four-year-old sheep turning up their great heavy fat
rumps to him to admire their mutton. He indulges the
idea that he is to have a splendid avenue of Pole beans
from the front gate to the cottage, and his bungalow, as
he calls it (for he has been in the East Indies), is to be
covered with Virginia creeper and the multiflora rose ; and
he fancies an arbour in his garden shaded with hops,
where he can invite an old sea-sarpant of a captain like
himself, who has doubled Cape Horn and the Cape of
Good Hope times without number, to come and converse
with him (which means swapping lies and getting half
drunk). Then he sees in the picture he has drawn, some
little harpooners such as he was once himself, with rosy
cheeks and curling locks hanging down their backs
(before the horrid quaker sheep-shears clip them off),
running about him, asking to sit on his knee and listen to
his yarns about the flying Dutchman, savages that eat
naughty children, the rivers of Jamaica that are all pure
rum, and the hills that are real clarified white sugar. Then
he prides himself on the notion that he is to astonish his
neighbours, that he is to have a sheep or two in the pasture from the Cape, with tails so heavy that they will
require a little pair of wheels to carry them, a Brahmin
cow that gives no milk, a Thibet goat whose fleece is
something between wool, cotton, silk, and hair, and a
Lapland deer that the natives use to draw their sleighs
with, while the hall of his bungalow is to be decorated
with stuffed birds, beautiful conch shells, Chinese idols,

South Sea weapons, and foreign pipes of all sorts, sizes, and tubes. Well, Jacob Coffin used to keep himself warm, when his ship was frozen up in the north, a-thinking of this ideal gall and all this castle building, and arter coming home with a'most a noble cargo of sperm ile and whalebone, and feeling rich and sponsible, and able to carry out his plans, he puts his affairs into a shipbroker's hands, and off he goes full chisel on a courtin trip to Philadelphia, (Pennsylvania, you know, is the headquarters of the Friends, tho' some on 'em are what we call wet Quakers, too; that is, not overly strict about dress,) and he picks out a'most a heavenly splice, and marries her right off the reel. She was too young for him by a long chalk, but he consaited he warn't too old for her, a mistake elderly gents often make; and this I will say, a more angeleferous critter was not to be found in all the universal United States. No, not even in Connecticut itself, which is famed all over the world for its galls and its pumpkins. Lick, warn't she a whole team and a horse to spare, making a man's heart beat so to look at her, as to bust his waistcoat buttons off. Oh, Jerusalem, what perfection of female beauty she was! You could have tracked her all the way from Philadelphia to Nantucket, for everybody was talking of the beautiful blooming Quakeress that old Dead Eyes the Whaler had married. Well, as soon as he got home, he bought a farm, and built his bungalow, and realized the visions that had haunted him during many a long voyage, and many a long night on the ocean. Well, things all went on smooth and comfortable as far as the world could see. She developed into a still handsomer woman, until she grew into an angel a'most; and he grew prouder and more pompous than ever, only folks thought he was more strict and more rigid, and a little grain crosser. He looked as sweet as ever tho',

when he showed in public; but even sweet cider will
ferment and turn so hard you have to hold your
breath while you swaller it, for fear it would cut your
throat. Well, what onder the sun is the use of dreams,
for in a general way they certainly do go by *contraries;*
at all events, it was so with Jacob Coffin. The verandah
he expected to have enjoyed so much was built of green
wood, and shrunk so like old Scratch, it leaked like a sieve,
and he couldn't make no use of it in wet weather; the
scarlet-runners only took to runnin' when the heat of
summer was over; the hop-arbour was so damp it gave
him the ague, and he couldn't sit in it; the roses and
Virginia creeper harboured ice, lice, and mice, and
turned out a regular-built nuisance; while his neighbour's
dogs killed his Cape sheep, and the Lapland deer jump'd
the fence and raced off due north, for them and wild
geese know the points of compass, by natural instinct;
the Brahmin cow had to be shot, for it had killed
one of his children; the brook took it into its head
to rebel, burst its bounds, and floated off his hay and
oats, and all his little water-wheels for turning his
grindstone, churning his butter, and so on; and his four-
year-old wethers were stolen by the steward of a New
York coaster that put in there for shelter. There was
no eend to his troubles. His young harpooner during
his absence made playthings of his idols, stuffed birds,
and other trophies; his wife had the ague when he got
home, and was so cold she did nothing but shiver and
chatter; and he was so cross-grained and unkind to her,
she gave up her "thee's and thou's," and took to calling
him an old Grampus, a spouting-whale, a black fish, a
solan goose, and a boatswain bird, with a marlin spike
stuck into him behind instead of a tail. The last time he
returned from Baffin's Bay he found the young Quakeress

had gone on a voyage of discovery on her own hook. She was on the boards at New Orleans, and had changed her name eend for eend from Coffin to Madam Fincoff; she was the *star* of the south ('And deserved the *stripes*,' said the Senator, sternly). Well, old Jacob had to gulp all this down, for he was *a Quaker ashore then*. If he had been to sea at the time, depend upon it he would have ripped out some words that ain't easy to translate into English, I can tell you. I can't say I pitied old Broadbrim much either, for youth is youth, and age is age, and they don't harmonize well together in matrimony. Youth has its pleasures as well as its duties; but age don't sympathize with the pursuits of the other. It wants to make it consider duty a pleasure; and that ain't in the natur of things to unite them in one. Duty first and pleasure after; or, pleasure first and duty after, just as you like. But come what will, relaxation and recreation must be allowed. Quakers, like Jacob Coffin, think women were made for them, and them only, and not for themselves at all. Now, Eve was made not to work for Adam, because things grew spontanaceously in their garden, but to keep him company and to talk to him; and if there was anything to do, depend upon it she coaxed or smiled, or cried or worried him into it. It was "Adam, put the kettle on" in those days, and not "Polly," as in our time. She had a tongue given her for the special purpose of beguiling his weary hours with chat, and one that could lubricate itself, and go on for ever without stopping. Now, Jacob ought to have thought of this before he married that gall. He might have known if you put a young colt into a stall, tie it up and feed it there, first its fetlocks take to swellin', and then its legs, and then its appetite goes, and it pines away to a skeleton. You must turn it out to grass, and let it kick up its heels.

It is innocent play natur intends for it. He ought to
have borne in mind what that poor thing had to endure,
that knew she was the queen of beauty and the queen of
hearts too, stored up in such an outlandish place as that.
If he had had a heart in him, he might have recollected
that he had transplanted that bloomin' rose tree from the
sunny banks of the Deleware, into the cold soil and un-
congenial climate of Nantucket; that he left her alone
there six months in the year to pine like a bird in a cage,
or to flutter against its bars, in a place, too, where
she only saw snuffy old olive-coloured men, or drabby,
grubby, weather-beaten old women — broad-brimmed
ongainly hats, or horrid old poke bonnets, only fit for cats
to kitten in, and where she heard nothen but the price
of sperm or whalebone, or sugar or molasses, or the dege-
neracy of the age, and the idleness of the maidens.   That
if she went into the town, she was nearly pysoned by the
crew of some newly-arrived whaler, whose clothes and
yeller cotton water-proofs smelt so of ile, she expected
the flames of spontaneous combustion to break out every
minute, while they, in their turn, stared at her as sailors
only can stare, who are accustomed to strain their eyes
lookin' out a-head for reefs, shoals, or icebergs.   Is it
any wonder she got out of the cage and flew off south?
To my mind it was the most nateral thing in natur.

'That is the pictur of *the Quaker ashore*, but when I
saw him he was "*a Quaker afloat*," and that's a critter of
another colour, you may depend.   I'll tell you how I came
to see him on board of his ship.   It was just arter the vam-
oosing of his wife. The Governor of the State of Maine, who
is a great lumberer on the Kenebec, and employs a regiment
of loggers in the winter a cutten and a haulen of spars and
pine butts to the head-waters of that river, and also the St.
John's (indeed the Timber vote put him in as governor),

o

wrote.to me to buy him some very peeowerful heavy cattle for his business. Having heard that old Jacob Coffin had two yoke of splendiferous oxen, away I went to Nantucket, as fast as I could, for fear he would be off before I could get there. As soon as I arrived, I went straight to his "bungalow." It was kept by his sister, an old maid, who looked like a dried apple that had been halved, cored, pipt, and hung in the sun to dry, to make her keep for winter sauce; stew her in cider, and she might become soft, and with the aid of Muscovado sugar, might be made (if not sweet—for that was onpossible) tender enough for a tart. Lord, what a queer-lookin critter she was, skin and bone was never half so thin. She wore a square poke bonnet as big as a coalscuttle, to avoid the stares of admiring young Quakers, and to save her complexion as a nigger wench does a parasol to avoid bronzin her skin. It was ontied onder the chin, and set loose to keep off the dust. Her skin was the colour of a smoked, dried salmon, and her teeth, which stod out apart from each other, as if each was afraid the other would make love to it, resembled rusty nails sticking into a fence-post arter the rail had fallen off from decay. Her nose was pinched as tight as if it had just come out of a vice; her chin turned up short and economical, like a napkin to protect her dress while eating. The pupils of her eyes were large and of a gray colour, and had the power of contraction like those of a cat. Her upper lip was graced with a few black straggling hairs that described a curve, and then looked as if they had taken root again, like the branches of a Banyan tree. Her gown was tucked up on each side into a wisp, and run thro' her pocket-holes, disclosing a shining green shalloon petticoat. Her stockings were home-made, with open worked clocks, that displayed to admiring eyes the red morocco skin underneath; while her shoes, manufactured at Salem (what Quakeress would wear one that warn't made there?), fitted tight, and had high heels (all small women wear them—they put them up higher in the world). Her breast was covered with transparent starched muslin, thro' which you could see a mahogany-coloured flat chest—she was a caution to a scarecrow, I tell you. Thinks I, "old gall, if you would take off your ongainly bonnet and stick it under your gown behind for a bustle, or stiffen out your petticoats like a Christian, or put on half a dozen of 'em, as the French galls to Canada do, it would improve everything but your mug most uncommonly, for now you look for all the world like a pair of kitchen tongs, all legs and no body, and a head that is as round as a cannon-ball." "How are you, aunty?" sais I. "I am not thy aunt," she said, "what does thee mean?" "It's merely a word of conciliation," sais I, "it's a way I have; I always use kind words to every one." "Thee had better use words of truth," she replied. There was no danger of any fellow running off with her to New Orleans, I tell you, for old Jacob, like many other fools, had run from one extreme to another. While I was a thinkin this intarnally, she began to talk to herself aloud—"What dirty people Jacob brings here," she said, "before he goes to sea—what a mess the house is in! it will take a week to clean it up and make it look tidy again: I must call the maiden Ruth, to set things to rights;" and she screamed out at the tip eend of her voice, "Ruth-ee — Ruth-ee-ee,"—in one long-continued yell, like that of a hyæna. Gracious! it rang in my ears for a week. Then she seized a broom and leaned on it as she stood in the middle of the sanded floor, which was covered with the eends of cigars, tobacco, broken pipes, and all sorts of nasty things, for she had no idee of defilin' her bettermost room, with its boughten carpets, by lettin' common folks into it. She was a parfect picture, I assure you, as she stood there on the centre of the room a restin' on her broom. "What may thy business be, friend?" she said. "I am not a friend," sais I, "but a stranger; thee had better use words of truth," giving her back her own imperance. "Well, stranger," then she said, not colouring up, for her natural complexion was deeper than blushes or blood rushes, "what may thy business be?" "To see the man the world calls Jacob Coffin," sais I. "Then thee had better make haste," she replied, "for he is going to sea, and is getting up his sails now. Look out of the window, and thee will see the ship." With that she began in an all-fired hurry to sweep away like mad, and she raised such a cloud of dust it was a caution to a whirlwind—it nearly choked me; so I walked up to her to shake hands and bid good by, but the dust got into my eyes and nose, and I sneezed like a buffalo in a driftin' sand. It was a rael snorter, I tell you. Lord! it blew her great dingy bonnet right slap off her head, loosened her hair (which was only twisted up and fastened with a comb), and let it down on her shoulders, like the mane of a wild Pampas horse. It nearly threw her over, for she staggered back till the wall fetched her up, and there she stood and glared at me like a tiger; but she was clear grit and no mistake; she never said a word, but bit in her breath and choked her temper down, and she didn't swear, tho' she looked uncommonly like doing so, and no mortal man will ever make me believe, when she was alone with her Quaker house-help, that she didn't let the steam off with a rush—at last, she called out again to the maiden, "Ruth-ee, Ruth-ee-ee." Her voice was as shrill as a railway whistle—it fairly pierced the drum of my ears. I couldn't stand it twice, so I cut stick and off hot foot for the harbour. She was in a blessed humour, I tell you, and if Ruth hadn't a tempestical time of it that day, then there are no snakes in Varginy. When I reached the harbour, I got a boat and pushed off for the whaler "Quahog," the anchor of which they were just heaving up. When I went below into the cabin, there was Jacob, the very pictur of Christian meekness, forgiveness, and resignation, a writing a letter for the crew of a shore-boat to take back with them. When he had written it, he turns to me and says, "Well, friend Peabody, what may thy business be?—be quick, for we are just off." So I ups and tells him I wanted his big black yoke of oxen, and the speckled pair also, and asked him the price. "Two hundred and fifty dollars a yoke," sais he, "thee can't ditto them nowhere in all the United States, for beauty, size, weight, and honest draught." "I can't give it," I replied. "No harm done," sais he ; and while we were chaffering he peels off his white choker and replaces it with a coarse yarn comforter, doffs his broad-brim and puts on a torpolin nor'-wester ; his drab vest and slips on a calf-skin waistcoat dressed with the hair on ; his straight-collared, cut-away drab coat, with large buttons, and mounts a heavy blue pea-jacket. It must have been made, I guess, by a Chinese tailor, for, tho' bran new, it had a large patch of the same cloth on each elbow ; then he slips off his olive-coloured breeches, and draws on a thick coarse pilot pair of trousers, and over them stout and monstrous heavy fisherman's boots. "Come, be quick," said he, "what will thee give for the cattle?" "Two hundred and twenty-five dollars a yoke," sais I, "and it's the final bid, and they are to be paid for on your return." "Done," said he, "write out the order for delivery, and I'll sign it." Well, then he onlocks a great sea-chest, and takes out a pair of " knuckle-dusters " and puts them on to his sledge-hammer fists——'

'What are they, Mr. Peabody?' I inquired, 'for in all my travels I never saw or heard of such gloves as those.'

'Why,' said Peabody, 'they are jointed iron things that strap on to the back of the hands, and extend over the knuckles, having knobby projections on them. Inside they are lined with leather to save your own bones when you strike with them. They are awful persuaders, I tell you, and leave your brand wherever you strike—skin, flesh, and cheek-bone give way before them, as if they were mashed by a hammer. Well, when he had fitted on those black kids, and buckled on a waist-belt, there he stood lookin' a plaguy sight more like a pirate than a Quaker, I tell you. Then he roared out in a voice of thunder—"Steward! steward!—pass the word forward there for the steward." Presently, in runs the critter, like a dog that's whistled for, answerin' all the way as he came—"Ay, ay, sir." "You darned lubberly rascal," said old Jacob, "what's the reason you ain't making ready for·my breakfast?" The fellow was dumbfounded and awfully taken aback, like a vessel under full sail when the wind shifts round on a sudden, and she is thinking of going down stern foremost. He was fairly on-fackilized; he couldn't believe in the transmogrification he saw, of the sleek, composed, neat-dressed, smooth-faced, *shore-going Quaker*, into the slaver-like captain that stood before him, dressed as a " *Quaker afloat.*" If he couldn't trust his eyes neither could he believe his ears, when he heard the good man swear. He stood starin' like a stuck pig, with his mouth wide open. "Do you hear me," said Jacob, in a voice that must have reached his sister's ears ashore, and he stamped on the cabin floor with his hob-nailed boot, in a way that you could see the print of it as plain as a wood-cut. "Friend," said he, a imitatin of himself when ashore, and lowerin' his tone, as he must have done when courtin', "let me wake thee up, for verily thee is asleep," and he hit him a blow with his knuckle-dusters under the ear that not only knocked him down, but made him turn a somerset; and as he threw up his legs in going over he fetched him a kick with the toe of his heavy boot that was enough to crush his crupper bone. "Cuss your ugly pictur," he said, "I'll teach you how to wake snakes and walk chalks, I know, before our voyage is ended." You may depend the steward didn't remain to stare a second time, but puttin' one hand where he got the blow, and the other where he got the kick, he absquotulated in no time, singing out as he mounted the steps, pen and ink, like a dog that's hit with a stone. "What do you think of that, old hoss?" said he, addressin' me. "I think the spirit moved you that time, and no mistake," sais I, "but it was the spirit of the devil; you are the first swearing Quaker I ever saw, and I hope I shall never set eyes upon another. Creation, man, what made you act arter that fashion, to that poor inoffensive crittur? If I was to take my davy of what I have seen when I went ashore, no livin' soul would believe me." "Friend Peabody," said he, "did thee ever see a ' *Quaker afloat* ' before?" "Never," said I. "So I thought, or thee would not be surprised." "Friend," he replied, "our sect is a religious denomination." "So I should think," said I; but he went on, "a meek, peaceable, passive, resistant, long-suffering people." "If that steward," sais I, "goes to Baffin's Bay along with you, he'll beat any Quaker in all creation in long suffering, and no mistake." He smiled, but went on, "It is a sect that pertaineth to the land and not to the sea. A ' friend ' is no more fit to command a ship than a bishop.

Both are out of place afloat. Lawn sleeves would first get covered with tar, and then be blown into ribbons, and a broad-brimmed hat would fly overboard in no time. When afloat we must dispense with our land-tacks, and lay aside our distinctive dress. We are among a different race from those who inhabit cities or till the land. We live amidst perils and storms, and reefs and breakers. A minute sometimes saves a ship or wrecks her. We have no time for circumlocution, and thee-ing and thou-ing. We must speak short, quick, and commanding, and use words sailors do, provided they are not profane. Without doing this no one would obey me. I never swear." " Why what onder the sun are you a-talking of, man?" sais I, " didn't you call that steward a damned lubberly rascal?" "Never," he replied; "that is an unbecoming word, if not a wicked one. I called him a darned lubber, which is a very different thing, and has a very different meaning. Nor do I ever strike a man; it's against my principles." "Well, if that don't cap the sheaf," sais I, "it's a pity that's all. Why, man alive, didn't you first knock that poor steward down, head over heels, and then kick him like a wicked hoss when he is just shod." "No," he said; "I only woke him up with a push, and shoved him forward, and what you call a kick was merely intended to lift him up on his feet. But come, have you written that delivery order yet?" "Yes," sais I; "'tis done, put your signature to it." Well, secin' what an old cantin scoundrel he was, I thought I'd take a rise out of him for fun, so I worded the delivery order thus—" Friend Peabody having settled with me for the black and speckled yoke of oxen, this is to authorize him to take them into his possession." He run his eye over the paper hastily and then signed it, and then said, "If thee don't want to go to Baffin's Bay with me, bundle up the companion ladder like wink, and be off, for we are onder weigh." So I ups quick stick, and he comes stumping arter me with his heavy boots, clamp, clamp, as heavy as a string of loaded jack-asses, over a plank bridge, make all shake agin. As I came near the side of the ship where the man-ropes were, he gave me a blow on the back (which he called a shove) that nearly dislocated my shoulder, and all but sent me head-first into the boat. Fortunately, the vessel was hove to for me by the mate, who was a towny of mine, or my boat would have been swamped, for there was a fresh breeze a-going at the time. "Fare thee well, friend," said he, as he leaned over the taffrel rail. "Peace be with thee, Jacob," said I, for my dander was up; "I hope I may never see your cantin', cheatin', hypocritical, lyin' face agin. Whether bears eat bears or not, I don't know, but, if they do, I hope a grizzly will chaw you up some fine morning for breakfast as a caution to sinners; but if you ever return, there is one thing I don't owe you, and one thing I do." "What may they be?" said he, in his blandest voice, that was so mild it would entice a fox into a trap amost. "First," sais I, "I don't owe you for the oxen, for the delivery order contains a receipt; 2ndly, I do owe you a quiltin, and I am the boy that's able to give it to you, too, that's a fact; if I don't dust your drabs for you, if ever I come across you, then my name ain't Peabody, that's all." Well if he didn't shake his knuckle-dusters at me, and swear, then I don't know what profanity is. As I pulled away from the ship, he turned round and gave orders to square the yards, and I saw him push two of the men to hurry them on, and it's very odd, both on 'em fell flat on their faces on the deck, and had to pick themselves up before they could go ahead; and that's the man you describe

o 3

" as more honest, honourable, and pious, than any Quaker you ever saw." '

'And pray,' said the Senator, ' what has this long digression to do with the subject we were talking of?'

'Why,' replied the other, ' this long lockrum was occasioned by your interruptin' and contradictin' me. You ought to know by this time—for you are a man of experience—that stopping a fellow in his observations is sure to lengthen his speech, argument, story, or whatever you call it. If you was to stop a preacher that way, he'd just take a fresh departure, square the yards, go off before the wind, and you wouldn't get out of the meetin'-house before dark. You was sayin' one year was like another in a general way, and I was showin' you that folks here thought they were going to the bad all the time, while we only travelled that road once in four years. I had got down as far as Bright, and I said a Quaker like him who had to bite in his breath, and choke down his anger, wasn't the best politician in the world, for he couldn't let off the steam by swearin. Well, *that's* the point at which you stopped me, and got that long rambling story for your pains. Now, I'll begin where I left off; but take warning,—don't stop me agin unless you want to be talked dead. Bright wants to give the poor all the right to vote, and the rich all the right to pay the taxes; and it is a prettier scheme than he is aware of. The experiment is in operation at New York at this very moment. The Irish and foreign emigrants have the majority in a general way, and unite in a body as one man. They vote the money, and the wealthy citizens have to pay it; and where does it all go? Why, in jobs. The cash is raised, but there is nothing to show for the expenditure. The taxes are fearful: if you was to add up the total amount of all the imposts, the result would astonish you, I can tell you.

And if Bright was settled there, he would, like an apprentice in a pastrycook's shop, soon get tired of the sweets of his own pet scheme—that's a fact. In addition to all this is the indirect tax levied at the Custom House. Our National Income, Senator, you know well enough, sounds small, and the expenditure economical, because we merely take the Federal Government account, and salaries of public officers which look as cheap as bull beef at one cent a pound; but add to that the taxes of all the separate states and corporations, and you will find it as costly a government as there is in the world. Bright takes the superficial view that all people do who don't understand the country. They pick out the cheap parts, compare them with similar ones in Europe, and say that is a sample of the whole. Well, timid politicians here that don't know much more than he does, are frightened to death at him, and Lord John Russell, and others. I say, give em' rope enough and they will hang themselves. Reform, as far as I can see, is the political bunkum of the House of Commons: nobody takes any interest in it but the members themselves. Wherever you go, people say the country is going to the devil. Well I have heard that cry to home long before I saw England, and yet we go ahead, and England goes ahead in spite of such critters; we can't help prosperin. The only difference between the two countries is, as I have said, people in England think they are going to the bad all the time, we only think so once in four years. I shall never forget what Uncle Peleg said to me once:—"Neph," said he, "I used to take great interest in politics once, but I have given it up now. It don't matter a cent I see, who is up, or who is down; there ain't much to choose among our political parties; pelf, pickings, and patronage, salaries and offices, is all either of them care for.

When Jefferson was elected, sais I to myself, the country is ruinated : here is a freethinker, a slave-holder, and a southerner, who has beat John Adams, the New England candidate ; he will spread infidelity through the land, he will sap the morals of our youth, he'll join in European wars, he will involve us with France, the British will slip in, conquer us again, and enslave us once more as colonists ; we are done for, we are up a tree, our republican flint is fixed, we shall be strangled in the cradle as an infant nation, and the crowner will find a verdict, 'died by the hands of Thomas Jefferson.' I sat up late that night at Springfield, with some patriots and heroes of Bunker's Hill, and the battle of Mud Creek, to hear the result of the election for President, for we were all for John Adams. It was eleven o'clock at night when the word came ; we were all excited, drinking success to Adams, and confusion to Jefferson, glory to the nation, prosperity to religion, perdition to freethinkers, infidels, and southern candidates, with other patriotic toasts, when in rushed Deacon Properjohn, his eyes starein six ways for Sunday, his hair blowin about like a head of broom corn, and his breath a'most gone. 'Hullo,' says I, 'Deacon, what is the matter of you ? who is dead, and what is to pay now ?' 'Why,' sais he, striking the table with his fist a blow that made all the glasses jingle again, 'I'll be darned if that old unbelievin sinner Jefferson hain't beat Adams by a majority of one,' and he burst out into tears. 'Our great nation is ruinated, swamped, foundered, and done for, for ever——' There wasn't a word spoke for the matter of two minutes, we were so flabbergasted ; at last we all gave lip together : 'Oh, gracious,' sais one, 'better we had never fought and bled.' 'Better,' sais another, 'if we had never resisted the British ; only think of that onprincipled man being elected over such a true patriot as Adams;' and then we all agreed the country was undone for ever. Then we consoled ourselves with drinking perdition to Jefferson, and set up a howl in chorus over the old Bay State, that took the lead, and bore the brunt of the revolution, bein chizelled out of its president this way. At last I fainted, as if I had been knocked down, was carried home by four men, and put to bed." "Are you sure you wasn't drunk, uncle?" sais I. "Quite certain," he said; "I might have been overtaken, I won't say I wasn't overcome like, for a very little will do that, you know, when you are excited, but I am sure I wasn't sewed up, for I remember everything that happened. When they brought me home, sais your Aunt Nabby to me, 'Peleg,' says she, 'what on airth is the matter; have you been runned over?' 'No,' sais I. 'Have you had a fall, dear?' 'No, it ain't that.' 'Then what is it, love?' 'The nation is ruinated, Jeff—Jeff—Jefferson is elected, and the rep—rep—republic has gone to the dev—vil.' 'Oh, I see,' said she, 'you are in a fair way to go to him yourself, acting in that prepostulous manner. Who cares whether Jefferson is elected or not?' she continued, 'I am sure I don't; what is it to the like of us? You are intosticated, Peleg, as sure as the world.' 'No I ain't,' sais I; 'it's only grief, Nabby dear, my heart is broke.' 'Is that all, you goney?' says she, 'it's lucky your precious neck ain't broke;' and she called the nigger helps, and hauled me off to bed, and the way she tumbled me in wasn't the way she put up her best chiney tea set, I can tell you. Oh, I couldn't have been drunk, nephy, for I recollected every word that passed. Well, next morning I woke up, none of the earliest I can tell you, with a thunderin headache, and my heart een a'most broke. I called, and called ever so loud, before I could make any one hear me. At last up

came your aunt, lookin as fierce as a she-cat facin a dog.
'What's all that noise?' says I.   'The girls at their
spinnin wheels,' said she.   'Stop them,' sais I, 'it's no
use now; Jefferson is elected, and the country is ruinated.'   Gracious, how her eyes flashed at that; she
stooped down, seized the bed-clothes just under my chin,
dragged them right off, and threw them all into the
corner of the room.   'Now get up this instant minute,
and go and look after the spring-work, or we will be
ruined in airnest.'   'It's no use,' said I, 'if Adams had
got in, the country would have been saved.   He was the
father of the country; but Jefferson!   Oh dear, the jig
is up now.   You thought I was drunk last night, but I
wasn't; and you see I am not tipsy now.   I tell you we
are done for.'   Well, she altered her course, and sat
down on the bed alongside of me, and said, 'Dear Peleg,
if you love me, don't talk nonsense.   Let us reason it
out.'   (And this, I think, Ephe, you must have found
out, that women, though they like to sail before the wind,
know how to tack too, when it's a-head.)   'Now,' sais she,
'Peleg, dear, suppose John Adams, the mean, stingy,
close-fisted, cunning old lawyer had got in—you know
you pay him fifteen cents a ton for the granite you take
to Boston out of his quarry, at Quinsey; suppose you went
to him, and said, President, I did my possibles at your
election for you, will you let me have it for twelve
cents?'   'No; I don't think he would,' said I.   'Well,
you owe neighbour Burford two hundred dollars, sposin
you went to Adams, and told him all your claims, and
asked him to lend you that amount to prevent Burford
suing you, would he lend it to you?'   'No; I don't think
he would, unless I gave him a mortgage, and paid ever
so much expenses.'   'Well, then, you see, *he* would do
you no good.   Now, Jefferson is in, and I won't gainsay

you about his character ; for though he talks liberal about slaves, it's well known he has sold some of his own half-caste children. Captain Card, of Red Bank, who goes every year to Charlestown, Virginia, with a cargo of onions, hams, and coffins, sais it's the common talk there.' 'Ain't that enough to ruin the risin generation?' sais I. 'No,' says she, 'but to ruin his own character. Well, now that he is in, what harm is he a-going to do to hurt you? Won't the corn ripen as usual?' 'Well, I suppose it will, if the airly frost don't catch it.' 'Won't the cows give milk, and the sheep wool for shearing, as they used to did?' 'Well, I can't deny that.' 'And won't the colts grow up fit for market as before? for every year we get more and more for our young horses.' 'Well, I won't contradict you.' 'Won't our children grow up as fast?' 'Ah, there,' I said, 'is the rub; they grow too fast now; nine children in twelve years, as we have'——I couldn't finish the sentence, she gave it me first on one cheek, and then on the other, like wink, and then she went to the wash-stand, got hold of the ewer, swashed the whole of the water into my face, and cut off out of the room, leaving me shivering and shaking, like a feller in the ague. Well, it was the month of March, which you know in New England don't give the sun-stroke; the bedclothes had been off for some time, and then came this cold bath, so I ups, dresses, and outs in no time. When I came down stairs, she was waitin for me in the entry. 'Peleg, dear,' said she, 'I want to say a word to you, come into this room; here is amost a capital breakfast for you, tea, coffee, smoked salmon, crumpets, doughnuts, preserved quinces, done by my own hands, and everything you used to like. There is one little favour, dear' (and she puts her arms round my neck, and kissed me; and who in the world can stand that, for I never could.) 'Granted,' said I, 'before you name it. What is it?' 'Never bother your head about elections; a vote is a curse to a man; it involves him in politics, excites him, raises a bushel of enemies, and not one friend for him, and makes him look tipsy, *as you did last night,* though you warn't the least in liquor.' 'I thank you for that, Nabby,' sais I, 'for I wasn't, I do assure you.' 'Of course not,' she said; 'I see I was to blame in thinking you was. Let us mind our own business, and let others mind theirn. Whoever hoes his own row, gets the most corn.' 'I will,' sais I; 'you will never hear me talk politics agin as long as I live, I can tell you.' 'Ah,' said she, 'what a sensible man you are, Peleg! your judgment is so good, you are so open to conviction, only place a thing before you.' 'As pretty as you, Nabby,' sais I, 'and it's all right.' Well, we had a sort of courtin breakfast that mornin, and parted on excellent terms. I was the most sensible man in all creation, and she the loveliest; and instead of fancying the country was going to the devil, we pitched both old Jefferson and old Adams to him. Since that, I have taken my wife's advice, and attended to my own affairs, instead of those of the nation. I observe that bankers, lawyers, merchants, and farmers grow rich; but that politicians are like carrion birds, always poor, croaking, and hungry, and not over particular as to the flavour of their food, or how they obtain it. If Jefferson had, arter our independence, taken to cultivatin the estate his father left him, he wouldn't have had in his old age to sell it, by a rascally lottery, as he did."'

'Ahem,' said the Senator, who took advantage of the momentary pause in this unconscionable digression to resume the conversation which the other had diverted. 'Yes, one year is pretty much like another, but the festivities of Christmas are in such close proximity to those of the new year, that the moral and religious reflections to which the period ought to give rise are in a great measure if not wholly overlooked. It is a serious thing to think that we are one entire year nearer the grave than we were on that day twelvemonths, and to reflect that the self-examination so appropriate to the occasion is postponed to what we are pleased to call a more fitting occasion.'

'Is Christmas kept with you as it is with us in England?' I inquired.

'Yes, I should say it was,' he replied; 'but in a greater variety of ways, according to the customs of the fatherland of the original emigrants. In a country like ours, and that of British America, where he who tills the soil owns it, and where industry and economy always insure abundance, you may well 'suppose that there are many, very many family reunions at Christmas, in which peace and plenty are enjoyed, and acknowledged by joyful and thankful hearts.'

'That's your experience, is it?' said Mr. Peabody.

'It is,' said Mr. Boodle.

'Well, then, it ain't mine,' rejoined the other. 'Of all the uncomfortable things in this world, an assembly of brothers and sisters, and uncles and aunts, and imps of children is the worst. They snarl like the deuce ; some is a little better off than others, and somehow that has a tendency to raise the chin, and make the upper lip stiff ; some is a little wus off, and then like soil that is worn out and poor, up springs the worst weed in the world ; some call it envy, and some jealousy, but I call it *devil weed*. Then some are pets of the old folks, and when they talk it into them, the others wink and nod at each other, as much as to say, " do you see *that ;* that's the way Tom got the yoke of oxen last fall, and Sally the side-saddle hoss." And then every one's child is handsomer or bigger than the other's baby, and it's hardly possible to award the prize to the one that cries and scratches the most. Save me from family parties; nothen in nature quals them. Give me the meetin where nobody cares a snap of a finger for nobody in particular, and has no interest but in a good feed, a good song, a good smoke, and chain-lightning to top it all off with.

'I never saw but one good family party in my life, or one in which all was pleased, and all kissed and shook hands together. It was at the readen arter old Deacon Tite's funeral. He was my uncle, so I attended to hear the will out of curiosity, to see what my mother was to get, though we all knew pretty well, for he had often said he would divide even among his sisters for he had no children. But he cut up better nor anybody could have guessed; he was a hundred thousand dollars richer than he was valued at, and he divided that like the rest, with some few little bequests. He gave my brother, Pete, his gold watch, and he left me his blessing; and do you know I offered to swap that with Pete for his watch, but the mean, stingy crittur refused, unless I gave a hundred dollars boot, which was more than the turnip was worth. I lost my bequest by giving my uncle lip one day. I told him he was Tite by name, and tight by natur, so I didn't expect nothen, and I wasn't disappointed. Oh, but didn't the rest all sing his praises, and then sing each other's praises — wern't they happy, that's all. We got into the cellar, got at his No. 1 cider, his old pine-apple rum, his port, that was in such earthy, spider-webby, dirty old bottles, you'd have thought it was dug out of the grave of Lisbon, when the earthquake filled it all of a sudden, old Madeira, bottled afore the Revolution, and old sherry that tasted nice-nasty of the goat-skins it was fetched to

market in, and then put into magnums. Creation! what
a thanksgiving-day we made of it! We cracked nuts,
cracked jokes, kissed our pretty cousins, told old stories,
and invented new ones. That was a happy day, I tell
you, and the only happy family party I ever witnessed.
But, mind you, it only lasted one day. The next mornin
the plate was to be divided, and aunt's trinkets, beads,
corals and pearls, bracelets and necklaces, diamond ear-
rings, and what not. So arter breakfast they was exhibited on the table. Then came the scrabble. Lord!
the women were a caution to hungry dogs with whelps.
The way they grabbled, and screamed, and yelled, and
talked, all at once, was astonishin. Mother was sittin in
the corner crying her heart out. Sais she, " I can prove,
Mr. Tite gave me that beautiful silver tea-urn, but I don't
claim it; I only want to have it in my share, for I have
a particular regard for it." " I'll get it for you," says
I. So I walks up to the table where they was all talkin
at the top eend of their voices, and I let off the Indian
warwhoop in grand style. First they all shrieked, and
then for a minute there was silence ; and sais I, " Mother
is it this old tea-urn you wanted?" " Yes," sais she, " it
is." "Then here it is," sais I, "as the eldest, you have
the first choice." She got it, and walked off with it,
leaving all the rest hard at it. The division of them
personal articles made enemies of all the relations ever
after! No, said he, rising, 'none of your family parties
for me; connexions at best are poor friends, and commonly bitter enemies. If you want nothing, go to them,
and you are sure to get it; if you are in want of any
assistance, go to a stranger-friend you have *made for
yourself*, and that's the boy that has a heart and a hand
for you. And now I will leave Senator and you to finish

your cigars; and as mine is out, and my whisky, too, by
your leave I'll turn in; so good night.'

'That is one of the oddest fellows I ever knew,' said
the Senator; 'but there is more in him than you would
suppose from his appearance or conversation.   He is
remarkable for his strong common sense and quickness of
perception.   But at times his interruptions annoy me; he
seems to take a pleasure in diverting the conversation you
are engaged in to some other topic, either by telling you
a story in illustration of, or opposition to, your views, or
by taking upon himself to converse upon some totally
different topic.   One can scarcely believe that a trite
observation, such as I made to you, about one year being
very like its predecessor, could by any possibility have
afforded him a peg upon which to hang all the stories with
which he has favoured us to-night.   I should have liked
to answer your inquiries fully, and to have given you a
description of the various ways in which Christmas is kept
in America.   On some future occasion I will do so; but
now the evening is so far advanced I believe I must follow
Mr. Peabody's example this once, at least, and retire.
Good night, and a happy Christmas to you wherever you
pass it.'

No. XI.

COLONIAL AND MATRIMONIAL ALLIANCES.

THE following day I strolled with my American friends
into the Park, through the narrow, dingy, and unseemly
entrance from Spring Gardens. A few minutes' walk
brought us in front of the Horse Guards, where we
paused for a while to witness a military review. We then
proceeded to the Serpentine, where we watched the gay
and fashionable throng, that, attracted by the crowd of
skaters, increased the number and brilliancy of the groups
that they themselves came to admire.

'The more I see of this great capital,' observed the
Senator, 'the more astonished I am at its population and
wealth. Places of public resort, of every description, are
thronged with people, and the crowds that frequent and
fill them do not perceptibly diminish the multitudes that
are usually seen in the fashionable streets or business
thoroughfares. The number of private carriages abroad,
during a fine day in the season, is almost incredible.
There are everywhere evidences of great opulence in this
metropolis that attract and astonish a stranger. The city
appears to him like a large estuary, receiving tributary
streams of wealth from all parts of the globe, and dis-
charging an increasing flood of riches in return; the
region between that and Bond-street as the emporium of

everything that is costly and rare, and the West End as
the stately abode of people of rank and fortune. All this
is perceptible at a glance, and a cursory survey fills his
mind with astonishment, but on closer inspection he finds
that he has seen only the surface of things.   As he
pursues his investigations, he learns that the city is a vast
warehouse for the supply of the whole world ; that its
merchants own half the public stock of every civilized
nation ; that there are docks and depositories underneath
the surface, containing untold and inconceivable wealth ;
and that the shop windows in the streets of fashionable
resort, though they glitter with gold and silver, or are
decked with silks, satins, laces, shawls, and the choicest and
most expensive merchandise, convey but a very inadequate
idea of the hoards that are necessarily packed into the
smallest possible space, and stored away in the lofts above,
or the vaults beneath. Pursuing his inquiries in the West,
he finds that the stately mansions he beholds there are the
mere town residences, during " the season," of a class
who have enormous estates in the country, with princely
palaces, castles, and halls, and that there are amongst them
one thousand individuals, whose united property would
more than extinguish the national debt.   Such is the
London, of which he has read and heard so much, the
centre of the whole commercial world, the exchange
where potentates negotiate loans for the purposes of war
or peace, the seat of the arts and sciences, and the source
of all the civilization and freedom that is to be found
among the nations of the earth.   But great, and rich, and
powerful as it is, it does not stand in the same relation to
England, as Paris does to France ; it is independent, but
not omnipotent ; there are other towns only second to it
in population and capital, such as Manchester, Liverpool,
Birmingham, Glasgow, and others, of which the wealth is

almost fabulous. Well may an Englishman be proud of his country. In every quarter of the globe, he finds that it is stamping the impress of its language, its institutions, and its liberty. You and I, who have travelled so far, and seen so much, have beheld yonder British soldier at Gibraltar, Malta, and Corfu, at the Cape, the ports of the East Indies, Hong Kong, Australia, and New Zealand, in the West Indies, and Newfoundland, Halifax, Quebec, and the shores of the Pacific. Great Britain fills but a small place on the map, but owns and occupies a large portion of the globe. Her first attempts at colonization, like those of other European powers, were not very successful, but the loss of the old provinces, that now constitute the United States, has taught her wisdom. She has at last learned that the true art of governing her distant possessions consists in imparting to the people that freedom which she herself enjoys, and in seeking remuneration for her outlay, not by monopolizing their commerce, but by enlarging it; not in compelling them to seek their supplies at her hands, but in aiding them to become opulent and profitable customers. She has discovered that affection and interest are stronger and more enduring ties, than those imposed by coercion; that there are in reality no conflicting interests between herself and her dependencies, and that the happiness and prosperity of both are best promoted and secured by as much mutual independence of action as is compatible with the undisputed and indispensable rights of each, and the due relation of one part of the empire to the other, and to the whole.'

'Do you not suppose,' I said, ' that in process of time, as our colonies become more populous and more wealthy, they will follow the order of nature, grow self-reliant, and become distinct and independent nations?'

'Some,' he replied, 'undoubtedly will, but there are others, that by judicious arrangements, may probably remain part and parcel of the Empire.   There is a vast difference between the colonies in the East, and those in the West.   The former are held by a very fragile tenure, and it is difficult to say how soon they may be severed from British control.   Australia perhaps will at no very distant period, claim its independence, and if the demand be made with unanimity, and appears to be the " well understood wish of the people," it will doubtless be conceded to them.   It is obviously neither the interest nor the wish of this country to compel a reluctant obedience, even if it possesses the power, which is more than doubtful.   The emigrant, when he leaves Great Britain for Australia, leaves it for ever.   In becoming a colonist he ceases to be an Englishman ; he voluntarily casts his lot in another hemisphere, and severs the ties, social and national, that bind him to his own.   While all is strange about him a feeling of loneliness and exile may oppress him, and cause him to cast a longing lingering look towards the land he has left.   During this state of mind, he finds relief in transmitting to his friends and relatives tidings of himself, and asking the consolation of letters in return.   By degrees the correspondence slackens, and finally ceases altogether ; new associates supply the place of his early friends ; and as imagination and hope are stronger than memory, the Old World soon becomes, as it were, a dream in the New. The interminable ocean is a barrier to the emigrant's return ; and although that is not insuperable in itself, the great expense of a double voyage precludes his entertaining the idea of ever revisiting his native land.   Where everything is new, the old is forgotten as soon as laid aside ; a change of climate, of habits, of wants, and of employments, requires him to accommodate himself to his altered circumstances; and the present occupies his thoughts to the exclusion of the past. Those among whom his lot is cast, have made the country what it is, and claim it as their own. He is among them, and of them; he is an Australian in thought, in word, and in deed. The history of his country is soon learned, for it has started into existence in his own lifetime. Although precocious, it has not outgrown its strength, and it gives promise of a still more rapid development. All that he beholds around him is at once the effect and cause of progress, and the dull monotony of the Old World contrasts strangely with the excitement of the New. Where everything is to be planned, adopted, and executed, the energies of all are put into requisition, and industry and ordinary frugality promise profit as well as remuneration. The land of his adoption has a future, the early dawn of which discloses nationality and greatness. It is self-supporting, and is not dependent upon the mother country; it has other markets besides those of Great Britain; it possesses a continental, a colonial, and a foreign trade of its own, and its commerce is already extending to the shores of the Pacific. It is the England of the East. The hostile attitude lately assumed by France has already raised the question of independence among the settlers, which is still engrossing public attention. " Ought we," they say, " to be involved in European wars, in which we have no direct interest, which are undertaken on grounds in which we have no concern, and are conducted and terminated without our assent. We are told that we must provide for our own defences. If we provoke attack, it is reasonable we should be prepared to repel it; but if the quarrel is between others, those who involve us in war, should, in common justice, shield us from its ravages. We

P

have everything to lose, and nothing to gain, by hostilities. If England is unable to provide suitable coast defences for herself, how can we do so with a far greater extent of seaboard, with a sparse population, and without an army or navy of our own? The sovereignty is nominal, the danger real. Our independence can do England no harm, because in proportion to our means, we shall always be among her best customers, while it will save our shipping from seizure, our seaport towns from bombardment, and our colonial and foreign trade from annihilation. We are too far removed from you to give assistance, or receive protection. The policy of the United States is not to intermeddle in European politics, a similarity of condition indicates the propriety of a like abstinence on our part.

'Such, my dear sir, I know to be the language of the Australians, and such, I foresee, will be the ultimate result. New Zealand is similarly situated. As respects the East Indian provinces, you have recently very nearly lost them by the rebellion of the natives. If France or Russia should be at war with you, either of them is in a condition to fan the smouldering embers of discontent into another outbreak, and the result would, doubtless, be most disastrous. The North American colonies are very differently situated in every respect; they may be damaged by either of those great powers, and especially by the former, but they can never be conquered. Unlike Australia, they have a vast inhabited back country, into which an enemy cannot penetrate, and they are only assailable in a few maritime towns, which constitute but a small part of their wealth, and contain a still smaller portion of their population. They are settled by a brave, intelligent, loyal, and above all, a homogeneous race, not very powerful for aggression, but fully competent, with very slight assistance to defend themselves;

and be assured, *we* should never permit any other European nation but Great Britain to hold them. It is a settled principle with us, that no portion of our continent shall ever again be subject to any foreign power. So long as the connexion lasts with England we shall respect it, and if they should become independent, we shall recognise the Government *de facto*, and welcome it into the family of American nations. With judicious management, I can see no reason why they should ever be severed from the parent country. Now, the inhabitants of Australia are emigrants, and not natives; they are a new people, suddenly elevated into wealth and political importance, exercising the novel powers of self-government, somewhat intoxicated with their great prosperity, and like all *novi homines* similarly situated, they exhibit no little self-sufficiency. They are impatient of control or interference, and can but ill brook the delay that necessarily arises in their official correspondence with the Imperial Government, from the immense distance it has to traverse before it reaches its destination. They think, and with some truth, that their condition is not understood, or their value duly appreciated; and that the treatment they receive from the Downing-street officials is neither conciliatory nor judicious. They feel that they can stand alone, and their language indicates a desire to try the experiment.

'The great bulk of the North American population, on the contrary, is of native growth,—the people have been born under the form of Government they now enjoy, and have practically known no other. They retained their loyalty during the trying period of our Revolution, and defended themselves with great gallantry during the war of 1812, when their country was invaded by our troops. Steam has so abridged the time formerly oc-

P 2

cupied by a passage across the Atlantic, that their principal men continually pass and repass between their respective colonies and Great Britain, and feel as if they constituted part of the same population. Daily packets have so facilitated correspondence, that three weeks now suffice for the transmission of letters and replies, while the telegraphic wire will soon place the people on both sides of the Atlantic within speaking distance. A passage from Quebec, or Halifax, to England, can now be effected in as short a space of time as was occupied, thirty years ago in a journey from the west coast of Ireland to London; and it is confidently predicted that the voyage will soon be accomplished in five days. Distance, therefore, constitutes no obstacle to a continuance of the union, nor do the wishes or interests of the people tend to a severance. It is a startling and extraordinary circumstance (but I am firmly convinced of the fact), that the colonists are more desirous than the Whig Government, for a continuance of the union. It has been the practice of that party, for the last fifty years, to undervalue the importance of their colonies, to regard them as incumbrances, to predict their inevitable tendency to become independent, and to use them, while the connexion continues, as a mere field for patronage for their dependents and supporters. Acting upon this conviction, they have been at no pains to conciliate the people, either by aiding them in their internal improvements, or admitting them to any share of the Imperial patronage, while they have carefully excluded them from any voice in that department which has the supervision of the vast colonial dependencies of the empire. This has been borne patiently with the hope that better counsels might ultimately prevail, but it will not be tolerated for ever. Political, like social alliances, can never be durable, when all the duties are on one side, and all the power and emoluments on the other.'

' With respect to the cumbrous and inefficient machinery of the Colonial Office,' I said, ' I entirely agree with you.   I have been in British America myself, and have heard the same complaints from leading men of all parties, in the several provinces.   They reprobate the constant change, as well as the uncertain attendance of the Minister, whose time is more occupied with the politics and interests of his party than the business of his own department, and whose authority is weakened and controlled by the action of the Chancellor of the Exchequer, the Board of Trade, and the Lords of the Treasury.   A friend of mine told me the other day, that a few years ago he came to this country to conclude some matters of great importance, that were in abeyance, and found, on his arrival, that the Secretary of State for the Colonies was attending a Congress at Vienna, and that after waiting some time, at great personal inconvenience and expense, he was compelled to return to America.   A second voyage to England, soon became indispensable, when after having made some progress in his negotiations, he learned with dismay that the Minister had retired from office, and the whole affair had to be commenced *de novo*.   Most men thus detained, have private or public duties at home that must necessarily be suspended during these interminable delays, and it is not unusual for a suitor to be compelled to leave the matter in an unfinished state, and re-cross the Atlantic.   The arrival of every steamer there, is anxiously watched, and at last his friends, or his agents, write to inform him that there is a change of Government and of policy, that it is difficult to say what views may be entertained by the new Secretary of State, but that before he can possibly decide, he must be informed of the facts of the case; that the ground must again be gone over, the same delays endured, and the same expense incurred as before. Nor is this all : they complain that, during the recess, they may call day after day in Downing-street, without being able to obtain an interview with the Chief. When he is inquired for, the answers vary, but are all to the same effect, " he is in the country, and not expected back till next week ;" or, " he is attending a Cabinet Council, and will leave town immediately afterwards ;" or, " he has not been at the office to-day." Nor is the applicant often more fortunate in obtaining an interview with the political Under Secretary. He, too, is frequently occupied elsewhere ; for instance, the former is now at his country residence in the north, and the latter is in Ireland.'

' But the clerks are there.'

' Yes, but clerks have no power, beyond that of receiving papers and transmitting replies ; and if they had, who would like to transact business with them ? Are the affairs of forty-three colonies of less importance than those of a private individual ; or are they governed by different rules ? What lawyer could retain his clients, if their interviews were restricted to his clerks ; or what medical man could maintain his practice, if his patients were referred to his apothecary ? A bank or a mercantile firm conducted in this manner, would soon become insolvent. The most irresponsible office in the kingdom, is that of a Colonial Minister. He makes no report to Parliament of his doings, and if he did, so intent are members on the business of their own party, or that of their constituents, that few would listen to it. His decisions are final in the distant parts of the empire ; for to whom can colonists appeal ? They have no representatives in the House of Commons whose duty it is to attend to their complaints, or promote their welfare ; and the public press, unless the grievance be most flagrant, is oc-

cupied with matter of greater interest to its readers. The
separation of a man and his wife in the Divorce Court,
will engross more attention than the severance of a colony,
and a police report, or an account of the Derby, appeal
more directly to the sympathies or pockets of the people,
than a squabble between a province and a Secretary of
State.'

'Yes,' said Mr. Peabody,—who had been silent for an
unusually long time, and who was evidently getting tired
of so serious a conversation,—' Yes, I guess the Derby is
more *racy*. Was you ever at the great American Circus
in Leicester square? 'cause if you were, you've seen Sam
Condon stand upon a pair of hosses, one foot on one, and
one foot on t'other, and drive two span of piebald cattle
before him, as easy as drinkin'. Well now, don't it look
as if it was a most wonerful feat? and don't people cheer
him and hurrah him as if he was taking the shine out of
all creation? Well, it's just nothen at all, it ain't him
that drives, but the horses that go; it's trainin' and custom in the cattle, and not skill in the rider; he ain't the
smallest part of a circumstance to it; he has as little to
do with it as the padded saddle he stands on. The hosses
do it all, for they are obedient, and go round and round
of themselves; but just let them two he stands on only
pull apart, and down he'd go lumpus, like a fellow atween
two chairs; or let 'em kick up, and away he'd go flying
over their heads, and like as not break his neck. Now
that's the case with your Colonial Minister; he don't
manage the Colonies, but they manage themselves, and in
general they go their circumferation quiet enough. But
neither Sam Condon nor he knows how to handle the
reins; nary one of 'em can do more than go through the
form. Lettin' cattle that know the road go of themselves
is one thing, and driving of them is another; any pas-

senger on the box can do the first, but t'other requires a
good eye, a strong arm, a light hand, and a cool head, I
can tell you. As uncle Peleg said when he went to
night-school arter he was grow'd up, "readin' and writin,"
said he to the master, "is easy enough, any darned fool
can do *that*, but spellin' is the devil." So any coach,
whether it is a state or a stage waggon, in a general way,
is easy managed, but when you slump into a honey-pot,
hosses and all, or get into a pretty frizzle of a fix, between
a pine stump on one side, amd a rut on t'other axle-tree
deep, or have to turn an icy corner sharp, or pass a
sloping, slippery, frozen glare, or to pull through a deep
ford that runs like a mill-race, with a team that's one-half
devils and t'other half cowards, it requires a fellow that
knows how to yell, to skeer, to strike, and when to do it,
and the way to steer to a hair's breadth, I can tell you.

'Lord, I shall never forget how I astonished a British
navy officer once. When I was a youngster, I owned and
drove the stage coach from Goshen to Boston; my team
consisted of six as beautiful greys as ever mortal man laid
eyes on; they were as splendid critters as was ever
bound up in hoss hide, I tell you, real smashers, sixteen
hands high, and trot a mile in 2-40, every one on 'em.
Oh, they were rael dolls and no mistake; I never was so
proud of anything in my life as I was of that six-hoss
team. Well, I had the British captain alongside of me,
and he was admirin' as much as I was a-braggin' of them,
when I showed 'em off a leetle, *just a leetle* too much, a
puttin' of them on their mettle, and pushing them a-head,
when away they went like wink', and raced off as if Old
Scratch himself had kicked them all on eend. The way
the women inside shrieked, was a caution to steam-
whistles, for they were frightened out of their seven
senses, and the captain was skeered too (for courage is a

sort of habit, and nothen else; clap a sodger on a fore-topsail-yard, and set him to reefing, and see if he don't look skywonoky out of his eyes.   Or mount a sailor on a mettlesome nag, and see if he don't hold on by the mane and crupper, or jump overboard; and yet both on 'em may be as brave as lions in their own line).   Well, it frightened the captain out of a year's growth, I tell you. He made a grab at the reins to help me haul 'em up. "Hands off," sais I, "leave them to me, it's only funnin' they are;" and I gave a yell loud enough to wake the dead in a churchyard we was passing, cracked the whip, and made 'em go still faster, right agin a long steep hill ahead of us, and when they reached the top of it, a little blown, I just held 'em in hand, and brought 'em down to a trot.   "Uncommon good, that," said he, "why, I thought they were runnin' away."   "So did they," said I, "but they forgot I could follow as fast as they could run."   Now hosses and men are more like than you'd think—you must know their natures to manage them.   How can a man govern colonies who never saw one, or onderstand the folks there, who are as different from old-country people as chalk is from cheese, when he never lived among 'em, and knows nothen about their wants, habits, train of thoughts, or prejudices?

'Why, it don't stand to reason, nor convene to the natur of things—Latin and Greek may do for governing Oxford or Cambridge, but Gladstone found Homer didn't help him at Corfu, where he made an awful mess of matters, and Palmerston will have to talk something better than he learned in Ovid, or Virgil, to the Pope. The Governor-General of Canada has written a book since he went there, and what do you think it is about? The Quebec and Halifax Railway?   No, that's trady.

P 3

The monopoly of the Norwest Company, that obstructs the settlement of a country as big as all France? No, that would bring down the great bear-hunter, and the Lord knows who upon him. The construction of a practicable route from Canada to Vancouver's Island, by which the China trade might be made to pass through the British territory? No, for that would involve expense and trouble, and he might get a hint he had better mind his own business. An historical, geographical, and statistical account of British North America? No, that country is growing so fast, it would require a new edition every year. Do you give it up? Well, it is a treatise on the words, "could, would, and should." Now he *could* write somethin' more to the purpose, if he *would*, and he *should* do it, too, if he held office under me, that's a fact. Yes, it takes a horseman to select cattle for the lead, or the pole, and a coachman of the right sort to drive them too, and it takes a man who knows all about colonies, and the people that dwell there, to select governors of the right sort, and to manage them, when he gets the collar on 'em. State-craft ain't larned by instinct, for even dogs who beat all created critters for *that*, have to be trained. It ain't book larnin that is wanted in Downing-street; if it was, despatches might be wrote like the Pope's allocutions in Latin, but it's a knowledge of men and things that is required. It's not dead languages, but living ones that's wanted. Ask the head Secretary what the principal export of Canada is, and it's as like as not he will refer you to the Board of Trade, as it is more in their line than his, and if you go there, and put the same question, it's an even chance if they don't tell you they are so busy in bothering ship-owners with surveys, and holding courts of inquiry, to

make owners liable to passengers for accidents, and what
not, that they haven't time to be pestered with you.
Well, don't be discouraged, go back to Colonial Office,
and try it again. Sais you to head clerk, " What's the
principal Canadian export ?" " I don't know any of that
name," he'll say; " there are so many ports there, but I
should say Quebec." " No," sais you, " not that, but
what's the chief commodity or production they send to
Great Britain ?" " Oh, now I understand," he'll say,
" it's timber, you ought to know that, for we have had
trouble enough about lumber duties lately." " Well,
what kind of timber ?" says you, " squared, or manufactured, hard or soft wood, which is the most valuable,
white, or black Birch, Hemlock or Larch, Cedar, or
Spruce; which wood makes the best trenails, and which
the best knees for a ship?" Well, I'll take you a bet of
a hundred dollars he can't tell you. " Then," says you,
" which is the best flour, Canadian or American? which
keeps sweet the longest? and what is the cause of the
difference? Have they any iron ore there? if so, where
is it, and how is it smelted? with pit or charred coal?
and which makes the best article? Well the goney will
stare like a scallawag that has seen the elephant, see if
he don't ! Now, go into any shop you like in London,
from Storr and Mortimer's down to the penny bazaar,
and see if the counterskippers in 'em don't know the
name, quality, and price of everything they have. Let
me just ask you, then, is it right that a national office
like that should be worse served and attended to than
them, and be no better than a hurrah's nest ? They have
little to do, are well paid, and ought to know something
more than how to fold foolscap neat, to write a hand as
tall as a wire fence, six orseven hurdles to a page, tie it
up snug with red tape, enclose it in a large envelope,

mark it "On Her Majesty's Service," and then clap a great office seal to it as big as a Mexican dollar, to make it look important.*

'The English regard this Colonial Minister as my sister Urania did her husband. She was as splendid a critter as you ever see, at eighteen or twenty, a rael corn-fed, hearty-looking gall. Well, she was uncommon dainty, and plaguy hard to please, and she flirted here, and jilted there, until she kinder overstood her market. A rose don't last for ever, that's a fact. It is lovely when in the bud, or expandin' or in bloom, or even full-blown;

---

* The following is the language of a French Canadian, Mr. Pothier, as reported by Dr. Bigsby in his 'Shoe and Canoe,' vol. i. page 204 :—

'I concede that the Colonial Office means well, but its good intentions are marred by ignorance. Your office people know nothing about us, and mismanage us, as they do all the other colonies. They seem to have neither sunlight nor starlight to guide them. We have had a hundred incontestable proofs of this. What good can an overtasked man, 3,000 miles off, do in my country? What does he know of its wants, modified by climate, customs, and prejudices, as well as by a thousand points in statistics and topography, distracted as he is with the cries of *forty-two* other colonies? These things are only known to him in the rough. He can direct and advise on general grounds alone, and, therefore, too often erroneously. Besides, he is like one of your churchwardens, only a temporary officer. He fears to meddle, and leaves the grief to grow. If we have a sensible, useful Colonial Minister to-day he is lost to-morrow. and we may have in his place an idle and ill-informed, or a speculative, hair-splitting, specious man to deal with, never feeling safe, and sometimes driven half-mad by his fatal crotchets. The blunders committed at home pervade all departments. The Lords of the Admiralty send water-tanks for ships sailing on a lake of the purest water in the world. The Ordnance Office (or some such place) send cannon to be transported from Quebec into the upper country in winter, one gun costing 1,700*l.*, to take it to Kingston, where, by-the-by, it never arrived, for it lies to this day in the woods, ten miles short of its destination.'

but there is a time for perfection and decay, that can't
be postponed, no how you can fix it; the colour will fade,
or wash out in the summer showers, and then it will
droop with the weight of its own beauty, and the wind
will deprive it, from time to time, of a leaf, till its size
and proportion is dwindled to a mere atomy; if not
plucked at the right time it's never gathered at all.
There it hangs pinin' on the parent stock, while younger,
and fresher, and more attractive ones are chosen by
fellers to put into their buzzums in preference to it, that
in its day was far sweeter and lovelier than any of them.
That was just the case with " Rainy ;" she woke up one
fine morning arter the marriage of her youngest niece,
and found she was an old maid, and no mistake. Her
vanity and her glass had been deceivin' her for ever so
long, without her knowing it, and makin' her believe that
some false curls she wore looked so nateral, no soul could
tell they weren't her own ; that the little artificial colour
she gave to her cheek with a camel's hair brush, was
more delicate and more lovely than the glow of youth,
and that the dentist had improved a mouth that had
always been unrivalled.

'Well, to my mind, looking-glasses are the greatest
enemies ladies have ; they ought all to be broken to eyer-
lastin' smash. It isn't that they are false, for they ain't;
they will reflect the truth if they are allowed. But, unfortunately, truth never looks into them. When a woman
consults her glass, she wishes to be pleased, she wants
to be flattered, and to be put on good terms with herself,
so she treats it as she would her lover; she goes up to it
all smiles, looking as amiable, and as beautiful as she
can. She assumes the most winning air; she gazes at
the image with all the affection she can call up, her eyes
beam with intelligence and with love, and her lips appear

all a woman could wish, or a man covet. Well, in course
the mirror gives back that false face to its owner, as it
receives it; it ain't fair, therefore, to blame it for being
onfaithful; but as ladies can't use it without deceivin' of
themselves, why total abstinence from it would be better.
Now, people may deceive themselves if they have a mind
to, but they can't go on for ever. Time will tell tales.
Whatever year a gall is born in, she has contemporaries;
when she looks at them and sees that they are ageing, or
the worse for wear, she tries to recall the days of her
youth, and finds that they are lost in the distance, and
when she sees her schoolfellows and playmates married
and parents themselves, all the glasses in the world fail at
last to make her believe she is still young.

  ' Well, the marriage of her niece startled Urania, as a
shadow does a skittish horse. She left the deep waters
where the big fish sport themselves, and threw her line
into the shallow eddies where the minnows are, and she
hooked little Tim Dooly, a tommy cod of a fellow, that
was only fit for a bait for something bigger and better.
It was impossible to look at the critter without laughing.
Poor thing, it was hard work to fetch her up to the scratch
at last, it actilly took three ministers and six bridesmaids
to marry her. She felt she had made a losin' voyage in
life, but she was clear grit, it didn't humble her one mite
or mossel, it only made her more scorny than ever, as if
she defied all the world, and despised what it could say.
I could see a motion in her throat now and then, as if
she bit in her breath and swallowed her pride down. She
actilly held her head so high, when the minister said to
Dooly, "Salute your bride," that the critter looked up in
despair, for he couldn't reach her lips. Sais I, out of
deviltry, "Stand on a chair, Tim." Lord! if you had
seen her eyes, how they flashed fire at me, it would have

astonished you, I know.   Age hadn't quenched *that*, at
any rate.   To prevent folks from noticing how undersized
he was, she just bent down forward and kissed him.
Thinks I to myself, "Old fellow, you have had all the
condescension you will ever get out of her, she has stooped
to marry you, and then stooped for you to salute her,
after this, look out for squalls, for there is a tempestical
time afore you."   And so it turned out ; *he* soon larned
what it was to live in a house where the hen crows.
"Rainy," says I to her one day, when she had been givin'
him a blowin' up, and was sending him off on some arrand
or another, (for she treated him, poor wretch, as if he had
been the cause of all her disappointments, instead of the
plaister to heal them), "Rainy," sais I, "I always told
you you carried too stiff an upper lip, and that you would
have to take a crooked stick at last."   "Well," says she,
"Eph, he ain't the tallest and richest husband in the
world, but he is a *peowerful sight better than none.*"   Now
the English seem to estimate the officer I am speaking of
the same way; they think if he ain't what he ought to be,
he is better than none.   But, unfortunately, colonists
think just the reverse, and say that it is far better to have
none at all, than an incompetent one, and to tell you the
truth, I think so too.'

' What remedy do you propose, Mr. Peabody ?' I said ;
' what substitute would you recommend for the present
establishment ?'

' Well,' he replied, ' it is a matter that don't concarn
me, and I have reflected but little upon it ; but I should say
the department should consist of a board wholly composed
of native colonists or persons who had resided in some one
of the provinces for a period of not less than fifteen or
twenty years.   It would not much signify then how often
they changed the minister, or who he was ; the main thing

is, the work would be done, and done right too. How-
somever, I must say this arrangement is nobody's fault
now, except for allowing it to exist any longer. It's an
"old institution," that was well enough fifty years ago,
when colonies were like children in leading-strings, but it
ain't up to the time of day now, and ought to be reformed
out.'

'That is quite true,' rejoined the Senator; 'if public
attention was once drawn to its inefficiency, no doubt a
suitable remedy would soon be found for the evil. It is the
duty as well as the true policy of the British Government,
to take the subject into its serious consideration. For
what vast interests are at stake, and what a noble heritage
is British North America! It extends in length from
Cape Sable, in Nova Scotia, to the Russian boundary in
the Arctic regions, and across the entire Continent, from
the Atlantic to the Pacific Ocean, and embraces an area of
greater extent than all Europe. The remarks I made to
you on a former occasion, upon the extraordinary facilities
for inland navigation enjoyed by Canada, by means of her
enormous lakes and numerous rivers, are equally applicable to the lower provinces. New Brunswick, as you
will see, by reference to a map, is intersected in every
direction by navigable rivers of great magnitude. The
St. John, which in size and beauty rivals the Rhine, is
more than four hundred and fifty miles in length, and
drains nine millions of acres in that province, besides
nearly an equal number in the state of Maine and
Canada, into both of which it extends to a great distance.
The eastern coast is penetrated at short intervals by
other rivers, varying from two to three hundred miles in
length, which afford facilities for settlement as well as
commerce, unequalled by any other portion of the continent beyond the English territories. In like manner,

there is no point in Nova Scotia more than thirty miles distant from navigable water. The whole of the borders of the latter province, and more than two-thirds of those of the former, are washed by the ocean, which in that region furnishes one of the most extensive and valuable fisheries in the world. Nova Scotia abounds with coal, iron ore, gypsum, grindstone, slate, lead, manganese, plumbago, copper, &c., which being recently liberated from the monopoly under which they have so long been excluded from public competition, will soon attract the capital and skill requisite for their development. It is the most eastern part of America, and of course the nearest to Europe. It is not too much to say that its wonderful mineral wealth, its noble harbours, its fertile soil, its extensive fisheries, its water powers, its temperate climate, arising from its insular position, and last, not least, its possession of the winter outlet, and through passage by railway, from England to New Brunswick, Canada, and the United States, all indicate that it is destined for an extended commerce, for the seat of manufactories, the support of a large population, and for wielding a controlling power on the American Continent. Assuredly it ought to be the object of government to draw together in more intimate bonds of connexion the two countries, to remove distrust, to assimilate interests, to combine the raw material of the new, with the manufacturing skill of the old world, to enlarge the boundaries, to widen the foundations, to strengthen the constitution, and to add to the grandeur of the empire.'

'Ah!' said Peabody, 'it ought to be their object, but it ain't; and arter all, English meddlin won't be no great loss, I can tell you. I don't think colonists will go into mourning for that, even if the Lord Chamberlain should order it. But I'll tell you what *was* a loss: you missed

having that most religious and respectable body of people—
the Mormons, as settlers. You know that when they got a
clearance ticket sarved on 'em at Nauvoo, and Joe Smith
was shot by the brothers and husbands of his forty wives,
they intended to vamoose the United States in toto, to
migrate to Vancouver's Island and settle there. But thinkin'
the English law agin bigamy might reach 'em some day
or another, they squatted at Salt Lake, in Mexican territory; for they knew they had nothen to fear from the de-
generate race of half-Spanish, half-Indian critters that
owned it. Well, as bad luck would have it, after our war
with that country, Salt Valley was ceded to us as part of
California, and the poor critters were boundaried under
Uncle Sam agin after all. Yes, I wish they had gone to
Vancouver, I should like to have seen what you would
have done with them, with your new-fangled divorce
courts. It's a great experiment that, Mr. Shegog, to try
polygamy out fairly in all its bearings, and see how it
works, not arter Turkish fashion, locking of the wives up, and
coverin' of their faces with veils, but arter Anglo-Saxon
way, making free niggers of 'em all. Utah is a place to
study human natur in, I can tell you. It's what the professor here calls a "new phase of life," where a man and
his ten or a dozen wives, each with a lot of children at
their heels, all live together in the same location, like a
rooster with his hens and chickens in the same poultry-
yard. For my part I have always thought one wife was
enough for any man to manage; and I have seen so many
poor fellows have the tables turned on 'em in matrimony,
and get lassoed and tantooned themselves, that I have
always been rather skeered to try the yoke myself. Whenever I see a poor fellow going to get spliced, it always
puts me in mind of a goney I met at Madam Toosore's
exhibition to London. There was a guillotine there in

the room of horrors, and a younker examined it most attentively, and after walking round and round it, and looking up at the knife and down on the block, what does he do but kneel down and put his head into the hole to try how it fitted, when he caught a glimpse, as he turned round, of the bright edge of the cleaver that was hanging right over him, suspended only by a string, and just ready to do the job for him. Well he was afraid to move for fear of slipping the string, and letting the cutter down by the run. The way he shrieked ain't no matter, it was the naterallest thing in the world, and so was the way he called for help. There was a crowd round him in no time. You never see such a stir as it made, for in a general way it's a stupid place that, with people going about as silent as if they were among the dead; but this set everybody a-talking all at once. They thought it was part of the show, and that he acted his part beautiful, just as a body really would if he was going to be beheaded in airnest. So nobody thought of helping him, but let him screech on as if he was paid for it, till at last one of the attendants came runnin' up—secured the knife—got him out, and was beginning to pitch into him, when the fellow saved him the trouble by fainting. I don't like puttin' my head into dangerous gear like that, without a chance of backing out again if I don't like the collar, I can tell you. I actilly couldn't get Mormon marriages out of my head, so I went all the way to Utah to see how the new scheme worked. Nothen ever raised my curiosity like polygamy, I couldn't see my way through it at all, though, in a general way, I must say (though, perhaps, it don't become me to boast of it), that I can see through a hole in a grindstone, as far as him that picks it.

'Will there be peace or war in the wigwam? sais I. I can understand a man bigamying, but I don't jist see

how it convenes to women. Will they all turn to, and
court their husbands, and try to be loved best in return,
each strivin' to outdo the other, or will they fight and
scratch like cats? Will they take it in turn to be queen,
and then be subjects (as fellows do when campin' out in
timber land, in the State of Maine, when each one cooks
in rotation, and attends on the rest), or will each have her
separate task, one to wash, another to bake, one to do
housework, and another to make and mend; or this one
to tend the children, and that the dairy and poultry, and
so on? Will the husband set their tasks, or will they
choose for themselves? And will they fight over the
choice, or take work in succession order? When a new
wife is taken what sort of a thing is the wedding, are the
other wives invited to it, and is it a jollification or a
mournin' time? Or does it go by default, like old Sam
Arbuckle's marriage?

'I must tell you that story, for it is a fact, I assure
you. He was the nigger butler to my brother, the member to Congress for Virginny. He had permission to
spouse Milken Sally, a slave on another plantation. A
night was fixed for the ceremony, the company assembled,
and the coloured preacher there to tie the nuptial knot.
Well, they waited and waited for ever so long, but the
bride didn't make her appearance. At last Sam grew
impatient, so sais he to the preacher, " Look here, Broder
Cullifer, it's no use waitin' for that darkey, I knows her
like a book, she's dropped asleep setting fore de fire—I'se
authorized to speak for her, so jest go ahead jest the
same as if she was here.' Old Cullifer thought it a wise
suggestion and proceeded with the service that united
them in the holy bonds of matrimony. When the ceremony was over off started the bridegroom in search of the
absent bride, and sure enough, when he reached her

cabin there he found her fast asleep by the fire, with some of her finery in her hands; and she was terribly riled when she heard the wedding had come off, and she was not there.

'Now, sais I to myself, does it go by default arter that fashion? or how is it managed? for it don't appear to me to stand to the natur of things, much less to the natur of women, that this sort of domestic arrangement can be just the most cheerful affair in the world. So I concluded, as I had nothen above particular to do, I'd go and take a look at the harems, and judge for myself. First of all I made for Nauvoo, where I wanted to see what sort of a city they had built for themselves, and to look at the ruins of their celebrated temple. It was there I first made acquaintance with our friend here, who was bound on the same errand ; and I'll tell you what, Mr. Shegog '—(and he gave me one of those sly winks that indicated he intended to excite and draw out the Senator)—'I must say that their founder, General Joe Smith, who was so barbarously murdered by the Gentiles, was a great man, and no mistake ; and if not a prophet, assuredly one of the best of men that ever lived on the face of the airth.'

Here the Senator turned round and regarded him with a look of the most unfeigned astonishment ; but he continued his panegyric with the utmost gravity.

'Everybody admitted his wonderful ability, as the editor of a paper called the *Times* said—(I don't mean the English *Times;* catch *that* paper praisin' a distinguished American ; no, not it, but a local paper of that name)—" Without learning," says he, " without means and without experience, he has met a learned world, a rich century, a hard-hearted and wicked generation, with truth that could not be resisted, facts that could not be disproved, revelations that could not be gainsaid or evaded; but, like the rays of light from the sun, they have tinged everything they lit upon with a lustre and livery which has animated, quickened, and adorned them !" That's what I call agreat picture, sir, drawn by a great artist.'

'I am perfectly astonished to hear you talk that way,' said the Senator. 'He was a vile impostor, in whom cunning supplied the place of talent, and hypocrisy that of true religious feeling. A proficient in roguery of all kinds from his youth, he was early instructed, and well skilled in practising upon the incredulity of the ignorant; and a popular manner, joined to a certain fluency of speech, enabled him to obtain a great influence over his hearers. To these powers he owed his ascendancy among his confidential associates in this wonderful imposture, who were men of more ability, but less tact and personal popularity than himself. It was in this way, that his very ignorance operated in his favour, for the language of a manuscript of a deceased author, which he had surreptitiously obtained, and palmed off successfully on the public as a revelation, was so much above what an unlearned man like himself could possibly have written, that it is no wonder that his dupes could only account for it, by attributing it to inspiration. You must recollect that among the many thousands of his followers, there was not one man of character or education. Mormonism is the grossest and most barefaced imposition of modern times. It was founded on folly and fraud; sustained by robbery and murder; and, under the sanction of a pretended revelation, it authorized and encouraged every species of licentiousness. It is too disgusting even for a topic of conversation. If Smith had been a good man, he never would have been the author of such a system; and if he

had been a man of talent, he would have moulded it into
such a shape as not to shock the moral feelings of all
mankind.'

'Well, Senator,' said Peabody, 'you may undervally
him as you please, but the world won't agree with you at
any rate. I should like to know, now, if there is a man in
Congress that could reply to Clay in such withering and
eloquent language as he did? Why, there is nothing in
Elegant Extracts equal to it; it's sublime,' and putting
himself into a theatrical attitude, he repeated with great
animation the passage referred to :—" Your conduct, sir,
resembles a lottery-vender's sign, with the goddess of
good-luck sitting on the car of fortune, astraddle of the
horn of plenty, and driving the merry steeds of beatitude
without rein or bridle. Crape the heavens with weeds of
woe, gird the earth with sackcloth, and let hell mutter one
melody in commemoration of fallen splendour. Why, sir,
the condition of the whole earth is lamentable. Texas
dreads the teeth and toe-nails of Mexico ; Oregon has the
rheumatism, brought on by a horrid exposure to the heat
and cold of British and American trappers ; Canada has
caught a bad cold from extreme fatigue in the patriot
war ; South America has the headache, caused by bumps
against the beams of Catholicity and Spanish sovereignty ;
Spain has the gripes, from age and inquisition ; France
trembles and wastes under the effects of contagious dis-
eases ; England groans with the gout, and wriggles with
wine ; Italy and the German States are pale with consumption ; Prussia, Poland, and the little contiguous
dynasties have the mumps so severely that the whole head
is sick, and the whole heart is faint; Russia has the
cramp by lineage ; Turkey has the numb palsy ; Africa,
from the curse of God, has lost the use of her limbs ;
China is ruined by the Queen's evil ; the Indians are

blind and lame; and the United States, which ought to be the good physician with balm from Gilead, and *an asylum for the oppressed,* has boosted, and is boosting up into the council-chamber of the government a clique of political gamblers, to play for the old clothes and old shoes of a sick world, and ' *no pledge no promise to any particular portion of the people* ' that the rightful heirs will ever receive a cent of their father's legacy." Is it any wonder, sir, that a man who could talk it into people that way, could draw converts from the remotest parts of the earth ?'

' The language,' replied the Senator, very coolly, ' is well suited for a grog-shop, where, no doubt, it would pass for eloquence, nothing could possibly be better adapted to his audience. Ah, Mr. Shegog,' he continued, ' I shall never forget the journey my friend and I took to Utah. As a member of Congress I was anxious to ascertain the true state of things at Salt Lake, by a personal examination, and also to inform myself of the condition and prospects of my countrymen in California, which promised to become one of the most important states in the Union. With this view I proceeded to Missouri, to avail myself of the escort and protection of the first band of emigrants bound for those places. From St. Louis, whence we started, the distance to Utah, *via* Council Bluffs, is more than sixteen hundred miles. The route passes over vast rolling prairies, unbridged rivers, sand hills, mud-flats, mountain ranges, and deep and precipitous ravines. The line of march was unhappily too well defined over these interminable plains for travellers to lose themselves in their unvarying and boundless expanse. So numerous and so frequent had been the caravans of emigrants, that had crossed this desert, that they had left melancholy traces behind them, of the sorrows, accidents, and misfortunes that had befallen them on their journeys. The track is marked by broken waggons, fragments of furniture, agricultural implements, cast-iron ware, and the bleached skeletons of oxen and mules, that have died miserably by the way, while unturfed mounds, of various sizes, afforded melancholy proof of the mortality that had attended the exodus of this deluded people. Some of them had been robbed of their contents by the wolves, and human bones lay scattered about on the short brown grass. The warning thus inculcated had evidently not been lost upon succeeding travellers, for I observed that some of the more recent graves were protected with heaps of stones, broken wheels of carriages, and other heavy substances. The train with which we travelled, did not escape similar casualties, for several women and children, victims to fatigue and exposure to the weather, were added to the number of the dead that reposed in that wild and dreary prairie. The buffalo hunts, the Indian encounters, the bivouacs, and the exhilaration of spirits caused by constant motion, were not new to me, who am so familiar with life in the North-west, and I was not a little pleased when the long and tedious journey ended, more especially as I knew that another, and no less fatiguing one, awaited me between Utah and San Francisco.

'The first glimpse we got of this far-famed Mormon valley from the Wahsach mountain, eight thousand feet above the level of the sea, was the signal for great rejoicing to our wearied and wayworn travellers. The women wept and the men shouted for joy at having reached the termination of their tedious journey. My first impression was one of sadness and disappointment. The distant prospect on which the eye naturally first rested, embraced a wild, desolate, and dreary country, and its loneliness, its silence, and its total isolation from the rest of the civilized world,

filled me with awe when I regarded it as the voluntary prison
of so many thousands of deluded human beings. Environed
on every side by lofty mountains, lay the vast plain which
the saints had selected as their home in the desert. The
great Salt Lake, as far as we could ascertain, extends
130 miles in length, and from 70 to 80 in breadth, lying
far away in the midst of a waste, uncultivated, and monotonous plain, suggesting the idea of the Dead Sea and its
melancholy and desolate shores. Withdrawing our view
from the distant scene, to that lying more immediately
before us, and which, from the great elevation of our
position, we had at first overlooked, we found that it fully
equalled in beauty the description we had had of it.
Beneath our feet, as it were, lay the object of our visit,
Utah, the Babel of the western world. We could look
down upon it as on a map spread upon a table. It was laid
out on a magnificent scale, being nearly four miles in
length and three in breadth, surrounded by a wall twelve
feet high, defended by semi-bastions within half musket-
range, and also protected by a wide, deep ditch. This
enormous work was constructed nominally as a protection
against the hordes of savages by whom they were surrounded, but in reality against the only formidable
enemy they had to fear—the idleness of the people.

'The streets were 120 feet wide, and the sidepaths,
20. A mountain stream, which originally ran through
the town, was distributed by conduits so as to irrigate
every garden and supply every house; and as the buildings were placed twenty feet back from the line of the street,
and the intervening space was planted with shrubs, the general effect was very agreeable. At all events, it made a
favourable impression upon us when emerging from the
boundless desert over whose unvaried surface we had been
journeying so long and so wearily. The site selected for

the city is certainly most beautiful, lying as it does at the
foot of the Wahsach mountain, whose snow-clad summit
is lost in the clouds. It is washed on the west by the
waters of the Jordan, and on the southern bounded by a
broad, level plain, extending to a distance of twenty-five
miles, and well-watered by numerous streams. This city
is certainly one of the most extraordinary instances to be
found in the annals of the world of what human per-
severance and industry can effect when stimulated
by fanaticism. It is unapproachable from any civilized
community, unless by a difficult and laborious journey of
nearly a thousand miles. In a severe winter it is wholly
inaccessible, and the cost of the transport of goods far
exceeds their original value. To overcome all these
difficulties, to erect such a city, and to bring into cultivation such a quantity of land as they have done in so
short a time, was to me a source of continued astonishment. I am not going to bore you with an account of
my explorations in the adjacent country (which, in a
scientific point of view, is exceedingly interesting), or to
describe Utah, but, as we were talking of polygamy, to
give you my opinion of its effects upon this community.

'Mormon marriages are the most wicked, as well as the
most impious, that can be well conceived. They are
twofold, those that are terminated by death, and those
that are to continue throughout eternity. The first are
ordinary marriages, conducted somewhat in the usual
form, but liable to be dissolved by mutual consent, upon
obtaining the approbation of the authorities. The other
is called *spiritual wifeism*. This can only be solemnized
in the temple, by the high priest in person, or by some
one of his associates to whom he specially delegates his
authority for that purpose. The forms and ceremonies
observed on these occasions, which are conducted with

great secrecy, and many mysterious rites, are of the most imposing character, and well calculated to leave a lasting impression upon the mind, while the oaths that are administered are of a most fearful description. In this manner a woman may be married to one man till death, and also *sealed* to another (as it is called) for all time to come. You have doubtless heard of these practices, for no man who has travelled as much in the United States as you have, has not been informed of them, therefore I need not enter into details. But the effect of all this is inconceivable, it must be seen, as I have witnessed it, to be fully appreciated. A polygamist has no home, and no wife; his women are idle and rebellious slaves, they are either indifferent to him, or hate and despise him; and his children, adopting the complaints of their respective mothers, inherit their hatred of their rivals and their offspring, and their disrespect for him whom they regard as the author of their wrongs, rather than their being. He grows sullen and severe, cold, selfish, and brutal; his wives sink into mere drudges, or are intemperate, or dissolute, or both; while the children, profiting by the bad example constantly set before their eyes by their parents, become early adepts in every species of vice. The mortality among *them*, caused by the very nature of this vile institution, is a melancholy proof of the viciousness of the system. As soon as the males are old enough to be useful, they are set to such work as is suited to their age, and thus the time that should be devoted to their education is occupied in earning their living, while the females, as soon as they arrive at maturity, are sold for wives to those who can afford to offer a suitable price for them.'

'Do the wives,' I inquired, 'live together in one house, assembling at meals and other occasions like members of the same family, or are they lodged and maintained in separate dwellings?'

'That,' said the Senator, 'is a matter of taste or convenience: sometimes they occupy detached abodes, but in general they are under the same roof.'

'Tell you what,' said Peabody, 'I was present at one of the drollest scenes I ever saw in all my born days; I thought I should have died a larfing. I lodged, when I was at Utah, with a feller who came from Connecticut, one Simon Drake; I know'd him long afore Salt Lake was ever heard of, by a long chalk, and seein that he and I were old friends, he took me in to stay with him, which was great luck, for the Mormons, like the Turks, don't like strangers to see the inside of their harems. Well, Sim had five wives, not counting the old one he brought along with him from Hertford, who was a broken-hearted lookin critter, that seemed as if she wouldn't long be an incumbrance to him. The rest were all young, goodlooking, rollickin hussies, as you'd see anywhere. As far as I could observe, they agreed among themselves uncommon well, for neither of them cared a straw about him, or anything else, unless it was the Theatre and the Assembly Rooms, of which they talked to me for everlastin. Sim was so overjoyed to see one from his native land, and to be able to talk of old times and old friends, that the whisky (which he drank like water, to drown past recollections or painful comparisons) gave him a return of delirium tremens, which I knew he had had when he was a young man. Well, one night he broke out all of a sudden, crowing like a cock, and making a motion as if he was a flappin of his wings. He actilly fancied he was one, and that his wives were hens, and he would make a dart at 'em to peck them, and bit them like anything. He ordered them to go to roost on the garden fence, to put their heads under their wings, and go to sleep, and the way he hunted and worried them into one corner, and then into another, and bothered and tormented them, was a caution to a dog in a poultry yard. The poor old wife, who had gone to bed airly, hearin the noise, put her head in at the door to see what was going on, and begged me with tears in her eyes to interfere, and keep him from doing mischief. So says I,

' " Sim, my old cock, let you and I go out first, and get on the fence to roost, and do you crow your best, and the hens will soon follow."

' So I takes him into the garden, and as I passed the water butt, I tript up his heels, and soused his head in, and held it there as long as I dared, and then let it up for him to breathe, and then in with it again, and so on, till I sobered him, when I took him into the house, gave him an opiate, and put him to bed. Arter this, we all separated, each to our own kennel, and just as I was a droppin off to sleep, I heard a light step on the floor, and a low voice, saying, " Are you asleep, Mr. Peabody?" "No," says I, "I ain't; but what in natur is the matter now, has he broke out agin?" "No, Eph," said the speaker (and I perceived it was the poor dear old lady), "he is quiet now; but I came to tell you this is no place for you. Those young women will get you into trouble; make an excuse in the morning, and leave this house to-morrow, and don't enter it again, except in company with the Senator," and she was off afore I could thank her. Thinks I, a nod is as good as a wink to a blind horse, I was thinkin the same thing myself. Edged tools ain't the safest things in the world to play with. In the mornin, Senator and I joined the caravan for California, and set our hosses heads towards San Francesco.

' Yes, it is a pity these birds hadn't lighted at Vancouver : most of them came from Wales, and it would have been better if they had returned to their allegiance again. It would give the folks something to do in Downing-street, and would please *you* too.'

'Please me,' I said, 'pray how could I be interested in the matter ?'

'Why,' he replied, with a laugh, 'you want to remodel the department here, and they could have taken down their sign, and put up a new one. They might call it a Government Office for " *Colonial and Matrimonial Alliances*." '

No. XII.

BIG WIGS.

THE Senator having expressed a wish to see the several law courts which are now sitting, we spent the morning in visiting them. He was more anxious, he said, to observe their arrangements and general appearance, the demeanour of the judges, lawyers, and officials, and the mode in which they discharged their respective duties, than to study the practical working of the machinery, for with that he was sufficiently familiar. He appeared to be much struck with the small dimensions of the apartments in which the courts were held ; with the limited accommodation afforded to the public; the number of the lawyers in attendance when compared to the audience ; and the little interest the proceedings seemed to excite among the people at large. Nothing, however, appeared to surprise him so much as the concise and lucid manner in which points of law were argued.

'Ah,' he said, 'I see your lawyers *do* give the court credit for knowing something ; I wish ours, would imitate their example. I do not mean to say that the bar in the United States undervalues the legal attainments of the judges, for that would be doing injustice to the common sense of the one, and the great learning and ability of the other ; but their arguments assume the form of dissertations. They begin at the beginning with fundamental

principles that everybody knows and can dispense with
hearing, and then trace the law, through all its branches,
down to the point at issue, where they ought to have
commenced. It is a very tedious and wearisome practice,
and much to be lamented. But it is partly the fault of
the judges, in not having the moral courage to check it,
and partly of the clients, who never think their advocates
do them justice, unless they exhaust the subject. A
pressure of business and a long arrear of causes will
ultimately convince the former that patience has its
limits, which, when exceeded, it ceases to be a virtue ;
and the latter, that long speeches are expensive superfluities that can easily be dispensed with. Lawyers are
also much to blame themselves, in being too pertinacious.
I observe that when a judge here interferes in an argument, and expresses a decided opinion, counsel at once
bow to his decision, and cease to press him further.

' There is more state and ceremony observed here than
with us, though not more order and decorum. We have
different modes of manifesting our respect for the administration of justice. Our people testify it by erecting
suitable buildings for the courts ; you, by robeing your
judges and lawyers. We might, perhaps, receive mutual
advantage by uniting the practice of both countries.'

' Well, I don't think so,' said Peabody. ' I call all
that sort of thing tomfoolery. What is the airthly use of
those nasty wigs, that are nothin' but a compound of
grease and horse-hair? Do you think there is any
wisdom hid away in those curls, that a judge can fetch
out by scratching, as an Irishman does an evasive answer
out of his shaggy, oncombed head ? They look like
Chicktaw Indians in council, sittin' with their hair pow-
dered with cotton fluff. It's a wonder to me they haven't
pipes in their mouths to make them look more solemn-

choly. It can't be possible that they want to resemble
venerable, old, grey-headed men, for *they* are bald in a
general way, and their hair is like the rim of a dish—all
round the edge. What awful things those wigs must be
in hot weather; why, the pomatum must run, like tallow
from new-made candles, and hang about their cheeks,
like the glass icicles of a chandelier! How a wise man
can put his head into a thing that's fit only for a door-
mat, and wear it in public, passes my onderstanding!

'It puts me in mind of my brother Peter, when he
went to Canton as United States Consul. He was major
of a regiment of volunteers at home, and he had a most
splendid suit of regimentals, all covered over with gold
lace, and sot off with an immense pair of epaulettes, each
as big as a ship's swob. When he arrived at Canton, he
thought he'd astonish the natives by wearing it as an
official dress. Well, whenever he strutted about the
streets in this rig, John Chinaman used to laugh, ready
to split his sides, and call out, "*too much foolo—too much
goldo;*" and he went by the nick-name ever after of "too
much foolo." Now, that's just the case with them ere
judges—there is "too much wigo and too much foolo.'
And, as for the lawyers, their noddles look, for all the
world, like rams' heads. I have heard tell of wolves in
sheep's clothing afore now, but I never knew what it
meant till to-day. If them horse-hair hoods is out of
place for judges, who are called Big Wigs, they are wus
for lawyers; for, what's the use of making a joker look
solemn, unless it's to take people by surprise, set 'em a
haw-hawhing right out, and then get 'em fined for contempt of court? A lawyer is chock-full of fun, like a
clown at a circus; it fairly biles up and runs over; and
when he cocks his eye and looks comical, you can't help
laughing—no how you can fix it. He can make a wit-

ness say anything he likes; he can put words into his mouth or draw 'em out just as he pleases; and keep the whole court in a roar. I never see one on 'em at that game, that I don't think of what I saw Signor Blitz, the great conjuror, do at Boston. He was a showing off his tricks one night at the Necromantic Hall, when he seed a countryman starin' at him with all his eyes and mouth, both of which was wide open. So he stopped short in the midst of his pranks and made a face at him, exactly like his, that set every one off into hystrikes a'most, it was so droll. When they had done laughing, he invited the feller to come upon the stage, and told him he'd teach him how the tricks was done. So up goes young Ploughshare, as innocent as you please. When he got him on the boards, he patted him on the back with one hand and put the other to his mouth, and, sais he, "You had potatoes for dinner to-day." "Yes, I had," said the gouey. "What makes you swaller them whole?" said Blitz, and he pulled ever so many potatoes out of his mouth and threw them on the floor. At last he picked one up, with a sprout on it six inches long. "Why, my good friend," said he, "looke here; they have begun to grow already. Do, for goodness' sake, chew your food; and, instead of swallowing it *holus bolus*, use your knife and fork to cut up your wittles, and he pulled *them* out of his mouth, too. Then he began to punch away at his stomach till he nearly doubled him up. "Hallo," sais Ploughshare, "what, in nature, is all that for?" "No-thin," sais Blitz; "I am only trying to break the dinner plates, for fear I should cut your throat in bringin' of them up." The feller thought he was in the hands of the Devil, and he turned and took a flying leap clear over the orchestra into the pit, and nearly broke his unques-tionably ugly neck. The shouting that followed beat

election cheers all to chips, I tell you. Now, lawyers can
bring any answer out of a witness's mouth as easy as
Blitz fetched potatoes, and knives, and forks out of that
countryman's, and set folks a roarin' as loud, too; for, in
a general way, it don't take much to make a crowd laugh
—*mobs like rotten eggs better nor sound ones.*

'What's the use of puttin' wigs on lawyers, when all
the horse-hair of a dragoon regiment, and all the grease
of all the bears in the world would never make 'em look
like sedate men? Why, they are as full of tricks as
Blitz, have just as much sleight of hand, and are quite as
much in league with the Devil as he or any other conjuror ever was. It don't convene to common sense, that's
a fact. And then if the judges must put on them outlandish wigs, what in the world is the reason they keep
on their red dressing gowns? Have they any clothes
under them, or do they wear them to hide the naked
truth? As for them white bands under their chins, as
they represent beards, why don't they wear real or artificial ones? They would look a sight better, and more
nateral too. Them sort of things do well enough in a
play-house, but it kinder strikes me, it's out of place in a
court of justice. If it's to awe common folks, and frighten
them out of their seven senses, why there's better ways of
doin' it by a long chalk. I should like to tell them a
story—that is, what they call a "case in point," or as they
say in lawyers' slang, that goes on *all fours* with it.
There was a squatter in Tennessee, when I was on a visit
to my uncle Reuben, who was a perfect outlaw of a
fellow, and a terror to the whole *vi-*cinity. He had
always lived on the borders of civilization, and hung on
its skirts, as a burr does to a horse's tail. He was on
the rear, where he could not be seen, nor rubbed off, nor
pulled off, nor kicked off. He was a trapper that robbed

traps instead of setting of them himself; a dealer in
hosses he neether raised nor bought, and always went
armed with loaded dice, marked cards, and a capital
rifle. He was an ugly customer, I tell you. He could
outrun, outride, outswim, outshoot, and outlie any white
man or Indian in all Tennessee; he could out-Herod
Herod if he'd a been there. He used to say he was the
only gentleman in the country, for he was the only man
that never worked. Though he didn't raise none, he had
a large stock that he taught to forage for themselves. He
used to turn his cattle arter night into other folks' meadow
lands to eat up their grass; and his pigs into their fenced
patches, to yaffle up their potatoes, until they larned the
way to go right in of their own accord and help themselves; and if the neighbours went to him and talked of
law, he'd point to his rifle, and threaten to sarve them
with notice to quit, till they were skeered out of their
lives a' most. Well, one poor fellow, who had his crops
destroyed time and again, and could get no satisfaction,
and was tired out watchin' night arter night, chasing the
hogs out of his diggins, thought he'd set a bear on 'em.
So what does he do but catch the longest-legged pig in
the herd and sew him up in the skin of a bear, coverin'
him all over, head, body, and legs with it, and then, towards daylight, he lets the drove out first, and the dressed
one arter them. When they got sight of him, off they
set as hard as they could lay legs to the ground, took up
the road that led through the woods, and he arter them,
and away they went like all possessed. Well, the squatter,
when he got up in the mornin', went over to his neighbour's potato patch, to bring his pigs home as usual; but
lo and behold they were not there; and more than that,
the fence was whole and standing, as if they had never
been in at all. While he was starin' about and kinder

puzzled, the stage-coach came up, and he hailed the driver, who told him he had seen them runnin' for dear life, chased by a bear; two of them was dead on the road, and the rest had taken to the woods, as soon as they saw the coach and the bear arter them. "Waal," says he, quite cool, "the bears owe me a grudge, for many a one of their family I have killed in my day. And what surprises me is, that they should venture so near me, for I haven't been mislested by them these three years: I'm glad my psalm-singing neighbour had no hand in it, for if he had, I'd a sent him in search of that constable that came here last summer to sarve a writ on me, and has never found his way back yet. The bears and I will balance accounts some day, see if we don't." and he went into the house as cool as if nothin' had happened.

'Now, if these judges are dressed to scare the crows, it appears to me bearskin would answer the purpose better nor horse-hair and powder. What do you think, Lyman?'

'I think,' replied the Senator, 'you don't know what you are talking about. It is the judicial dress, adopted ages ago, and preserved to the present day. It is well suited to an aristocratic country, in which there are various orders and ranks, with their peculiar robes and dresses, that are worn on state occasions. They may not be so appropriate to a republican form of government like ours, but there is no reason why they should not be worn even with us. Although, in theory, all men are equal in the United States, we do not pretend that all officers are, and of these the judges are the highest in public estimation, and the most exalted in rank. Why should they not wear a distinctive costume? Their duties are grave and important, and some of them, especially in criminal courts, of a solemn and awful character, affecting the lives of those who are tried before them. As they are not the everyday business of life, and judges are set apart to discharge them, the paraphernalia of the court ought to be in keeping with the sanctity of the law, and the importance of its due administration. Dress is an arbitrary matter ; but everywhere, on public occasions, propriety dictates, and custom sanctions the practice of suiting our habiliments to the occasion. In a court of law, as in a church, everything should be done decently and in order. We have not this particular costume in our country, but we have adopted others of a similar nature for various officers of the public service. The military have a dress peculiar to themselves, and so have the navy, whilst many Christian sects, especially the Episcopalians and Romanists, have their own distinctive vestments. Collegiate, municipal, masonic, and other institutions have also their prescribed robes and badges, and they occasion no animadversion, because we are accustomed to them ; but they are as open to remark as those of the English judges which you have just been ridiculing. A gold epaulet, and a cocked hat and feathers, which I have seen your brother sport, when at the head of his regiment of volunteers, are adopted, and approved on the same ground as the wig and the ermine of these judicial officers.'

'I assure you, Mr. Shegog,' he continued, 'that I regard the English bench with great veneration ; we owe to it a deep debt of gratitude. Although I have not the honour of knowing those gentlemen we have just seen, my studies have made me tolerably familiar with their predecessors, and I have no doubt they display as much talent, learning, and impartiality as those to whom they have succeeded. When we dissolved the connexion with Great Britain, it was not because we disapproved of, or quarrelled with its form of government, but with those who administered it at that time ; and when we had to frame one for ourselves, we adopted as much of yours as was at all applicable to a country in which there was no royal family, no nobility, and no established church ; and I think I may add, without exposing myself to the charge of national vanity, that the constitution we finally adopted was, under all the circumstances, the best that could be devised. Monarchy was out of the question. In the absence of the three great institutions I have just named, it was wholly inapplicable to the people or the country· Necessity, therefore, gave us no option ; a republic was the only alternative we could adopt. The office of chief magistrate became elective as a matter of course. The difficulty (and a very great one it proved) was how to construct an upper branch of the legislature, where there was no class in any way corresponding to the peers, or even the landed aristocracy of England, that could operate as a check on the House of Representatives. The manner in which this was effected reflects infinite credit on the framers of the constitution. If both senators and representatives were chosen by the people at large, though nominally divided into two separate chambers, they would in effect be but one body, for they would have the same feelings, be clothed with similar powers, and responsible to the same constituency. They, therefore, arranged that the members of the House of Representatives should be elected by the people ; but those of the upper branch by the legislatures of the several states, and to secure a careful and judicious exercise of the important functions of the Senate, they established the age of thirty years, as the earliest period at which a member could be eligible for election, while that of a Representative was fixed at twenty-five years. To increase the respectability of the body, it was made more select by restricting its numbers, and making its basis State Sovereignty; while that of the lower branch was regulated by population; thus, New York furnishes but two senators, while it sends to the other branch more than forty representatives. To invest it with dignity it was constituted an Executive Council of the nation, no treaty being valid without its ratification, and no appointment legal without its approval. To insure its independence, and qualify it for these important duties, the term for which senators are elected was extended to six, while that of the representatives was limited to two years. Where the supreme power rests in the people, who are theoretically and politically equal, perhaps no better or wiser provision could be made for the construction of this body.

'Having thus established the three branches of the legislature, it became necessary to erect a judiciary, a very delicate and difficult task, considering that every state possessed its own courts, and was jealous of any authority that should over-ride them. They accordingly created a tribunal, called the "Supreme Court," and invested it with the sole power over all cases, whether in law or in equity, accruing under the enactments of Congress, and also with an extensive appellate jurisdiction. It possesses powers far beyond those of the English courts or, indeed, of any other country in the world, for it controls not only the local legislatures, but the president, and the Congress itself. In England, Parliament is politically omnipotent; in America, the people are the source of all power, and by a constitution of their own making, have created a Chief Magistrate, a Senate, and a House of Representatives. By that written instrument certain powers are severally delegated to them, which they cannot extend or diminish. It is an organic law, and, like every other law, must be interpreted by the judges. If Congress passes an act in contravention of it, the Court declares it to be unconstitutional and void, and will not enforce it.

'In England Parliament can alter the succession, limit or enlarge its own jurisdiction, and change even the form of government. In America, Congress cannot make the slightest alteration of the kind. This is a novel and immense, but salutary power, that is lodged in the Supreme Court. It curbs the impetuosity and arbitrary will of a party, and forms a safeguard for the liberty of the people. To render the Constitution as permanent as possible, the people, while they reserved to themselves the power to amend it, very wisely guarded it against their own interference, except in cases of great urgency, by surrounding its exercises with restrictions of a most conservative character. They precluded themselves from taking the initiative in altering it, by enacting that appeal must be made to them either by two-thirds of the members of the Congress, or by a vote of two-thirds of the assemblies of the several States. Without this preliminary sanction they have left themselves no power to meddle with this sacred document. If they were to attempt to do so the Court would decide their action to be illegal, as it would in the same manner if Congress were to undertake to exceed its constitutional limits.

'Thus, the Supreme Court absorbs the whole judicial authority of the nation, for the Senate, unlike your House of Lords, has no appellate jurisdiction. It can indeed try an impeachment preferred by the House of Representatives, deprive the accused of his office, and declare him ineligible to serve the public again; but it belongs to the legal tribunal alone, to convict and punish him criminally. The judiciary takes cognizance of all offences on the high seas, and of all matters of international law, as well as of the relations of one State to the other or to Congress. It is the sheet-anchor of the State, and we are mainly indebted to it, under God, for the stability of our institutions. In no country is the avenue to the Bench so well guarded as with us. The chief magistrate has not the power of appointment to it, he can only nominate, and the Senate, composed, as I have said, of members from each State, indiscriminately brought together from every part of the Union (for one of the qualifications of a Senator is residence within his own State), must approve of the recommendation before the commission can issue. All parties, without distinction, however much they differ on other points, concur. in the importance of upholding the authority, and maintaining the respectability and efficiency of the Bench, and although there, as elsewhere, political feeling pervades and influences public patronage, it has never been known to operate in the selection of a judge—unless, perhaps, where the choice lay between two candidates of equal pretensions, when congeniality of opinion has turned the scale. More than this can scarcely be expected from the infirmities of human nature. From the first establishment of this tribunal to the present time, the selection of the judges has been such as to satisfy the just expectations of the public. They have all been able, learned, upright, and impartial men, and have discharged their duties in a manner alike honourable to themselves and their country. They had great and good models before them in the judges of England, and a never-failing source of instruction in their recorded decisions. When they commenced their judicial labours, the principles of law, civil, criminal, and maritime, were well established, and they may both be said to have started at that time from the same point. It is impossible for us to conceive how

much our two countries owe to their respective judiciaries.
You must, however, excuse me for saying that I think
our government defers with more respect to the decision
of the judges, and is more ready than yours to uphold
their authority. The Whigs, who are expert at removing
land-marks, to enlarge the sphere of their own action, have
more than once shown a disposition to take the law into
their own hands. Lord John Russell was prepared on a
recent occasion to admit the Jews to the legislature, in
defiance of the law, by a mere resolution of the House, to
which he wished to give the effect of an Act of Parliament, utterly regardless of the collision it would produce
between the House of Commons and the judges; and,
in the late case of Dr. Smethurst, Government have set
aside, upon grounds altogether unsatisfactory, the decision of a Court, solemnly pronounced after a patient investigation of a most painful nature. Nothing could be
better devised to weaken the authority of a judge, or to
destroy the confidence of the public in the verdict of a
jury than such a course of procedure. In ordinary cases,
when an application is made to the court for a rule to set
aside a verdict, the grounds of the application are distinctly
stated, and before it is made absolute, it is fully argued
in public. In this case the application was made in
private, the parties consulted were not sworn, nor sub-
jected to cross-examination, nor any opportunity given to
the prosecuting officer to rebut their evidence, either by
argument or the production of other persons equally competent to form an opinion on the subject. If there must
be an appeal in criminal cases (I do not mean a new
trial, for that is out of the question), it should be heard
before a competent tribunal, in a formal and legal
manner, and the proceedings conducted in as public a way
as the original trial. There are cases in which the pre-

rogative of the Crown to pardon, may be exercised with great propriety, but in general, it ought to be confined to those instances in which the law, under which the trial takes place, is involved in doubt; or where additional evidence has been discovered, which, had it been known at the trial, might have produced an acquittal; or where the verdict was not in accordance with the charge of the Court, or was influenced by party, personal, or religious feeling. But where both the judge and the jury who tried the cause, arrived at the same conclusion, and the former has subsequently, on mature reflection, seen no cause to change his opinion, and more especially when the latter, as in this instance, have declared that their decision was formed from the evidence, even before they heard the charge, which confirmed, but did not influence, their verdict, I can see nothing to justify the Secretary in interfering to prevent the course of justice, especially as he is an unprofessional man, and *was not present at the trial.*

'Mr. Justice Story, one of the most eminent lawyers among us, was an intimate friend of mine, and he told me that a judge's notes or a short-hand writer's report of the trial of a cause, although verbally accurate, could not be depended on in a review of the case for a new trial, on the ground of the verdict being against evidence, because it was necessary to *see* and *hear* a witness examined in order to know what weight to attach to his testimony. The jury, in considering the witness's evidence, estimate also his credibility. They alone can judge from the manner in which he gives his testimony, whether he understands the subject, is cautious in his replies, and free from personal or professional bias. Facts positively attested, and opinions distinctly given (where they are admissible), are all that appear in a written report; but there is no record of the hesitation, the flippancy, the indifference, or the manifest ignorance of the witnesses, and yet they have perhaps left an impression on the mind of the jury, that such witnesses were not worthy of credence.

'This was a case of murder effected by poison. After the verdict was given, and the sentence passed, the Home Secretary refers the whole subject to a *surgeon*, who was not present at the trial (and therefore incompetent to estimate the value of the testimony), nor under oath, nor cross examined, nor confronted with those upon whose evidence he was called to judge. Nor was his report submitted to the prosecuting officer, for his remarks thereon, but it was adopted as conclusive, not because the Secretary of State was more competent to judge of a question of medical science than a question of law, but on the extraordinary ground, that as the only man he had consulted, differed in opinion from those witnesses that were examined for the Crown, there must be a doubt, and that consequently it was his duty to set aside the decision of the Court, and to pardon the convict. If the conclusion that he has thus arrived at, is correct, it should form a precedent to be followed in other cases; and if it be so regarded, there will be an end of executions for murder by poisoning, where there is a difference of opinion between medical witnesses and the reviewer; for in no case will there be any difficulty in finding a doctor of sufficient scepticism, or conceit, to doubt the infallibility of medical science, or the accuracy of the opinions of his brother practitioners. There is an immunity in confidential communications, that makes the exercise of humanity an agreeable duty; and the offer of an appellate jurisdiction over the professions of law and medicine, is too great a temptation to a man to elevate himself at the expense of both, to be successfully resisted.'

'Ah, now you are talking " dic," ' exclaimed Peabody, 'and I can't follow you. When I talk '——

' You use the *vulgar tongue*,' retorted the Senator.

'You may take my hat,' replied the other; 'I cave in, I owe you one, but you needn't chalk it up, for I'll be sure to pay you back before long. What I was going to say was, I wouldn't mind Smethurst gettin' off, if they had only hanged one of them tarnation onfackilized goneys of doctors. I never see a case yet, in which they were called as witnesses, that they didn't make super superior fools of themselves. Nothen they love so dearly as to differ, and they never give a positive straight up and down opinion, except when they get a chance to contradict each other. There is no brotherhood atween them, as there is among lawyers: thieves have too much honour to peach on each other: doctors convict one another always. They are like moles, each critter burrows in his own hole in the dark, and as they can't see no track but their own, they swear there ain't any other. They dabble so much in chemistry, they treat truth like a compound substance; and they get so bothered with their analysises and tests, that it has neither cohesion, nor unity, nor colour, when they have done with it. They may be very good doctors, 's far as I know, but they are the worst witnesses under the sun; they swear that everything *may be*, but that nothen *is*; that you can judge of a disease by its symptoms, but that the symptoms of any given number are so much alike, you can't tell what ailment a person died of. That's the way Smethurst got off. Sir Brodie, who was made a judge of the Appeal Court in criminal cases, and sat for the first time in this case, rapped his snuff-box before he opened the lid (the way Pat knocks a feller down, to have the pleasure of pickin of him up, for one good turn deserves another), sat down in his arm-chair, put one leg over the other, laid his head back, looking woudrous wise, took out a pinch of rappee, and said, " This is a law case, and it's very odd

I am the rap*por* and the snuff is rap*pee*," and then he
sniffed it up, and felt good all over. " It's the first legal
opinion I ever gave—'who shall decide when doctors
disagree?'—I won't pronounce judgment at all." So he
took up his pen, and wrote, " Medical science is in its
infancy" (which means there was none when he was in
practice), " and you can't expect wisdom from the mouths
of babes and sucklings. Therefore, whether Smethurst
was, or was not guilty of poisoning, not knowing, can't
say."

'Now, if that ain't a farce, then the murder of that
poor gal warn't an awful tragedy, that's all. They are
gettin' on here, Lyman, that's a fact, when an old retired doctor upsets judge and juries, and sais there is no
dependence on medical science. What in the world have
the halt, the lame, and the blind been dependin' on for
1860 years? If he has pretended to cure all his life
"secundem artem," and there *is* no art, couldn't folks
recover back their fees from him, on his own con-
fession? Yes, they are gettin' on here; they'll soon
appeal to the wise woman, old Liddy Lonas, that tells
fortins by cards, and the lines in the hands, and the vein
in the forehead, and the stars, and so on. Let them ask
her if a verdict is right or not, and people will credit her,
though they won't a doctor. They darn't doubt her, and
if they did, she'd soon find a way to make 'em believe, as
Titus Cobb's ghost did his son Eber. Eber Cobb, who
got a great fortin from his father, went to a spirit rapper
at Albany, to have a talk with the old gentleman, just
out of a lark, for he no more believed in it than you do.
Well, he was soon put into communication, as they call
it, with the old bill broker, who answered all his questions
quite satisfactory, and then gave him some advice he
didn't quite like, when he broke out into a loud laugh, and

said it was all tarnation nonsense; that they couldn't take
him in that way, and that he warn't born in the woods to
be skeered by an owl, and so forth. Well, he had hardly
said this, when the table began to turn slowly, and then
to spin round like a teetotum, when it ran right up agin
him like a mad bull, and fairly kicked him right out of
the room, "Hold on, for marcy's sake," cried Eber,
lookin' as white as a sheet, and most awfully terrified;
"hold on, I believe it now, that's 'xactly like the old man,
he's as violent as ever, oh, that's him to a dead sartinty;
he never could bear contradiction at no time, without
gettin' into a'most an all-fired passion." From this day
forth, I believe in spirit rapping.

'Yes, let Cornwall Lewis consult old Liddy Lonas in
the next case of a man that's convicted of murder, and
he'll satisfy the public a nation sight better than by referring it to Sir Brodie. Liddy knows as much of life as are
a doctor in creation does of death, and twice as much of
women as he does; and she'd have told Secretary, if he'd
asked her, whether that onfortunate, beguiled, and simple
gal died from nateral causes, or by the hand of a murderer.

'I'll tell you what I've obsarved here in England.
The people never forget what they are taught at school;
they larn that the masculine gender is more worthy than the
feminine, and they act on that through life. If a man
murders his wife, they say, "sarved her right." But if
she does for her husband, she may as well go to work to
knit a large stocking to put both her feet in, to die decent
—for hanged she'll be, as sure as income-tax! They
may laugh here at Judge Lynch as much as they like;
he never hanged an innocent man, or let a guilty one
escape, as far as ever I could hear; and it's my opinion, if
he had visited Richmond, when this Smethurst affair happened, he'd a given universal satisfaction. He's a man

R

that never eats his own words, as some English folk do, though he has often made others gulp them.

'And talkin' of that puts me in mind of Sir Brodie. I met him the other evening to dinner, and sais I, "How do you do, Judge Brodie?" "I am not a judge, sir," said he, looking all abroad, "but a medical man." "Beg your pardon," sais I, "they told me Chief Baron and jury tried Smethurst for murder, pronounced him guilty, and sentenced him to death, and that you turned the tables on them, tried *them*, and found them all guilty of a conspiracy to murder an innocent man! It's the best joke I ever heard since I was raised. Well! I never in all my born days!" sais I, "it takes the rag off the bush quite, that, if you didn't row them all up Salt River, it's a pity!" He didn't know whether to take it up or not, but steered between both pints, looked comical in his eye, but grave in the face. Sais he, "Mr. Peabody, I have a great respect for a judge, and if it were a matter of law, I should bow to his decision; but this, sir, was a question for our profession, and '*medical science is in its infancy.*'" Sais I, "If it is in its infancy, there are some whopping big sucking babies of students in it— that's a fact, and no mistake." "What a droll man you be!" sais he; "I admire the Americans uncommonly. They not only take a common-sense view of everything, but they catch its ridiculous points too; and sometimes I am puzzled to know whether they are in earnest or in jest. But let us drop the subject of the trial, for here comes a Q.C." "Does that mean, 'Queer Cove?'" sais I; "for it's like what I used to call my brother. I gave him the title of Q.C.F., and always put it on his letters arter his name, for he was for everlastin' a-talking of trespass, and *quare clausum fregit*, as he called it."

'Well, up comes Q.C., and shakes hands with Doctor.

Sais he, "So Gladstone has put off his budget till Friday.
What's the matter with his throat?—is it influenza?"
" No," sais Doctor, "it is a sort of Parliamentary diph-
theria. He has had to eat so many of his own words, in
leaving Derby to join Palmerston, that his swallow was
affected, and sore throat supervened. Several members
of the Government are affected more or less by the same
complaint." " Well," sais I, "one's own words are hard
to gulp—that's a fact, especially when swallowed dry ;
but when they are taken with the sweets of office they go
down as slick as mint julep."

' But to get back to Judge Lynch, as I was a-sayin'.
He never eats his own words. What he says he means,
and there is no appeal from him. Execution follows his
sentence as thunder does lightning. He ain't a military
man, that declares martial law, holds a drum-head court,
is as savage as a meat axe, and don't valy life more nor
a fig of tobacco, but a plain, homespun citizen, that
declares common-sense, holds a neighbourly court, and,
though starnley just, is a marciful man, and never leaves
a feller in suspense a minute longer than can be helped.
There is no pomp, nor toggery, nor tomfoolery about him.
No one can point to him as they did to my brother, and
say, " too much goldo, too much foolo." He wears
neether wig, nor gown, nor white-choker; he don't sit
with closed doors, in some hole or corner, like those
English Big Wigs, as if he was afeared people would see
or hear what he sais or does. But he holds his court
under the broad canopy of Heaven. He don't sit on
a bench, and give the Russia leather cushion the meek
and lowly title of " *the woolsack*," that hypocrites might
think him humble. Nor has he a figure of Justice stuck
up behind him, with a bandage over its eyes, and a pair
of scales in its hands, to show that it is so blind it can't

see whether it weighs even-handed or not. But Judge Lynch sits on a stump, like a patriarch of old, in all the native dignity of a patriot judge, with a simple wide-awake hat on his head, a halter in one hand, and a revolver in the other—emblems and implements of justice—lays down the law of natur to the jury, and if they convict a feller, strings him up to a nateral gallus—the first tree near hand—whistles " Possum up a gum tree," and then says, " Come, boys, this here court is adjourned, let's liquor." A doctor would think it a nation sight better for his precious hide to save his breath to cool his broth, than to meddle with *him*, I can tell you. If Judge Lynch had been at St. George's-in-the-East, the other day, he'd a saved the Bishop the trouble of suspendin that are onfackalized '——

' Don't let us enter upon that subject,' said the Senator, ' it is a most painful one ; both parties are very much to blame—extremes meet. Too much form and ceremony naturally breaks down with its own weight, and produces a revulsion that ends in total destruction of both. But this is not a matter that should be treated with levity.'

To assist him in changing the conversation I asked him what he thought of the new Divorce Court we had just visited.

' I have heard and read a good deal about it,' he replied, ' and am bound to say I do not think it open to the objections that have been raised against it. You must recollect that it is regarded from very opposite points of view, according to the peculiar notions of people on the subject of divorce. These opinions it is not necessary to discuss, it would lead us into too wide a field for mere conversation ; but assuming that the principle upon which it is founded is correct (upon which I do not wish to offer an opinion), the court appears to me to work well in practice. I do not wonder that the public is alarmed when they see the great number of cases that are brought before it for adjudication; but it must be recollected, that when the House of Lords was the sole tribunal that could decide upon them, redress was confined to the rich man and the mere pauper, as a divorce could only be obtained by the expenditure of a very large sum of money, or by the gratuitous services of lawyers. The consequence was, that a vast deal of obloquy was thrown upon the aristocracy, as they were, with very few exceptions, the only parties who figured in these trials; and an impression prevailed, not only among the people of this country, but among foreigners, that the upper classes were distinguished from the middle and lower orders, as much by their profligacy, as their wealth and social rank.

'It would now appear, that so far from this being the case, they furnish fewer instances of depravity than those in an inferior station, which, considering their great wealth, their leisure, and other circumstances, does them infinite honour. Indeed it is said, and I believe with some truth, that while a better and sounder tone of morals prevails in the higher ranks, there is by no means a corresponding decrease in the rest of society of those offences that are the special objects of adjudication in this court. Since I have been in England, I have perused with great attention the reports of cases tried before this tribunal, and I have met with no instance in which a divorce has been decreed on insufficient grounds, or where there was any reason to suspect collusion between the parties.

'The House of Lords was a very objectionable tribunal. No man, however high in station, or eminent for ability, is fit to try a cause unless he is professionally trained for the exercise of judicial functions. A judge is naturally

cold and impassive; his prejudices and his imagination
are carefully eliminated from his mind; he is accustomed
to deal with testimony, to analyze, weigh it, and estimate
its real value.   An unprofessional judge, such as a member of the House of Peers, is a man of feeling as well as
honour, his impulses are good, but they are not chastened
like those of a lawyer. He does not very readily perceive
the difference between an equitable and a legal claim, or
between what is expedient and what is strictly lawful.
He relies more on the purity of his intentions than on his
knowledge of principles, or the rules of evidence, and
frequently decides more in reference to what he thinks
ought to be, than what can be done.   The absence of a
jury lessened the value of their decisions in the eyes of
the public—not that jurymen are more intelligent or
more honest than the Peers—but because the popular
element was wanting in the tribunal.   The fiat of the
court was the judgment of an order of men far above the
common in station, for which they alone were responsible
who pronounced it; it was open to criticism, and often condemned, because, though the members of that house were,
from their high station and character, beyond the suspicion
of partiality, they were not exempted from the imputation
of unconscious bias, in consequence of their not possessing
those attributes of judges which I have just named.   The
present Court of Divorce will be more satisfactory to the
public, because its decrees are founded upon verdicts;
and as the decisions of juries are those of the people, the
judge derives a support from their concurrence, far
beyond the intrinsic value of their opinions.   Suspicion is
apt to attach to irremovable functionaries, from the natural tendency of established authority to become arbitrary.
Juries are fluctuating bodies, and cannot be easily acted
upon. If a verdict be unsatisfactory, the certainty that

the same jury will never again be assembled together, reconciles us to the evil, and induces us to hope for more intelligence and superior discretion from the next. Their chief value is to make the people bear their own share of the responsibility of administering justice, and to elevate the judge in public estimation, by placing him beyond the reach of those imputations, that ignorance and vulgarity are so prone to fasten upon their superiors. I differ, therefore, *toto cælo* from Mr. Justice Cresswell, as to the expediency of sitting with closed doors. Nothing can be more disagreeable than to have to listen to the disgusting details usually given in evidence in suits for divorce, more especially as they attract the lowest and most depraved audiences. Of this, however, he has no right to complain, for when he accepted the commission, he knew the nature and incidents of his duties. It is essential that these causes should be heard in public for reasons similar to those I have already assigned; the evil does not consist in open trials, but in the publicity given to these offensive matters by the daily press. It is to be hoped that the good sense of its conductors may induce them to omit all details unsuited for general perusal, and that the repro-bation of the public will punish any infraction of propriety in this respect.'

' 'Zactly,' said Peabody, 'there ought to be an Aunt Debby in every family, as there was to our house, to hum, to act as a reader, and see if there was anything improper in the newspapers, or in the new books we took in from the circulatin' library. Lord! how prim and precise she was. I think I see her now a-standin' afore me as neat and nice as if she was just taken out of a bandbox that was brought home from the milliner, with her black silk dress fittin' as tight as her skin; her white, clear-starched, stiff kerchief crossed over her breast, and

tied behind; and her little, beautiful, crimped muslin cap,
that was edged with short, stiff, hair curls, like tassels on
a fringe. When she stood up to receive a stranger, in
the second position (as dancin' masters call it), with one
little tiny foot just far enough out to show her ankle that
she was so proud of, crossed her hands in front, and half-
bowed, half-curtsied, she was a pictur worth framin', I
tell you. Everything about her seemed new except her
face, and that looked as if it had been took good care of,
and had wore well, too. She was as formal and perlite
as you please, and really looked as good natured as an
aunt can that has to govern other folk's children, for no
woman knows how to bring up juveniles, except one that
has none of her own. But when she put her spectacles on,
it was time to close reef and keep an eye to windward for
squalls, that's a fact. They made her look old and feel
old; they told tales of eyes that was once bright, and
bygone days when she was young, and she scolded every
one that came near hand to her, as if it was their fault
she warn't young still. I don't think she had an idee
that there was anything good onder the sun, except
herself and her presarves; she saw evil in everything.
This warn't proper, and that warn't delicate; this wasn't
decent, and that was downright wicked. Whenever she
read anything funny in a paper she'd look as black as
thunder, and 'jaculate, "Well, I wan't to know!!! If
this don't beat general trainin'!!" and so on; and then go
and hide away the paper, and say nobody but father was
to read it. Well, in course the moment she turned her
back, the gals raced off, ransacked the desk, pulled it
right out, and read it, for it set their curiosity a-goin',
and when a woman gets that up, nothin in natur will stop
her. Eve couldn't, nohow she could fix it. If she hadn't
a-been ordered not to eat the apple, it's as like as not·

she never would so much as have seen it, there were so
many more temptin' lookin' fruits in Paradise. But no,
there was a secret, and if she was to die for it, nothin would
stop her from tryin' to find it out. Well, anything that
Aunt Debby forbid was sure to be read. One day father
sent home a book called "Peregrine Pickle:" I dare say
you have heard tell of it, it's one of the greatest and
funniest books ever written, it is so full of human natur.
Sister Phemy picked it up and began to read it, when
Aunt Debby came in and snatched it right away from her.
"What in natur is this?" sais she. "What! reading a
novel," and she turned up the whites of her eyes, and
fairly groaned. "I never saw anything so shocking in all
my born days," sais she, and out of the room she flounced
like anything, crying, "Oh, oh, oh; what is this wicked
world a-comin' to? I will go upstairs and pray for you!"
Well, hour followed arter hour, and they waited and waited
for ever so long, and still no Aunty came back. At last Phemy
grew awful skeered, and she crept upstairs to old Debby's
room, and as the door was ajar, she pushed it gently open,
and peeped in, and there sat Aunty by the window in her
rockin' chair, a-readin' of the very identical horrible book,
and a-shakin' all over with laughter, the tears of fun
actilly a-runnin' down her cheeks, till she was most off in
hystrikes. Arter a while Phemy slips in a tip-toe, taps
her on the shoulder, and says, "Aunty, dear, what a protracted time you've had of it, haven't you, and all on account of my sins, too! But, dear Aunt, what in natur is
the matter of you? Ain't you well? What makes you
weep so?" " Weep," sais she, pulling a face as long as
the Moral Law. "Weep, is it? I guess I am weepin',
this wicked book would make anybody shed tears. Oh,
to think that your father should send such an awful work

as this home!!" Well, in course Phemy stole it away the first chance she got, and all the gals read it.

'Now, which do you think did most mischief in our house, Peregrine Pickle or Aunt Debby? Tell you what, delicacy is one thing and squeamishness another, but they ain't commonly found travellin' arm and arm together, for there never was a squeamish woman that had a delicate mind, that's a fact.'

'It is not necessary,' said the Senator, 'to settle their relative demerits; but it is quite clear that Miss Peabody was but an indifferent instructress for young ladies, and "Peregrine Pickle" an unsuitable book for them to read. But, be that as it may, no newspaper ought ever to be admitted into a house, the columns of which are defiled by the recitals of these disgusting trials.'

' Well, I am glad I have seen this Divorce Court, too,' said Peabody, 'not on account of the philosophy of the thing, because I don't onderstand that, but because Britishers are for everlastingly a-tauntin' us, and sayin' we tie the nuptial knot so loose that half the time it comes undone of itself. Well, if they fix it tighter here, there are them that know how to loose it, at any rate. Parsons think they can tie the fisherman's knot, but lawyers are up to the dodge, and can ondo it as quick as they can fix it. There is nothin in natur equal to *them* except a parrot, and he (no, I won't say he, for there is no such thing as a male parrot, they are all Pollys)—and she can loosena link as quick as you can put the chain on her. Now, I'll tell you the difference between our divorces and yours: we dissolve matrimonial partnership sometimes because it don't convene to the parties to continue it. It's a matter of what they call incompatibility—a long word that means when two naturs don't assimilate or mix pleasantly, like ile and water. Here it is a matter of

crime. Our folks try to perform what they promise; and
when they find it onpossible, they give it up as a bad job.
A woman vows to love, honour, and obey, and, praps, she
finds she has been most awfully taken in; she can't either
love or honour, and when that's the case, in course she
can't obey. Well, when all these combine, what's the
use of goin on snarlin, bitin, and scratchin for everlastin?
When you match a pair of hosses, if one is honest in
draught, goes well up to the collar, and has spirit and
bottom; and t'other is tricky, won't do its share of work,
has no go in it, and gives in arter a few miles—what do
you do? Why, get rid of the bad one, and get a better
mate in its place. Or, if one stays quiet in its pasture,
comes to its oats when called, and lets you put the bridle
on easy; and the other, the moment it is loose, jumps
the fence, races over the country, gets into your neighbour's field, and when, arter a thunderin long chase, you
pen it up in a corner, it turns tail to you, lays down its ears,
and kicks like all possessed, so that it is as much as your
life is worth to get up to it, and, when you do, it holds
its head so high you can't reach up to put the bridle on,
or won't loosen its jaws to take the bit, or, if it does open
its mouth, bites like a pair of blacksmith's pincers—what
do you do? Why, just send it to vandue, or swop it
away for a better one, for it don't convene to keep it
always tied up in its stall.

‘ Well, it's more difficult to choose a human mate than
a hoss match by a long chalk. A hoss don't pretend to
be better than it is; it is no hypocrite—once a devil, always
a devil. They never try to look amiable; but a woman
ain't so easy judged of, I can tell you. She can look like
an angel, be as gentle as a lamb, and talk as sweet as
honey; her face can be as sunny as the heavens on a
summer's day, and if you ain't up to tropical skies, you

wouldn't believe it could ever cloud right up, be as black as ink in a minute, and thunder and lightenin come out of it, hard and sharp enough to stun and blind you. Well, you put to sea with this confidence, the storm comes, she won't answer her helm, and you are stranded in no time; there ain't no insurance office to make up the matrimonial loss to you, and what are you to do? Are you to repair damage, launch the wreck again, and be drove ashore a second time; or, are you to abandon the ship, leave it there, and have nothin more to do with it?'

'Then, do you mean to say,' asked the Senator, 'that it is always the fault of the female?'

'No, I don't,' said Peabody. 'It's oftener the fault of a man, in my opinion, than of a woman. It ain't the lady that proposes, but the gentleman. "Caveat emptor," as my brother Gad, the lawyer, said, in a suit I had with a feller, about the soundness of a hoss I sold. (Father called him Gad, because, like Jacob, he see'd there was a troop of us a-coming.) Well, that law phrase means the buyer must cave in if he a'n't wide awake. If a lovier can read faces—which is as necessary for a man to study when he goes a-courtin as any book that is taught at school—he will see the marks of the temper there. A company face, like a go-to-meetin' dress, ain't got the right sit; it's too stiff and too bright, and you can see it ain't put on every day; there is an oneasiness about her that wears it; it don't seem nateral. The eyebrows are lifted arch-like—they don't stay up sponteneously; the smiles are set—they don't come and go with the rise and fall of the tide of the spirits. The mouth is kinder lengthened to take the droop out of the corners, and that pushes up the cheek, and makes a dimple in it. And the upper lip, instead of curling up sarcy, swells ripe and plump at the mouth. A gall with a face of that kind looks as if she had come into the world singing, instead of cryin' like a young kitten. Courtin is bad for the eye-sight you may depend; a feller is apt to get parblinded by it; if he didn't stare so much, he'd see better. Let him get a look at her when she don't know it, and then he'll see the nateral expression; he'll find the brow puck-ered close, the mouth curved short at the small eend, the eye contracted, and the lips half their former size, and puckered in tight. And if he can't get a chance to see her that way, if she has a rival, set her a talkin about her; or if she has ever tried it on to a feller, and got the cold shoulder, steboy her at him, and he'll soon find the set smile has set like the sun—gone out of sight till next time, and the angel mask has dropped off, and the shrew face left, looking as large as life, and twice as nateral. Now, if he ain't a judge himself, let him do as he does when he buys at an auction—ask the advice of them that are, and if his friends have as much of the fool about 'em as he has, let him remember every gall, like every other created critter, has a character, good, bad, or indifferent. Everybody is known among their neighbours for exactly what their valy is. This one is a termagant, that one a flirt, this is imprudent, and that discreet, while t'other is as good-hearted, good-natured a gall as ever lived. Well, if a man won't make use of his common-sense—and he is took in, all I can say is, it sarves him right.'

'No,' said the Senator, 'that's not what I mean. Do you think a man is oftener taken in, in matrimony, than a woman?'

'No,' he replied, 'I don't. I think it's the other way. As I said before, recollect it's him that proposes; in a general way he gets spooney, goes right up to her head, and marries. Sometimes it's the gall he admires, and sometimes her money or rank; but he commonly plays the first card, and leads off for her to follow suit. I say commonly, for women know how to put it into a man's head, and make him think it's all his own doings. Well, havin' made up his mind, nothin ever stops him; he flatters, not with homœopathic doses, but draughts that would choke a camel; he swears as false as the feller did who deposed to knowing a fusee ever since it was a pistol, when he heard it was called a "son of a gun." He vows eternal love, and takes his davy he'll die of a broken heart, or drown himself, if he's refused. Men know what liars men are, but women don't; and how should a poor gall tell, who ain't permitted to look at men's faces, to see if they are stamped with deceit or not? How can she study physiognomy? She is all truth herself (if properly brought up), and confides in others. She knows she was made to be loved; and when a man vows he does adore her to distraction, and she knows that word adoration is only applied to angels, why shouldn't think she is one, and believe the man who worships her? No! poor critter, she is oftener took in than the false lover is. Now, when the fraud is found out, whichever it was that cheated (sometimes both are let in for a bad bargain), and when contempt, and then hatred, and then squabblin and fightin comes, ain't it better for both to cry quits?'

'Don't talk nonsense, Ephraim,' said the Senator, 'you know better than that. Matrimony is not a partnership to be dissolved by mutual consent. "*Whom God has joined, let not man put asunder.*"'

'Yes,' replied the other, 'but those that the world, the flesh, or the devil has united——'

'We'll drop the subject, if you please, Mr. Peabody,' rejoined the Senator, with some warmth.

'Now, don't fly off at the handle arter that fashion,' said Peabody, with provoking coolness, and a comical expression of countenance; 'it ain't safe. When I was chopping at our wood pile onct, the axe flew right off tha way as quick as wink, and took the ear off of old Jabez Snow, our black nigger help, as slick as a knife. The varmint thought when he felt the blood runnin' down his cheek that his skull was split, and his brains oozing out, and he gave a yell so loud they heer'd him clean across the river, which was more nor the matter of a mile wide there, and then he fell down in a conniption fit. It spoilt his beauty, I can tell you, for nothin looks so bad as a half-cropt nigger; it gave his head a lop-sided look ever arter. So don't fly off at the handle that way; it's dangerous, that's a fact.'

'Well,' said the Senator, 'we ought not to be angry with you, for men eminent for their ability and station in the British Parliament have talked as loosely and absurdly as you do. It is grievous to hear a man like Lord Campbell dispose of the arguments derived from Scripture against the remarriage of divorced parties; and the scruples of learned and pious men on the subject, with a flippancy that betokens either ignorance, or indifference, or both. As I said before, I will not enter into that wide field of controversy, although I entertain a very strong opinion upon the subject, founded, not like that of his lordship, on a superficial view of it, but after mature consideration and anxious investigation.

'Leaving untouched, therefore, the interpretation, Mr. Shegog, which your legislature has put on those passages of Scripture, on the subject of divorce, I will content myself with saying, that I cannot approve of the enactments of the recent law. Nothing can be worse than that portion of it which makes a marked distinction between the rights of husband and wife. The former can procure a divorce "a vinculo," upon the proof of adultery, the latter can only obtain a similar relief, when that offence is coupled with bigamy, or incest, or cruelty, or desertion for a period of two years. How a Christian legislature like yours, composed of a body of English gentlemen, of peers spiritual and temporal, and above all, with a Queen constituting its first and highest branch, could thus degrade woman below the level she has held for centuries, in this and every other civilized country, is to me altogether unintelligible. If their rights are thus rendered unequal, so are their respective punishments. The husband may be mulct in damages for his offence ; but the wife, by the usages of the world, is for ever banished from society, and her punishment terminates only with her life. It is deeply to be regretted that the suggestion of the Archbishop of Canterbury, to restrain the guilty party from remarriage, and that of the Bishop of Oxford, to visit the offence with imprisonment, were not adopted. As the law now stands, it is unscriptural, impolitic, and unjust.'

Here our conversation terminated, and I was compelled to hurry to the station to be in time for the train. The term of my 'pass' on the South Western line expires to-night. Whether I shall renew it, or accept the invitation of my American friends, from whom I have derived so much amusement and instruction, to accompany them on a short tour into the country, I have not yet decided, but this sheet completes the memorabilia of my present 'Season Ticket.'

LONDON: PRINTED BY W. CLOWES AND SONS, STAMFORD STREET.